MǪLAZHA

(CHILD OF A WHITEMAN)
A MEMOIR

RICHARD I. HARDY

One Printers Way
Altona, MB R0G 0B0
Canada

www.friesenpress.com

Copyright © 2022 by Richard I Hardy
First Edition — 2022

All rights reserved.

No part of this publication may be reproduced in any form, or by any means, electronic or mechanical, including photocopying, recording, or any information browsing, storage, or retrieval system, without permission in writing from FriesenPress.

Excerpt(s) from THE COMPANY: THE RISE AND FALL OF THE HUDSON'S BAY EMPIRE by Stephen Bown, copyright © 2020 Stephen R. Bown. Reprinted by permission of Doubleday Canada, a division of Penguin Random House Canada Limited. All rights reserved.

ISBN
978-1-03-912667-1 (Hardcover)
978-1-03-912666-4 (Paperback)
978-1-03-912668-8 (eBook)

1. BIOGRAPHY & AUTOBIOGRAPHY, NATIVE AMERICANS

Distributed to the trade by The Ingram Book Company

Table of Contents

vi   **AUTHOR'S NOTE**

viii   **DEDICATION**

xii   **ACKNOWLEDGEMENTS**

xiii   **FOREWORD**

xv   **INTRODUCTION**

PART I

FUR TRADERS, MISSIONARIES, AND THE ESTABLISHMENT OF A MACKENZIE RIVER MÉTIS FAMILY

1   **CHAPTER ONE**
ANCESTRY

4   **CHAPTER TWO**
SHÚHTA GOT'INE

11   **CHAPTER THREE**
EUROPEAN ROOTS

19   **CHAPTER FOUR**
THE GAUDETS

52   **CHAPTER FIVE**
THE GAUDET BOYS GO TO SCHOOL

64   **CHAPTER SIX**
THE HARDISTYS

PART II

GROWING UP IN FORT NORMAN

77   **CHAPTER SEVEN**
MY EARLY LIFE

81   **CHAPTER EIGHT**
THE BELT

97   **CHAPTER NINE**
GROWING UP

109   **CHAPTER TEN**
MÉTIS SETTLERS

114   **CHAPTER ELEVEN**
END OF CHILDHOOD

126   **CHAPTER TWELVE**
SPORTS DAY AND YELLOWCAKE

134   **CHAPTER THIRTEEN**
FIRST BIG TRIP

PART III
STUDENT RESIDENCES AND THE DEVILS OF GROLLIER HALL

145 **CHAPTER FOURTEEN**
FIRST STEPS TO HELL

160 **CHAPTER FIFTEEN**
INTO THE ABYSS

172 **CHAPTER SIXTEEN**
SERENDIPITY

183 **CHAPTER SEVENTEEN**
THE AFTERMATH OF GROLLIER HALL

PART IV
DIFFICULT YEARS

195 **CHAPTER EIGHTEEN**
THE CROSSROADS

204 **CHAPTER NINETEEN**
WANDERING

PART V
FINDING MY CALLING

217 **CHAPTER TWENTY**
ACADEMIA

225 **CHAPTER TWENTY-ONE**
PRACTICING LAW

PART VI
STARTING OVER

239 **CHAPTER TWENTY-TWO**
RETURN TO THE NORTH

247 **CHAPTER TWENTY-THREE**
MARYANN

260 **CHAPTER TWENTY-FOUR**
NÁÁTS'IHCH'OH

268 **CHAPTER TWENTY-FIVE**
VANCOUVER ISLAND

269 **CONCLUSION**

275 **EPILOGUE**

285 **BIBLIOGRAPHY**

287 **APPENDIX A**

288 **APPENDIX B**

289 **APPENDIX C**

291 **APPENDIX D**

311 **APPENDIX E**

AUTHOR'S NOTE

Mǫlazha was a nameless concept
for about three decades. There were
a number of false starts when I
would get about three to four thousand
words down on paper and then run out of
anything else to say. It was only when
I decided to sell the family property in
Fort Norman, in 2019, that the ideas
began to coalesce. I hope that readers find
some value and some enjoyment in the stories
that have been included. One of the main
difficulties that I faced while researching
and writing this book is that most of that
time was during the COVID-19 pandemic.
This made it difficult to access various archives,
to say the least. Thank you for taking the time
to read my life story.

Richard I. Hardy – March 31, 2022

Rick Hardy with a moose-hide jacket made for him by his Mama in the mid-1970s.
Credit: Maryann Hardy

DEDICATION

I dedicate this book to the memory of my parents, Jack and Alice Hardy. Mama was born and raised in the Mackenzie River District, and Daddy came from Nova Scotia. They met in Fort Norman in the early 1930s and were married on July 16,1934. They remained dedicated to each other all their lives, and they rest together, for eternity, in our family section of the old Anglican graveyard in Fort Norman. When they met and married, Canada was still in the grip of the Great Depression. The year they were married, they pledged what they owned to the Hudson's Bay Company (HBC) for fifty pounds of flour, moved to the bush on Bear Island, and lived in a tent for a year. Daddy had a contract cutting firewood for the HBC steamboats. Their first child, Leo, was born on the island the following spring. Their lives were filled with hard work and struggle. Notwithstanding that, they raised me well and gave me values that I struggled to live up to. Without them, I would not have found what successes I have been blessed with in my life.

Hədɛrı ʔedıhtł'é, seyıghǫnéke Alice hé Jack Hardy kuk'éts'əhdlı gú kuráhdı gháré kugha bəńdéńtł'e. ʔamá Dehchogá begǫhłı gú ʔeyı réyǫ, ʔabá Nova Scotıa gots'ęyá ʔayı́t'e. 1930s ʔegúhyɔ́ ʔala Tułıt'a ʔələhdzı́né keyıʔa, gú 1934, July k'e ʔehghákuyęya. Dánéhwá dene keyıle gots'ę ʔelehdıkədəwíle gú dene keyılé hagú hıdú dugolaodəwı gots'ę Tułıt'a raxégot'ıne ńkuyęya gota, ʔələhk'ú shukıya. ʔelehts'ę kákeyıʔa, lekı́shu ʔegúhyɔ́, Canada góyə ʔareyǫ́né kehé súré yuwé godéhw'e godéwé yıle. Lekı́shu ghái yerı kuts'ę k'éyıhxa, Legóbę

Yúkǫ́ hé kugha ʔedútł'e gha ʔakéja gú łıhfań lak'e horéno dadıdlu kughaʔedádı hé Sah Dúwé łıe xaı gots'ę deshıta nóbaléyə ʔakeyı́t'e. ʔabá Legóbę goʔeláshó gha tse dúfı gogha beńʔedętł'e. Godowe ʔuyálélé ʔala kuya Leo Sah Dúwé begǫ́hłı. Goshó godəyı ʔeghálakeyı́da hé tsı́keyıwe. ʔekáht'é kółı gonezǫ́ sekeréhshǫ gú dene nezǫ wóhle gha gásekuréhtǫ, ʔeyı gok'éhtá dene wóhle segha godəyı kółı ká rásodéle. Dánéwá dene həhłı yerı he gonezǫ ʔedegha ńgóńʔǫ haı kududzıne nídé dódı gha yıle.

Jack and Alice Hardy in front of their first house in Fort Norman in 1934.
Credit: Hardy Family Collection.

The Fur Trade World of Charles Phillipe Gaudet

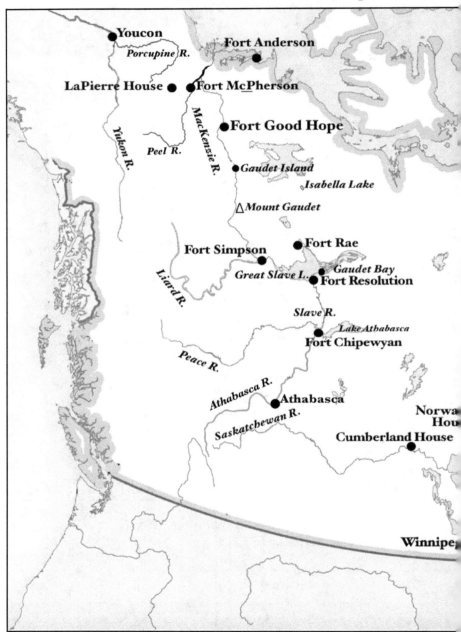

1851~C.P.G. travels from Montreal to Norway House where he meets James Anderson, and signs a five-year contract to become a POSTMASTER. **1851**~Travels to Fort Chipewyan, Fort Simpson and on to Youcon for his first Outfit. **1852**~Transferred to LaPierre House. **1852**~Makes a country marriage with Natalie, and Eliza is born in 1853. **1853**~Transferred to Great Slave Lake, Fort Rae. **1854-1857**~Transferred back to Youcon. **1857**~Transferred to Big Island, Fort Good Hope. **1858**~Marries Marie Fisher in Fort Simpson. **1858**~Transferred to Fort Resolution. **1859-1863**~Transferred to Peels River, Fort McPherson. **1863**~Promoted to CLERK. **1863-1878**~Transferred to Fort Good Hope.

1866-1868~C.P.G. takes a two-year sabbatical, and with Marie and five children, travel to Ottawa to visit his mother. One daughter, Sara, dies there. On the return trip, two more daughters, Eliza and Marie, die at Cumberland House. **1878**~Promoted to CHIEF TRADER. **1878-1911**~Serves in Fort Good Hope as CHIEF TRADER, and makes contact with the Inuvialuit at Fort Anderson. **1911**~Retires as Chief Trader and remains in Fort Good Hope until 1917, assisting the HBC. **1917**~Leaves Fort Good Hope to return to his birthplace in Montreal but dies on the way in Winnipeg. Place names that Charles Phillipe Gaudet left on the maps of the present day Northwest Territories: Gaudet Island, Mount Gaudet, Gaudet Bay, and Isabella Lake (named for his daughter).

ACKNOWLEDGEMENTS

With regard to the many photos that I have used to help tell the stories in this book, I would like to acknowledge the following: the Gaudet family in Montreal, who saved the photos that had been taken by their patriarch—Joseph Leon Gaudet (the family photographer) of the family in Fort Good Hope and elsewhere; Mama, who took many photos during her lifetime and gathered others so that we would know from where we came; my wife, Maryann Hardy, who at one point in her life was a professional photographer and has continued taking pictures during all the years that I have known her—Maryann also prepared all of the photos and other documents that are presented in the book; Elizabeth Hardy, my late sister-in-law; as well as all of the other individuals and institutions who have so generously agreed to allow me to use their work.

I thank Lucyann Overvold for providing the Dene translation of the Dedication and the correct words for the various place names used throughout the book. Lucyann cautioned me that she would be using the Fort Good Hope dialect and I agreed. The dialects used in the Sahtu are similar enough to be understood by all Dene speakers there. Besides that, the Gaudet presence in the Sahtu did start in Fort Good Hope.

With regard to research, I would never have been able to gather as much detail as we have on the first Gaudet family, Marie and Charles Phillipe, without the years of hard work by Diane Payment. A true friend and a Métis patriot, if there ever was one.

Also, with regard to research, I want to acknowledge the help and cooperation of the various archivists who are mentioned in the book.

Thank you to my friend Sheila McPherson for the inspiring words in the foreword.

With regard to funding for the project, this book would not have been possible without the generous financial support of the Fort Norman Métis Community. I thank them for that as well as their ongoing encouragement.

Finally, to all the good folks at Friesen Press. Thanks for being there and showing all the patience that you have with me.

FOREWORD

Sheila MacPherson

Rick Hardy's memoir, *Mǫlazha*—child of a white man—is a powerful story of a journey of pain, challenges and ultimately healing and personal reconciliation. Rick's stories of his largely happy and blissful childhood growing up in Tulita, NWT (formerly Fort Norman) provide a rare glimpse into the day-to-day dynamics of family life in a small northern community. The beauty of his childhood stands in stark contrast to his first-hand experience of physical and sexual abuse when he was sent away to residential school at the young age of twelve. The raw description of the abuse suffered by Rick, and so many vulnerable students, shook me to my core. Like Rick, I also grew up in the North and lived in Inuvik at the same time that Rick was attending school. At that time and for many years thereafter, I was completely unaware of the huge gulf between my school experience and Rick's experience, and the experience of so many of the indigenous students with whom I was growing up. The abuse suffered by Rick (and other's) is horrific enough, however, perhaps ultimately even more damaging was the complete disregard of the abuse by others in authority, coupled with a shocking lack of any support to assist Rick in healing from this trauma. Rick's ability to survive the horrors of residential school and sexual abuse and to go on to an illustrious legal career as the first Metis lawyer in the NWT is a testament to the resilience of the human spirit. Notwithstanding his strength and fierce determination, the legacy of his residential school experience haunted Rick, as did (and does) the fact such damaging behaviour appeared to be tolerated and condoned by those in positions of power within the Catholic church. Rick candidly acknowledges his struggles with anger and alcohol abuse and the damaging role that both played in his life, particularly in the early years after his residential school experience.

In addition to shedding light on Canada's shameful residential school experience, *Mǫlazha* also explores some of the political developments of the seventies and eighties, flowing from the Berger Inquiry and the developing body of case law supporting indigenous rights to self-determination. Rick was one of the leading architects of the modern political institutions in the NWT and his first-hand knowledge of the struggles—and excitement—of this era makes for fascinating reading. Rick's stubbornness and tenacity played no small role in the modern land claim negotiations for his people.

Mǫlazha should be required reading for anyone who wants to understand the impact of the residential school experience on so many as well as for those who wish to understand the deep roots and interrelationships of indigenous northerners.

∞

Sheila MacPherson is a lawyer who practices law in Yellowknife as a partner in the law firm of Lawson Lundell, LLP. Sheila has a BA (HONS) from Carleton University (1982) and an LLB from Dalhousie University (1987) and was called to the Bars of the Northwest Territories in 1988 and Nunavut in 1999. She is the past President of the Federation of Law Societies of Canada and a former Commissioner of the Canadian Human Rights Commission.

∞

Sheila's father, Gerry MacPherson, taught high school in Inuvik, NWT and Iqaluit, NT, for many years. Rick recalls "Mr. MacPherson" teaching him Mathematics and Social Studies while he was in high school in Inuvik. Rick also recalls "Mr. MacPherson" being one of the best teachers that he had in high school and inspiring his life-long interest in history and politics.

INTRODUCTION

As I was getting to the end of the first draft of this book, I saw a story on the CBC North website. The report was about the memoir being written by Mister Justice Murray Sinclair. I have not yet had the opportunity to meet this good man. I hope he does not take umbrage with me for using some of his words. He said:

> Four questions inspired this memoir: Where do I come from? Where am I going? Why am I here? Who am I? I didn't invent these questions. I first heard them when I was studying philosophy at the University of Manitoba, just prior to law school.

I realized that similar questions were informing what I was doing by writing this book. Justice Sinclair went on to say that his family had endeavoured to give him answers to those questions:

> But they were answers that were greatly prejudiced by the residential school experience, which was such a dominant force in our family. I didn't have complete access to all the information that I felt I needed in order to be able to answer them. So I set out on a road to discover what those answers were.

Prior to seeing Justice Sinclair's words, I realized that I was also writing to find out who I am and why I am here. I will endeavour to answer those questions by writing this book. However, in many instances, the "I" in the questions becomes "we." I am also very much aware that I am from the third generation of my family that was an attendee at a residential school.

The first question, "Where do I come from?", is most appropriate for me because of my Métisness. I am Métis. Having made that declaration, I acknowledge that there is, sadly, no common definition of who or what a Métis is. I was raised as and spent all of my adult life believing that I was Métis. In fact, as will be shown in this book, I consider myself to be from a very distinct group of Metis known as the Mackenzie River Metis. Who is and who is not Métis is a controversial question? This should not be so.

This question can easily expand to the "we," meaning the Mackenzie River Métis. I believe the best way to explore this question is to search as far back as possible to find the individuals, both European and First Nations, who joined together to create my family in the Mackenzie River District of the Northwest Territories. The answers that I find may apply, in part, to other families. However, my intention is to find my roots only, which, of course, will extend to my children and grandchildren, if they so choose. From time to time, I will use old terminology and refer to First Nations people as Indians, and Métis as Half-Breeds.

The second question, "Where am I going?", is more difficult for me, as I have, basically, already lived my life. Perhaps it might be appropriate for me to substitute "we" for "I," with the "we" being my family and the Mackenzie River Métis who we are part of. It is probably okay to add, "Where have I been?"

The third question, "Why am I here?", is an excellent one. It is a question that most people in this world, Indigenous or not, ask. I will explore what I believe to be the reasons that I am in this world.

The answer to the fourth question, "Who am I?", at this point in time, seems obvious. I am Richard Irving Timothy Hardy, a Métis from the historic Métis Community of Fort Norman in the Mackenzie River District of the Northwest Territories in Canada. Perhaps I will have a more philosophical answer once I am finished writing this book. Fort Norman is now called Tułít'a; however, I prefer to use the name that I grew up with.

Exploring these questions will require a lineal timeline approach, starting with my bloodline, my birth, and my life. How does the beginning influence who I am today? Of course, there will be the occasional side trip to delve into some issues that don't fit within a lineal approach.

Not all readers of this book will be familiar with what is called the Mackenzie River District. Prior to the establishment of Canada by England in 1867, the lands that drained into Hudson's Bay were ruled by the Hudson's Bay Company by way of a royal charter granted by the king of England in 1670. The geographic area was extended in 1821 to include the rest of the western and northern areas of North America, which are now part of Canada and the USA. Of course, someone will immediately cry out that the king of England had no authority to do this. That is correct, but he did do it. As a result of the extension, the monopoly and rule of the HBC was extended to lands that the Dehcho, or the Mackenzie River, flowed through. This was thirty-two years after Alexander Mackenzie's journey to the Arctic Ocean.

Trading posts were being established in lands that were new to the Europeans, and the owners of the HBC wanted the same rights that they held in the original geographic area of its charter. This geographic area was called Rupert's Land. The law over this vast area was administered by the HBC.

An example of this administration of justice is the case of Baptise Cadien. I first heard about this case many, many years ago in Fort Norman. It was, and is commonly referred to, as the Métis Massacre. Later, after I became a lawyer, I was asked by a prominent author from northern Canada if I knew anything about the case and if I knew where to get written information about it. The author knew that I was from Fort Norman and, being a lawyer, that I might have some knowledge about the case. I did not, but over the years, I continued searching for information. Eventually, the thesis by Allan Lloyd Patenaude, *The Administration of Justice in Canada's Northwest Territories, 1870–1990: A Case Study in Colonialism and Social Change*, appeared online. The paper included three pages on the Cadien case, and this formed the baseline for future discussions. Since then, the NWT Archives Library has posted a reproduction of the report of the case published in 1838.

Without going into all of the details of the case, the report outlines how Cadien and his companions, who were employees of the HBC, murdered eleven Hareskin Indians from Fort Norman, in 1837, over a dispute about a Hareskin woman whom Cadien had a previous relationship with. Cadien and his companions were arrested by HBC employees in Fort Norman and sent to Norway House, then London, England, and finally to Three Rivers, in present-day Quebec, where the trial was held. Only Cadien was found guilty of the murders and was sentenced "to be taken, & c. and on the . . . he be hanged by the neck until his body be dead." After many interventions and petitions, the sentence was commuted and, instead, Cadien was sentenced to be sent to the penal colony in Tasmania. Cadien perished on the way to Tasmania.

The area under the rule of the HBC was so massive that the HBC organized the lands into districts. The HBC Archives includes a glossary that has a description of what "districts" were. Without quoting the entire text, it ends with "District names, boundaries and headquarters altered over time." The trading posts established in the districts were ruled by a hierarchy of chief factors, chief traders, factors, traders, post managers, and so forth. Generally speaking, the Mackenzie River District included the Mackenzie River and tributaries draining into it. Because the Mackenzie River District was the largest of the districts, it had a headquarters in Fort Simpson and a sub-headquarters in Fort Good Hope. The districts were eventually folded into the Fur Trade Division and then the Northern Stores Division in 1959, as the HBC expanded its department store businesses in the emerging cities in Canada. The Northern Stores Division was eventually sold to the North West Company in 1987, which operates the stores today as "Northern." This company is publicly traded on the TSX and

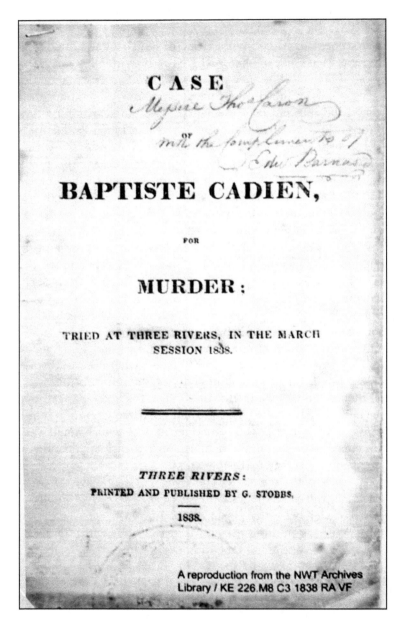

Cover page from the report of the *Case of Baptise Cadien for Murder*.
Credit: NWT Archives Library/KE 226 M8 C3 1838 RA VF.

is not related to the original North West Company, which was taken over by the HBC in 1821.

When Canada decided to make treaties with the Indians, as they were then referred to, living in what was then called the Northwest Territories, the boundaries of the Athabasca and Mackenzie River districts were generally followed, excluding the area of the Yukon Territory. Treaty 8 generally followed the boundaries of the Athabasca River District. The commissioner for the making of Treaty 8 also acted as the commissioner for the Athabasca District Half-Breed Commission. Treaty 11 generally followed the boundaries of the Mackenzie River District, and the commissioner for Treaty 11 also acted as the commissioner for the Mackenzie River District Half-Breed Commission.

The geographic reach of the Mackenzie River District, and the name, continues to have much meaning for the descendants of the Half-Breeds, who established the families that continue to live in and use the lands that made up the district. Lying within the Mackenzie River District is Shúhta Got'ıne Néné— Land of the Mountain Indians. That is where my Indigenous ancestors lived.

In chapter six I introduce a "nature vs. nurture" concept, but I find the need to make references to it prior to fully explaining it. My apologies to the readers for any confusion this might cause.

PART I

FUR TRADERS, MISSIONARIES, AND THE ESTABLISHMENT OF A MACKENZIE RIVER MÉTIS FAMILY

Filming of *Alexander Mackenzie: Lord of the North*. Walter Hardy is second from the left.
Credit: Hardy Family Collection.

PART I

1

CHAPTER ONE

ANCESTRY

The blood that flows through my veins comes from a mixture of North American Indigenous and European ancestors. My North American Indigenous ancestry is primarily from the people who lived along the Dehcho (the Mackenzie River). The territory that they lived in extended from the headwaters of the Raven's Throat and Redstone rivers, following the Mackenzie Mountains north to approximately the Carcajou River, then to the Mackenzie River and then south along both sides of the Mackenzie to the junction of the Redstone and Mackenzie rivers and west back to the starting point. The centre of this area was the Begádóh/Gravel River. Those ancestors were commonly known as Shúhta Got'ıne or Mountain Indians. Boundaries were flexible, and the Shúhta Got'ıne sometimes extended their land use south into what is now called the Dehcho Region and west into what is now called the Yukon.

The Shúhta Got'ıne lived a nomadic life, moving with the seasons. There are no written records of the time prior to the Europeans' arrival, but the nomadic life did continue for at least a century after contact. I am fortunate enough to be able to remember when the Shúhta Got'ıne still made the treks west from Fort Norman into the foothills and the mountains. There are also the written records of the traders and the missionaries, which can give us glimpses of life as it was. In my case I am also fortunate that my father, Jack Hardy, who was *Mǫla* or White, travelled with the Shúhta Got'ıne and observed how they lived and what their practices were while away from the influences of the towns.

There are two known sources of my Shúhta Got'ıne ancestry, and both of them flow to me through my mother, Alice (Gaudet) Hardy. The first source, in time, is from her grandmother, Marie (Taupier) (Fisher) (Houle) Gaudet, who was born on June 24, 1843 "in the vicinity of Fort Liard/Fort Simpson." I am thankful to Diane P. Payment, who researched Marie's ancestry when she wrote "Une Femme En Vaut Deux – Strong Like Two People," which was published in the anthology *Contours of a People – Métis Family, Mobility, and History.* She wrote of Marie's mother as follows: "Elise Taupier was one of the few Métis women hired by the HBC as a 'bully' (disciplinarian) on the boats between Fort Liard and Fort Simpson."

Payment also wrote, "Taupier was the daughter of a French Canadian voyageur and an unidentified Aboriginal woman of Beaver or Slavey ancestry." I have since received some information from Albert Lafferty, a prominent Métis from Fort Providence. The information included scrip records for Elizabeth Hyslop (claim no. 178), which indicate that Hyslop came to that name through marriage. The records disclose that she was born in 1840 and was the daughter of Elise "Toutpied" and Francois Houle. "Toutpied" is described as being a Chipewyan woman.

Unfortunately, I have not been able to find anything more on Elise Taupier's ancestry. Was she Métis, or was she an Indian? If she was Métis, I would like to know if her Métisness stems only from a Mackenzie River Métis or if she was also from Red River, through her father. Was she actually born in what we call the "country," or was she sent north by the HBC? We know that she had other children besides Marie, but how many? Payment also wrote that it is not known if "Taupier" was Elise's father's or her mother's name. Nevertheless, we do have a recognizable starting point, albeit incomplete. When we say the "country," we mean the land we were born on and use. For example, my country would be centred in Fort Norman and extend out from there as far as my family's use extended. Of course, there are no boundaries.

The second source of my Shúhta Got'ıne ancestry is from my grandmother, Sarah Jane (Hardisty) Gaudet. Sarah Jane was Mama's mother. Although Sarah Jane was educated, a Christian, and took Half-Breed scrip in 1924, she was a full-blooded Shúhta Got'ıne. Sarah Jane's parents were Allan and Mary Hardisty, who were also both Shúhta Got'ıne. Allan Hardisty was a catechist for the Anglican Church and was given the name "Hardisty" by a chief trader for the HBC who was stationed in Fort Simpson. I have no doubt that Allan and Mary's ancestors came from the people who occupied and used the land that makes up the Mackenzie Mountains and environs from time immemorial, and their grandparents or great-grandparents would have been present when contact with the Europeans took place.

To be clear, contact with the Europeans by the Indigenous peoples took place across South and North America centuries before it took place along the Dehcho, which makes the experiences different, in many aspects.

European contact with the Shúhta Got'ıne took place starting in the summer of 1789. It is well known that the contact was led, for the Europeans, by Alexander Mackenzie, while looking for a water route to the Pacific Ocean. Stephen R. Bown, in *The*

Sarah Jane (Hardisty) Gaudet, one of the daughters of Allan and Mary Hardisty. Credit: Hardy Family Collection.

PART I

3

Company – The Rise and Fall of the Hudson's Bay Company, describes the departure of Mackenzie's voyage to the ocean as follows:

> *On June 23, 1789, he [Mackenzie] led three cargo canoes with five eastern voyageurs and Six Chipewyan across the water from Fort Chipewyan on a grand adventure that he later claimed was sponsored by the North West Company.*

Mackenzie himself provides a more detailed picture in *The Journals of Alexander Mackenzie*, as follows:

> *We embarked at nine in the morning, at Fort Chipewyan, on the South side of the Lake of the Hills . . . in a canoe made of birch bark. The crew consisted of Four Canadians, two of whom were attended by their wives, and a German; we were accompanied, also by an Indian, who had acquired the title of English Chief, and his two wives, in a small canoe, with two young Indians; his followers in another small canoe.*

I include the above detail to compare it to the National Film Board's *Alexander Mackenzie: The Lord of the North* production from the early 1960s. The importance of the production to me and the members of my community is that it was filmed on the Dehcho, primarily between Fort Norman and Fort Good Hope, with most of the local actors being from Fort Norman. One of those local actors was my brother, Walter, who played one of the "four Canadians," along with Alfred Lennie, Napoleon Kenny, and Paul Baton, who played the others. The dust jacket of the film states: "This film follows the path outlined in Mackenzie's journal." The film is true to the facts, as written by Mackenzie, with one exception. They only used one "cargo canoe," which was most likely a budgetary issue and not one of wanting to depart from the historical detail. The "star" of the film was Don Franks, who was a well-known Canadian actor of that era.

Within twenty years of Alexander Mackenzie's "grand adventure," fur-trading posts were established along the Dehcho. With that development came the Europeans, who provided their part of my bloodline.

CHAPTER TWO

SHÚHTA GOT'INE

As I said earlier, I need to do more research on the background of Elise Taupier, who is my great-great-grandmother. If Elise was not Shúhta Got'ine, as I previously thought, then that bloodline would not have started until the Hardistys joined with the Gaudets in 1899. Whenever the bloodline started, it would not have changed the fact that the Shúhta Got'ine were migratory and occupied that part of the country commonly known as Shúhta Got'ine Nene.

In the east was the Dehcho and its tributaries, flowing from both east and west. From the east flowed the Blackwater River and the Great Bear River. From the west flowed the Raven's Throat, Gravel (Keele), Little Bear, Carcajou, and Mountain rivers. In the west were the Mackenzie Mountains and their foothills and lakes. There were also a number of trails that followed these rivers into the mountains. The tributaries that flowed from the east into the Dehcho were used mostly by the K'álǫ Got'ıne (Willow Lakers) and the Sahtú Got'ıne (Bear Lakers). The users of Shúhta Got'ıne Néné travelled extensively to the south and interacted with the Indigenous people who, today, populate communities such as Nahanni Butte, Fort Liard, Trout Lake, Jean Marie River, Fort Simpson, and Wrigley. They also travelled over the mountains that, today, form the boundary between the Yukon and the Northwest Territories and formed relationships with people who, today, live in Ross River and Mayo, Yukon.

The area is described on page two of *Spirit of the Mountains*, which was produced by a number of entities with core direction from the Tułit'a District Land Corporation.

Individual families and groups had their own preferred routes to and from the mountains. The last people that I remember making the trek were David and Blandine Wright in the late 1950s. They left Fort Norman, on the east side of the Dehcho, in the late fall and paddled downstream to the mouth of the Little Bear River, on the west side of the river. They would likely have cached their canoe or simply abandoned it, with the intention of constructing a new one the following summer. From there they would have walked on their trail into the foothills of the mountains. It would have been a beautiful time of year with some snow on the ground and other hints of winter to come, tempered by the warm sun during the day. Berries would still

PART I

Map of Shúhta Got'ıne Néné. Credit: Tulít'a District Land Corporation/NWT Protected Areas Strategy.

have been readily available, and the animals would also have been busy preparing for winter. I don't know how long the walk would have taken, but I speculate that it would have been a few weeks. They likely had some dogs, which were used to pack supplies. Of course, David and Blandine would have carried packs as well as their guns. In addition to staples, such as dried meat, dried fish, tea, sugar, flour, and salt, they would also have been carrying ammunition and snares. They likely killed small game to eat on the way to their wintering area. The dogs likely carried the tent, traps, and other heavy or bulky items.

David and Blandine Wright, last of the old-timers. The picture would have been taken in the early 1960s. Credit: Chief Albert Wright School and Judith Wright Bird.

Once they reached their wintering area, they would have settled in for a stay, started hunting bigger game for food, and set fishnets once the lakes froze over. They would have likely left the sled and harnesses for the dogs from the previous winters' stays. This allowed them to use the dogs in the winter. The dogs would have been used to haul wood to the camp for the fires that kept them warm. They would also have been active every day harvesting food for themselves and the dogs as well as setting and checking snares and traps and pulling the nets for fresh fish. Life was good for this old couple, as it had been for the ones who came before them.

As I ponder what I am writing, I wonder if the Shúhta Got'ine had dog harnesses and carioles before the Europeans and the Métis came to the country. It is likely that they would have travelled by walking with pack dogs, year-round, prior to contact. The carioles and dog harnesses would have been brought to them by the Europeans and the Métis. I do not say this to disparage the Shúhta Got'ine. I say this in the hope that we can find the truth about how they really lived. I don't doubt that once this exchange of technology took place, the Shúhta Got'ine would have improved on it. There have been many suppositions about this, usually through the lens of the time that the supposition is being written.

The fur bearers they trapped were to earn cash when they returned to Fort Norman in the spring/summer of the following year. I have a modest collection of northern books, and one of my favourites is *Son of the North*, by Charles Camsell, whose family we will see more of later in this narrative. Camsell spent two years in Fort Norman, starting in 1895. He was the teacher at a small school run by the Anglican Church. He was born in Fort Liard and was raised there and in Fort Simpson, so he knew his way around the bush. Chapter seven of his book is titled "Native Life." It is one of the best descriptions of life in the North at that time that I have read. I first read the book when I was quite young. It was loaned to me by Mama, who was an avid reader. Camsell described a trip that he made to the Mackenzie Mountain foothills from Fort Norman by dog team in February or March 1896:

> *I remember a winter visit that I made out of Fort Norman to the camp of the Mountain Indian Chief, Little Dog. I remember it largely because of one observation that I made at that time and which has always remained with me. Little Dog belonged to the old school, and he never wore trousers, either in winter or summer. His ancestors had never done so, and he was not going to adopt any whims of the fashion makers of the outside world.*

Camsell tells his readers that Little Dog was around sixty years old at the time and then provides further detail of his clothing:

> *On his feet he wore moccasins, over socks consisting of a square of blanket material. His legs were partly covered with cloth leggings decorated with coloured yarn or bead work and reaching a little above his knees. His thighs were bare. The upper part of his body was covered with a shirt which hung loose. Over this was the black cloth Hudson's Bay capot which overlapped his leggings by a few inches and was held in place by leather strings and by a decorative "assumption" belt about his waist. The capot was surmounted by a hood, usually thrown back on the shoulders except in the coldest weather. His head was bound with a red cotton handkerchief to keep his long black hair tidy. Outdoors he wore mooseskin mittens which were attached to a worsted cord slung around his neck. He had no pockets but tucked under his belt was his tobacco pouch, which carried his knife, his pipe and the old fashioned flint and steel with a piece of touchwood for starting a fire.*

> *With this outfit one would wonder how could he possibly survive the temperatures of forty and fifty degrees {Fahrenheit} below zero*

quite common in that country, but he did. His hunting grounds were in the deep woods and he could always find shelter and make a fire to get warm.

I still shudder when I think of Little Dog and his haberdashery! I have been out in the weather that Camsell describes, and I can tell you that I would not go without long johns, denim pants, and snow pants to keep my nethers from freezing. My feet would be covered in two pairs of wool socks, heavy duffels, and mukluks tied tightly to keep the snow and cold out.

Once the longer, warmer days began in March and April, Little Dog and his people would, as would the Wrights, start moving south toward the banks of the Begádǫh/Gravel River to prepare for the return to Fort Norman after the rivers broke up. The return to Fort Norman would be by moose-skin boats. Preparation for the boat trip would include hunting and killing many moose. The hides, after the hair had been scraped off, would be wrapped around handmade spruce frames to build the moose-skin boats. These boats would bring them, their families, their dogs, and some dried meat and preserved fat to Fort Norman. Camsell tells us that the return to Fort Norman, in his day, would have been in early July for a quick bit of trading.

The Shúhta Got'ıne would then return to the mountains by going up the Begádǫh/Gravel and spending the summer hunting and killing big game, mostly moose. They would dry the meat and prepare the fat with wild berries for storage. In September they would return to Fort Norman with more moose-skin boats loaded with bales of dried meat, pounded meat, grease, and fat and trade that with the HBC for goods to get through the winter. Everything that Camsell wrote rang true with me. However, I was and continue to be saddened by having seen the last of this lifestyle, including the return of the last true moose-skin boats to Fort Norman from the mountains in the late 1950s. These boats were made entirely of biodegradable materials, which could be put to other uses.

Included in my art collection is a wood-block print by Maurice Cloughley that I treasure—83/200. It is of what I call the last real moose-skin boat trip. One of the reasons I treasure the print is because it is from a photograph taken by Cloughley in 1959, which triggers a fond memory for me. Although we had nothing to do with the photo, my friend, Mike Gladu, and I found a way to the water and went swimming in the Mackenzie River at that time. It was very cold—those are giant ice blocks behind the image of the moose-skin boats.

PART I

"Moose-skin canoes at Fort Norman."
Credit: Maurice R. Cloughley (*The Spell of the Midnight Sun*).

Again, I ponder as I write. I do not intend in any way to call into question the resourcefulness of the Shúhta Got'ine in the construction of these boats. However, if one looks at pictures of York boats, one will see that the design of the moose-skin boat is very similar to the York boats. The resourcefulness of the Shúhta Got'ine lay in using the materials that they had available to them to create what they did, even if it was modelled on what was brought to them.

York boats. Credit HBC Heritage.

The York boats were used on the Mackenzie River starting not long after Mackenzie's trip to the Arctic Ocean until the advent of steam boats on the Mackenzie River after 1885. The Prince of Wales Northern Heritage Centre says this about the moose-skin boat: "From the late 1800s to the 1950s, mooseskin boats were built by the Shuhtahgot'ine (Mountain Dene) to carry large amounts of cargo along dangerous mountain rivers."

The boats were built to get to Fort Norman to trade with the HBC. One of Mama's stories is about this trade. What the Shúhta Got'ine had to trade were furs, fresh moose meat, dried moose meat, pounded moose meat, fat and grease. To get sufficient quantities of these goods to Fort Norman, they needed large boats. Mama said that they would bring large amounts of these trade goods into Fort Norman in September and then return to Begahdeh by foot up the Gravel River. The trade goods would be exchanged with the HBC for items that the Shúhta Got'ine did not have—ammunition, steel traps, tea, sugar, flour, and so forth.

The Shúhta Got'ine would then return to Fort Norman by dog team around Christmas time with furs, which they would exchange for more manufactured goods, as well as the moose meat products that they had exchanged for southern goods earlier in the year. The HBC was, in effect, used as warehousemen. Coincidentally, they would also attend Christmas services put on by the Anglican Church.

Although Allan and Mary Hardisty were Shúhta Got'ine, they mostly remained in Fort Norman, where Allan carried out his duties for the Anglican Church. These duties included hunting and fishing in the winter, so Allan was able to keep these skills honed. Even though they were, by nature, Shúhta Got'ine, they were, by nurture, adopting a new lifestyle that would be assumed by the Métis, or Half-Breeds, as they were then known, over time. Allan and Mary had many Half-Breed grandchildren, many of whom we will meet later.

They would have known Camsell, as he was there at the same time that they were. It appears that Camsell may have been sent to Fort Norman to take over the teaching duties from Allan, freeing him up to carry on his other responsibilities such as preaching to the Dene in their own language.

I find it very interesting that both of my antecedent Indigenous roots are from people who were adapting to the changing lifestyle that had started in the North in the first half of the nineteenth century. One family was changing through the fur trade with the HBC. This family was Catholic. The other was changing through the missionary activities of the Anglican Church. They were, of course, Anglican. Interestingly, both roots merged into one family to give rise to the Half-Breeds who, with other families, over two generations, became known as Mackenzie River Métis.

CHAPTER THREE

EUROPEAN ROOTS

My first European ancestor to enter the Mackenzie River District and live there, for two years, was Alexander Munro Fisher. I want to acknowledge the work done by a Fisher relative, Art Fisher, of Regina, Saskatchewan, who put together extensive research on the Fisher family. He sent me a copy of that work in February 1998. Art is a descendant of Alexander's brother, Henry Munro Fisher. The Fisher and Munro families are both from Scotland. They came to North America in 1757 and 1759, respectively, to fight for the British against the French and the Indians. They settled in what is now New York State after that war. Then came the American Revolution, and they chose to remain loyal to the British Crown. As a result, the families became United Empire Loyalists and moved to Montreal. At about the same point in history, in 1776, Donald Fisher married Elizabeth Munro in New York State. In 1783, Elizabeth gave birth to her second son, Alexander Munro Fisher.

Alexander was born and raised in Montreal and likely started out life working for his father, who became a tailor in that city. Alexander eventually joined the HBC. Although he reached the level of chief trader, a level he retained until his retirement in 1845, he was not particularly popular. He seemed to have been despised by Sir George Simpson, as set out in Simpson's "character book." An entry from the character book is included in Fisher's biographical sheet, maintained by the HBC Archives, which says he was, "a trifling thoughtless superficial lying creature . . . becoming so much to liquor that I found it necessary to remove him . . . to one of our most Sober Stations." I assume the sober station was Fort Good Hope.

Based on what I have been able to read about Alexander, I would say that he was an unsavoury character. But, for better or for worse, he was my great-great-grandfather. He spent time in Fort Good Hope as the chief trader for approximately two years: 1841/1842. He had left his "country wife," Angelique Savard, in Fort Chipewyan the previous summer. When she finally arrived in Fort Good Hope, she was pregnant by another man, and Fisher "turned her off" and left her in Fort Chipewyan in 1843 on his way back to Montreal. In the meantime, Fisher had a brief tryst with Elise Taupier while in Fort Simpson, which resulted in the birth of Marie Fisher. Payment tells us that we know very little about Marie's youth, but it seems clear that Alexander Fisher acknowledged her as his daughter and, as a result, she was able to use his name. Payment speculates that Fisher probably provided for her before he left the North for good. Fisher died on April 2, 1847, in Montreal, two years after his retirement. Having been a chief trader for twenty-two years, he likely died a wealthy man.

I use two terms in this book that not all readers will be familiar with. The first is "country marriage" or "country wife." This form of marriage was generally between a European fur trader and an Indigenous woman. First, it was a reference to the lack of church blessing. Today it is called "shacking up." Second, it was used as an indication that the European man only meant it to be a marriage while he was in the "country." The phrase "turned off," or variations thereof, indicates an end to a relationship. It indicated a divorce, without the "husband" having to worry about any legal or religious niceties. The "wife" was usually left to fend for herself.

Marie would have been approaching four years old when her father died. It is almost as if Alexander Fisher came and planted his seed and then left, never to be seen again. Marie's mother, Elise, married Francois Houle, a Métis interpreter for the HBC, in the aftermath. Francois became Marie's stepfather. It seems clear that Francois Houle was a Red River Métis, and Elise was, at least, a Mackenzie River Métis, so it would be natural to assume that Marie was raised as a Métis. It is also safe to assume that she spent time as a child in Red River while Francois was on a two-year leave (called a "retirement" in the HBC records). The retirement would have been necessary as Houle was not an officer of the HBC and, therefore, not entitled to the two-year sabbaticals that officers were. When he returned to the Mackenzie River District, he rejoined the HBC. At the time Francois was in "retirement" in Red River Country, he, Elise and Marie went to Saint Boniface, and Elise was baptized as a Catholic. It seems reasonable to surmise that seven-year-old Marie would have also been baptized at the same time.

I was surprised to find a certification of birth issued by Father Robin in Fort Good Hope on July 12, 1915, in the material that Julien Gaudet, her cousin, had sent to Mama. The certificate confirms the baptism of Julien's father, Joseph Leon Gaudet, in the year he was born, 1875. Joseph Leon was the youngest son of Charles Phillipe and Marie. Like his older brothers, Joseph Leon also went into the service of the HBC when he completed his education.

The surprise in the certificate is that Joseph Leon's godparents were Francois Houle and Elise Taupier. This finding explains the references by Payment to Marie's parents being close by for support. Payment goes on as follows:

Marie Fisher's parents had a fishing camp at some distance from the fort, and Marie liked to accompany them on hunting and trading expeditions. Like other local Métis and Slavey women, she filleted and dried fish—an important food staple—snared rabbits, trapped small fur-bearing animals, and cultivated a large root garden.

Charles Phillipe Gaudet, in his "Indian outfit," taken while the family was on a trip to Ottawa to visit his mother in 1867 and 1868.
Credit: Montreal Gaudet Family.

Until I found Payment's references and then the certificate, I thought Elise Taupier had disappeared from our story. She likely became known as Elise Houle, having married Francois.

If we apply the nature measurement against Marie, she would be one quarter Shúhta Got'ıne. Of course, this assumes that her grandmother, Elise's mother, was Shúhta Got'ine and not from some other First Nation. However, if we apply the nurture measurement, then it would be fair to say that she was Métis without reference to any blood quantum.

My second European ancestor to "settle" in the Mackenzie River District was Charles Phillipe Gaudet. Charles Phillipe was born in Montreal on May 1, 1828. A family tree prepared by our late cousin, Julien Gaudet, son of Joseph Leon, sent to Mama in 1982, with years and full names adjusted by me, shows Charles Phillipe's parents being Joseph Timothee Gaudet (1791–1841) and Dorothee Elizabeth Short (1790 -?). Dorothee would have lived at least until 1868 when Charles Phillipe, Marie and their children visited her in Ottawa.

Payment, in a note to *Une femme En Vaut Deux,* says: "The Gaudet family was of Acadian origin. The first male ancestor arrived in Port Royal from France in 1632, and the descendants suffered the expulsion of the Acadians by the British in 1755." Charles Phillipe joined the HBC in 1851 and was sent to the Mackenzie River District that same year, where he spent sixty years in the service of the HBC, with the last forty-eight of those years in Fort Good Hope. He spent fifteen of those years, from 1863 to 1878, as a clerk, and thirty-three years, from 1878 to 1911, as a chief trader. He stayed in Fort Good Hope for an additional six years as a retiree, from 1911 to 1917. During his years as a retiree, his son, Frederic Charles, was the clerk in Fort Good Hope for what appears to be three outfits. It seems that being a retiree entitled the employee to retain possession of the house they had lived in. This was also the case with my grandfather, Charles Timothy Gaudet, in Fort Norman, after he retired in 1930.

The HBC had many categories of employees, as described in a document from the HBC Archives. It seems that the ranks, in order, were as follows: chief factor, chief trader, factor and clerk. There is also another category called post master, which, as near as I can figure, was a step below a clerk. Only the chief factors and the chief traders were officers and shared in the profits of each outfit. An outfit would be what is today called a fiscal year. An outfit lasted from June 1 of one year to May 31 of the next. Although all four of Charles Phillipe's sons "joined the service," none rose above the rank of clerk. I have often wondered about this. Looking at pictures of the sons, I think that Frederic Charles, at least, had the presence to rise to the rank of an officer. Frederic Charles finished his career at the HBC warehouse in Montreal as a warehouseman. To be fair, I should acknowledge that the company stopped appointing "officers" after the council meeting of 1887 in Winnipeg. But still, a warehouseman?

Even though the HBC had abolished the system of officers it still had a normal management structure, as most other businesses in Canada did. As far as I could determine, the "native sons" did not advance very far within the company after 1887.

Marie (Fisher) Gaudet, holding her dead child, Sara, who died in Ottawa during the 1867/1868 trip. Two other children, Elizabeth and Marie, died in Cumberland House on the return to Fort Good Hope in June 1868.
Credit: Montreal Gaudet Family.

PART I

15

As I was nearing the end of the penultimate draft of this book, I came across a thesis by Denise Fuchs to the Department of History at the University of Manitoba. I was actually looking to see if I could find anything at St. John's College about Allan Hardisty, who had received some education in Winnipeg. I did not find anything on him, but I did find a plethora of information about William Lucas Hardisty, who had adopted Allan. Fuchs's thesis is titled *Native Sons of Rupert's Land 1760 to the 1860s*. To me it was a fascinating read for two reasons. The first was the discovery that William Lucas Hardisty was of mixed blood. His father was Richard Hardisty Sr., and his mother was Margaret Sutherland, who was "of mixed descent." William Lucas also married a woman "of mixed descent" named Mary Allen. However, Fuchs says: "William Lucas . . . was another native son who appeared virtually non-native in the records and whose attitudes toward Indians reflected those of his European counterparts."

The second point of interest for me was the extensive review done by Fuchs of the prejudice that the "Native Sons" faced in the service of the HBC. Fuchs concluded that:

The examination of the attitudes that informed the manner in which they were depicted in the records and their educational achievements and careers within the fur trade reveals that cultural and racial biases affected their lives, in both subtle and direct ways.

Fuchs's coverage ends in 1870, but I believe that the biases continued well into the twentieth century.

My aunt, Jane Gaudet, worked for many decades at the store in Fort Norman and, in fact, earned a retirement pension. However, there is no mention of her in any of the HBC records, including the biographical sheets. My speculation is that the HBC had some sort of a bias against women working in what was then called the Northern Stores Division.

The Anglican Church leaders were avid supporters of the HBC and vice versa. It seems clear that the same attitudes that were prevalent among the "non-mixed descent" employees of the HBC were also present among the same group in the Anglican Church. That likely explains why I could not find anything about Allan Hardisty in the Anglican Church Archives. It is a terrible legacy that we contributed to ourselves. From Charles Phillipe right to, and including, my generation, we would have been very happy if we could have passed ourselves off, as William Lucas Hardisty and his brothers did. However, that did not happen, and we have all become stronger as Mackenzie River Métis.

Charles Phillipe and Marie were married in Fort Simpson in 1858. Marie was fifteen years old at the time. Thus, my European bloodlines, Scottish and French, and my Indigenous bloodlines, were merged into one, in the children of Charles Phillipe and Marie. Based on the foregoing, we can surmise when we became Métis. While there was no big boom, might there have been a bit of a hiccup in the universe at that moment?

Payment refers to Elise as Métis. Like the big boom of science, our little hiccup is murky. Based on the facts that we do know, mostly provided by Payment, it is reasonable to speculate that Elise would have been born around 1815 or so and had a career as a Bully before she met Alexander Fisher and gave birth to Marie in 1843. We can accept that Elise was Métis, and her husband, after Fisher, Francois Houle, was clearly Métis.

That, from my point of view, makes it clear that Charles Phillipe Gaudet married a Métis. Two of their sons, John Peter and Charles Timothy, applied for and were granted scrip. The first to do so was John Peter. His application was made under the Athabasca District Half-Breed Commission on June 22, 1899, with the payment of $240 being made on August 28, 1899. In his application, John Peter described his mother as a Half-Breed and called her Mary Houle. At the time, John Peter was not married and was a clerk for the HBC at Lesser Slave Lake.

Charles Timothy made his application, along with those of his wife and children, to the Mackenzie River District Half-Breed Commission on July 15, 1921, in Fort Norman. The family was paid $2,640 in June of 1924. Charles Timothy described his mother as a Half-Breed and used the name Mary Fisher. The amount of $2,640 would be worth $41,155 in 2021.

Whether anyone likes it or not, the Government of Canada was the government of the country at that time and continues to be so to this day. The scrip applications of John Peter and Charles Timothy, and the approvals by Canada, are authority enough for the descendants of John Peter and Charles Timothy to be clearly acknowledged as "Métis" under section 35 of the Constitution Act, 1982. To be clear, it is common knowledge that the term "Half-Breed" has long fallen into disuse, being replaced by "Métis."

I gave a private talk to lawyers from my old law firm, Davis & Company in the summer of 2021, and among a variety of topics, I tried to explain the origins of the Métis. The foregoing is an excerpt from the notes I prepared for that talk.

Many will ask who are these "Métis"? Aren't they just Indians? Sometimes the answer is that Métis are Indians in a hurry!

PART I

17

In order to properly answer the question, we need to go back to the origins of mankind. I believe in the science that tells us that all human beings originated out of Africa. I am sure that it is commonly accepted that when we originated out of Africa, we did not come out as the many, many races and nationalities that currently inhabit the earth. No, we emerged as one people.

As this one people spread around the world, many different races and nationalities developed and continue to develop. Where did the Scots come from? Where did the French come from? And so on and so on. The Métis emerged, as did the Scots and the French, as a developing and then as a distinct people. The difference being that this only happened very recently for the Métis, relatively speaking. Primarily, the Métis resulted from unions between European fur traders and Indigenous women. As the number of these mixed-bloods increased, they coalesced into what they are today—the Métis. It is interesting that there is no group of Métis that originates with the Inuit. There are many mixed-blood Inuit, but they overwhelmingly identify as Inuit and not as anything else.

I would suggest that this is a result of acceptance by the Inuit of the mixed-blood progeny into their families. On the other hand, neither the Indian nor the European families were, usually, very accepting of the mixed-bloods that they produced. I should know as I have been called a "Goddamned Half-Breed" often enough by both the Dene and the White people here in Canada. There is no hard and fast rule that says the mixed-bloods must be Métis. I know mixed-bloods who have chosen to identify as Indian. In some cases it is a genuine feeling that they are Indians and not Métis. In other cases it is a simple economic choice. If you are an Indian or an Inuit, you get many benefits from the Government of Canada that Métis don't get. These benefits include extended health benefits, post-secondary education support, and business support. This is part of the emergence and growth of a people to choose, individually, what is important.

The story will continue to be written for many generations to come. The descendants of some people who are thought of as Métis today will merge into the Indian group that they live amongst. In those cases there will be no Métis amongst them, as there are no Métis amongst the Inuit. We are on the shakeout cruise.

Two or three generations ago, many mixed-bloods chose to identify as European, mostly French. This was a result of the shame and prejudices that they had to live with, primarily from those of European descent. Many people in my extended family faced this situation when they moved from the North to cities in Canada.

I went on to say that the reverse is true today. Many of the Métis of today are embarrassed by their European heritage, so they tend to join the Indian group that they are descended from. Perhaps the day will come when these individuals will realize that they are neither, and they will also be proud to say, "We Are Métis." I, for one, will be happy to welcome them home.

While I am on the subject of our European ancestors, I have to say this. I get a good laugh whenever I hear, or hear of, the many young Indigenous people and the many ignorant journalists who complain about cultural appropriation by non-Indigenous people in Canada. Give me a break. Take some time to thank the Scots for bringing us bannock. Take time to thank the French for bringing us fry bread. Take time to thank both the Scots and the French for bringing us the fiddle and the jigs and reels that we now claim as our own. There are so many other things that are claimed to be "traditional" but really have their origins with our European ancestors. To me, "traditional" means, in the case of the Mackenzie River District, anything that Indians or Inuit made or did prior to the arrival of the Europeans' and the Metis.

PART I

19

CHAPTER FOUR

THE GAUDETS

"Old man, he die." Those were the words that Theresa Campbell, out of breath from running, shouted to us early in the day on Friday, July 18, 1952. This was how we learned that my grandfather, Charles Timothy Gaudet, had died. My memories of this sad event are partially actual recall and partially from stories told to me by Mama. My sister, Diana, was born three and half months before Granddad's death. My brothers, Rod and Leo, were still in hospitals with tuberculosis, away from the community. I don't recall my other brother, Walter, being around when this happened, but he would have been. He was twelve years old at that time.

The evening before he died, Granddad came to visit us at our home. In 1952 there were no moving vehicles in Fort Norman except for a few tractors. There were no telephones, no television, and few distractions. The one constant connection to the outside world was AM (called longwave at the time) radio, which we listened to on large battery-powered sets. The reception for the radios was not that good in the summertime. As a result, most people did a lot of visiting early in the evening before the card games began. Aunt Christine, Aunt Cecilia, Aunt Jane, Uncle Fred, and their families all owned properties adjacent to each other at the south end of the community. We lived at the other end of the community. Granddad's house was at the centre of the community, right beside the HBC compound. The evening of July 17, 1952, must have been our turn for a visit from him.

I do not remember this, but Mama told me the story so many times that I may as well have. Mama and I were in our yard with Granddad, and a storm was starting to form over the Mackay Range, to the west of us. The sky was turning dark and ominous, and there was rain in the air. Our yard had a well-kept lawn, flowerbeds, and a picket fence. I kept pulling on Granddad's pant leg, telling him to hurry up and go home or else he was going to get wet from the rain. He turned to Mama and, in his heavy French accent, said, "Well Aleees, I guess Reechard does not want me here, so I better go home." He said this jovially with a smile on his face and then headed off to his house on the second bench of the community. Grandparents have many favourite grandchildren over the years, and I was, apparently, having my turn. That was the last time we saw him alive.

Gaudet House in Fort Norman, 1932. Credit: NWT Archives/R. E. Howell photograph collection.

We called him Granddad. Some people called him Old Tim, and others called him CTG or the Old Man. Having spent his entire life in the service of the HBC, he was likely called other less pleasant names as well. He was born in Fort Good Hope in the Mackenzie River District on May 5, 1872. He was eighty years old when he died from a sudden stroke while he was hoeing the potatoes in his garden. His house and his garden overlooked the Anglican mission. The property is now owned by the Tulít'a Dene Band. They have built an arbour where his house used to be, and the Robert D. Clement Building, where the Band has its offices, is built on the ground where the garden was. Band Council members complain, from time to time, about a ghost, possibly his, in the building. Like his father before him, Granddad was an HBC pensioner and continued "assisting" the company to the end of his life. Assisting meant taking the hands of the new breed of managers, mostly from Scotland, and keeping them from making too many mistakes. It also meant being language interpreters for these new managers.

∞

I do remember the immediate period after Theresa got to our house and delivered the news. Everyone in the house began wailing and crying. This was quite confusing to me as I did not know what "He die" meant. Theresa spoke pidgin English. We had an upstairs in our house, and I was sitting on the top step of the narrow staircase all alone. I didn't know why, but I joined the wailing and crying, as what was happening made me feel very sad. Although I didn't know what it was, I did know that something very bad had happened. My tears rolled freely.

Theresa Campbell was Sahtú Got'ıne, originally from Great Bear Lake. She was widowed. She lived with Granddad and his spinster daughter, Aunt Jane Gaudet. Theresa was more or less the maid for the household. She was also Aunt Jane's hunting and trapping partner. As with many English names, Theresa's was given a Dene inflection, and she was called "Darazha." Of course, two of my older brothers, Walter and Rod, couldn't resist teasing the poor woman by calling her "Tarzan." At least that is what I was told. This, of course, would anger Theresa, but the two scoundrels could always outrun her—little buggers. Tarzan movies were big in the community at that time. As there was no theatre, the movies were shown in the school classroom.

Even at the age of eighty, Granddad was still the dominating figure in Fort Norman. He had married Sarah Jane Hardisty in 1899. They made their lives between Fort Norman and Fort Wrigley as Granddad was shifted back and forth by the HBC. They had thirteen children. Granny, as she was called, predeceased Granddad in 1943. Unfortunately for me, I never met her, as I was not born until 1947. However, based on Mama's and Aunt Jane's stories, I felt like I knew her.

Leo Hardy and Rod Hardy, on one of their dad's horses in front of the Gaudet House in Fort Norman, c. 1947. Credit: Hardy Family Collection.

Six of their children predeceased Granddad and Granny— George (b. 1900), John (b. 1901), Mary (b. 1903), Rosie (b. 1905), Leon (b. 1915), and Charlie (b. 1918). Seven of the children were still alive at the time of Granddad's death—Cecilia (b. 1904), Bella (b. 1907), Frederick (b. 1910), Alice (Mama) (b. 1911), Jane (b. 1914), Christine (b. 1920), and George (b. 1921).

Of the seven children still alive, five of them made their homes in Fort Norman in 1952.

Tim Gaudet, c. 1898, in Fort Norman, proudly wearing the hat and button of a HBC manager. Credit: Provincial Archives of Alberta 0614149.

The sixth child still alive, Aunt Bella, had married Ted Trindell and was living in Fort Simpson, where they made their home. Interestingly, Ted Trindell had married the oldest Gaudet daughter, Mary, first, but she, unfortunately, died about three years after marrying him as a result of childbirth complications. Unfortunately, the baby also died. Bella, with two daughters from a previous relationship, married Ted a few years later, and he adopted her two daughters. The first daughter was born in December 1934, and the second was born in September 1935.

Uncle George, the seventh child, was working for Imperial Oil in Norman Wells and spent most of his time there. He returned to Fort Norman a year or so after Granddad died.

PART I

Granddad was reputedly a tyrant over his family. He would only allow his children to marry other Half-Breeds or White people. At least that was the way that "rule" was passed on to our generation. It is likely that the "rule" came from his parents. The anomaly being that Sarah Jane Hardisty was neither a Half-Breed or a White Person but was a full-blooded Shúhta Got'ıne. She was also educated and was a Christian, as was her father. I think this was what the "rule" meant. Unfortunately, it got couched in the wrong terms. Hindsight can help understand anomalies of this sort.

∞

As I did the research for this book, I came to see a different picture of Granddad than the one some of his descendants have of him being a hard-nosed bully. He and Sarah Jane were married on July 15, 1899. He was 27 years old and she was 18. He was the clerk (manager) of the post in Fort Norman. She would have recently rejoined her family in Fort Norman after having attended the Anglican residential schools in Fort Resolution and Hay River. I imagine him seeing her for the first time, a sixteen-year-old beauty, disembarking the steam boat on a beautiful warm and sunny day, looking radiant and pure. I imagine that he fell in love with her on the spot. Marrying her would mean opposing his own mother who was rabidly Catholic. Not only would he be marrying an Anglican, he would be signing a contract committing all of their children to the Anglican church and the wedding would take place in the Holy Trinity Anglican church in Fort Norman.

He was faced with choosing to be with the woman he was madly in love with and incurring the wrath of a domineering mother. He chose love. Sarah Jane became pregnant and their first child, a son named George Alexander, was born on June 21, 1900. George died that same year. A second child, a son named John, was born in 1901 and also died shortly after his birth. I can only imagine the agony that they felt by this point in time. We know that George was accepted into the Anglican church a few days before he died. However, we don't know if John was received as well. I can imagine the pall that fell over the lives of Tim and Sarah Jane. I can imagine both questioning their decisions to marry someone not of their faith.

I am attaching a copy of the "contract" that Granddad signed in order to marry Sarah Jane.

Marriage contract signed by Tim Gaudet. Credit: Anglican Church of Canada, General Synod Archives.

Besides marrying a person who was uneducated, having a child without being married was also unacceptable to Granddad. When Aunt Bella committed her indiscretions, as discussed earlier, she was expelled from the Gaudet household and had to fend for herself. Mama told me that the RC Mission had a small shack on its property, and Bella was allowed to live there. The father of the two girls was a free trader, competing with the HBC in Fort Norman, and was already married. Additionally, he was not a Half-Breed or a White man. He was, in fact, from either Syria or Lebanon. His name was M. T. Jomha, and he traded in Fort Norman from 1927 to 1937. Now, he is simply another person who has disappeared from our story.

Bella eventually found employment at the hospital in Fort Simpson and moved there with her children. It is likely that this was when she and Ted decided to marry.

Granddad and Aunt Bella must have reconciled after she married Ted. After all, she was now properly married and had a man who would be a father to her children. Bella told me a story about the huge batches of bannock that she would cook for Granddad whenever he passed through Fort Simpson on his river trips.

Nine of the thirteen children were still alive during the scrip period from 1921 to 1924. Six were Catholic. The other three were, to the best of my knowledge, Anglicans. The thirteenth child, Uncle George Gaudet, was not born until a month after the scrip applications were made. Consequently, he could not be included because the Order in Council that established the Mackenzie River District Half-Breed Commission, specified that an applicant had to be alive on the date that Treaty 11 was made in Fort Providence. That date was June 27, 1921. Uncle George was born on August 10, 1921. Thus, he missed the scrip cut-off by forty-four days. That probably didn't matter as all of the scrip money went into the purchase of a schooner by Granddad. Mama told me that she and the other children were not happy about this, especially when the schooner sank!

I am not absolutely sure if Mary was actually a Catholic. We have the wedding picture of her and Uncle Ted, taken in 1929. The bridesmaid is Aunt Bella, and the best man is Uncle Joe Hall. I have a hard time imagining Uncle Joe in a Catholic Church, so it may have been an Anglican wedding.

L to R: Joe Hall, Bella Gaudet, Ted Trindell and Mary (Gaudet) Trindell at Ted and Mary's wedding in 1929 in Fort Simpson.
Credit: Hardy Family Collection.

As earlier described, the Gaudet family origins in the present-day Northwest Territories started in 1851 when young Charles Phillipe Gaudet, who was already in the service of the HBC, was posted to Fort Youcon. To get there he had to travel from Norway House and follow the trading routes into the Mackenzie River District. He then followed the open water in 1851 down the Mackenzie River and up the Peel River by York boat. He was twenty-two or twenty-three years old at the time. Fort Youcon was in Russian territory at that time.

MOLAZHA

The HBC Heritage website describes the invention and history of the York boats used to service all of the HBC inland posts. The boat could carry about three times as much freight as the largest canoes. The name "York" is from York Factory, on Hudson's Bay, where the boats were built by Orkney men specifically recruited for this purpose. The York boats were still in use along the Mackenzie River and its tributaries in the mid-1880s. The coming of steamships eventually replaced them. Coincidentally the beginning of the use of moose-skin boats coincided with the HBC no longer using the York Boats.

I understand that Charles Phillipe entered into a country marriage with a Gwich'in woman while he worked in the Gwich'in territory, first at Fort Youcon and then at La Pierre's House. I also understand that there was a child, a girl, from this relationship. Payment says that her name was Eliza, and her mother's name was Natalie. The 1911 census shows an Eliza Denezouli, age fifty-eight, and a Loucheux (Gwich'in), as the wife of Denezouli, age sixty, and also a Loucheux (Gwich'in). The census reported that they were living in Fort Wrigley at the time. This woman was likely the country child of Charles Phillipe. I understand that Eliza lived with the Gaudet family until she formed her own family. I don't know if she left any descendants. Interestingly, Charles Timothy was the post manager in Fort Wrigley in 1911. I would assume that he acknowledged Eliza as his sister. Who knows?

If the information found in the 1911 census is correct, Eliza was born in 1853. Charles Phillipe was the post master in Fort Youcon in 1851/1852 and in La Pierre's House in 1852/1853. He returned to Fort Youcon for three more years, starting in 1854/1855. After he married Marie Fisher in 1858, he was sent to Fort Resolution for one year and was then sent to Fort McPherson, which at the time was called Peel's River, for three years. After that, he and Marie and Eliza moved to Fort Good Hope. Charles Phillipe was posted to Gwich'in country for a total of eight years and spent much more time there while he was the chief trader in Fort Good Hope, with responsibility for the Gwich'in country. Interestingly, Fort Youcon is in Alaska now but was still Russian territory while he was posted there. It is now spelled "Yukon."

Payment alludes to Eliza being at the wedding in Fort Simpson. Perhaps I have read too much into what she has to say. However, it still begs the question: how did the Gaudets come to raise Eliza and maintain what appears to be a lifelong relationship with her? Did her mother, Natalie, die while Eliza was young?

PART I

27

Charles Phillipe was known to have been a devout Catholic. However, there are records showing that he converted to the Anglican Church on August 24, 1858, while in Fort Simpson, under the guidance of Archdeacon James Hunter. He likely did this for business purposes. This "conversion" took place four days after he and Marie were married in the Catholic church in Fort Simpson. Being French and Catholic at that time was not a good combination for advancement in the HBC. Payment writes that he forced Marie to go through a second wedding in the Anglican Church after already being married in the Catholic Church. After that happened, he would have been able to say to his superiors that he was baptized as an Anglican and was married in the Anglican Church.

Martha McCarthy also explored the religious travails of Charles Phillipe in *From the Great River to the Ends of the Earth.* She had this to say:

> *One of the supporters of the Anglicans at this early stage was Charles P. Gaudet. Gaudet had been the only Catholic, and the only French-Canadian, in the upper ranks of the HBC of the Mackenzie District. Upward mobility in the company seemed to demand acceptance of the anti-Catholic and pro-Anglican stance of those in charge of the district. Archdeacon Hunter received Gaudet into the Church of England in 1858; Mr. Kirkby performed his marriage service at Fort Simpson in 1859.*

I wonder why Charles Phillipe did not do a better job of preparing his sons for the prejudices and biases that they would face in their careers with the HBC. This is especially relevant in light of his difficulties resulting from being French and Catholic with a Half-Breed wife and children. Perhaps he was simply an optimist.

∞

As referred to earlier, Alexander Munro Fisher, Marie's father, served as chief trader in Fort Good Hope in 1841 and 1842. While he was in charge of the northern Mackenzie River District from the post in Fort Good Hope, the Indians and the Whites of the area suffered from famine. Fisher wrote a report on the famine for the HBC. The report is in his handwriting and is available online from the HBC Archives. It is written in the style of those days. My wife, Maryann, has done her best to put the words into today's fonts. Because of the controversial nature of the content of the report, I am presenting it in its entirety.

On the 10th of Oct' /41 I reached this fort and found it well stocked with 4 Bastions, Good Houses, Stores, Many Houses and Mr. C.M. Hector M.Kenzie, a man and Mr. Satuno family consisting of five children were the only persons in the Fort, four other men were absent & at the Fisheries if they so may be called.

The Ramparts about Six miles from the Fort gave 1300 White Fish, the other Fishery La Rocques Lake four days travel from the Fort gave 230 fish, Total for the Winter 1530 fish with 1300 lbs Dried Meat in Store was all that of men 3 women & 6 children had to depend on, and at the usual rations food for 64 days. Fortunately, I brought down with me, 4 bushels Barley which Mr. Lewes intended for Mr. C.T. bell & myself but I took the whole and seeing at once that it required some great chance of Providence to save us immediately, I began to disperse my men first I sent Mr. M.Kenzie with three Indians to cut out the new road from Peels River and on the 20th Nov sent back four of my men to Ft Norman keeping only 3 men with the two families, the latter in a state unmoveable.

I then put all hands at the Fort on half allowances to (????) out the time as far as possible but at last in Febr the famine was so great and dreadful both for the Indians & Whites, that tho greatly reduced in strength I wast obligated to save myself by undertaking a voyage to Ft Norman to seek food & then persuaded Mr. McBeath to send down provisions and fetch up one of these men with his family by the time they arrived I had recovered a little in strength and returned to my charge of Ft Good Hope and found 52 Indians men, women, and Children had fallen victims and perished by famine, all within 200 yds of the Fort and the surviving of them were living on the Carcasses of their relatives. These Indians, men and women kept always their axe in hand for self-preservation and if any was found sleeping was instantly knocked in the head and as soon devoured by their best relations four perished in this manner the night after my arrival at the Fort _____ I found my man and his family living on *moose skins, pack cords, Bear Skins, Leather Sled wrappers etc.*

The little Provisions I took down from Ft. Norman saved us until the arrival of Game, Geese etc. On the 28th May Outer Land Indians arrived at the Fort and report that they have fallen on several Indian camps but found they could not distinguish who they were. All the Fresh Meat that was killed from 31st oct. to 27st May was of 68 lbs, caught 2 squirrels and one crow.

The returns were Number of Packs, 21. Amount of returns Value 1313.10.0 Apparent Gain 1113.16.0 And on the 31st Mr. C.F. Lewes arrived at Ft. Good Hope. Alex Fisher"

One of the reasons that I present the report in its entirety is because of the writings of Emile Petitot. Petitot was a Catholic priest who has attracted a great deal of controversy. Early on, Petitot was lionized for the work he did as a cartographer and linguist among the Dene people. However, when it became known that he was also a pedophile, he fell out of favour. The City of Yellowknife had named a park after him but changed it when the truth became known.

Petitot was nowhere near Fort Good Hope when the events that Alexander Fisher writes about took place. In fact, Petitot was three years old at the time and nowhere near North America. Petitot worked in Fort Good Hope from 1864 to 1878. He wrote his version of the events in 1889 after he returned to France, never to return to North America.

I found Petitot's version in a report titled "Notes on the Métis People of the North Extracted from the Writings of Emile Petitot O.M.I." by Donat Savoie, printed in September 1977. I thank my friend, James Christie, from Fort Providence for drawing my attention to this work. Savoie later completed "Land Occupancy by the Amerindians of the Canadian Northwest in the 19th Century, as reported by Emile Petitot." This work was published by Indian and Northern Affairs Canada in April 2001.

In his September 1977 work, Savoie reports that Petitot used a thinly disguised pseudonym for Fisher in his writing and put the entire blame for the famine and resulting cannibalism of 1841/1842 on Fisher, calling him debauched, immoral, licentious, and an Arctic Don Juan. While one can excuse literary licence to a certain degree, one cannot forgive outright lies. Petitot says that:

Flint [Fisher] therefore hastily prepared to flee from Fort Good Hope during the night; he and his entourage made their way to Fort Norman, then on to Fort Simpson; he later left for good.

The object of Petitot's vitriol, the one who was there, wrote a report that differs completely from Petitot's. Where did Petitot get his information? I suggest that Petitot was told some stories by Indians who might have been there thirty or so years earlier who twisted the facts to shift the blame for their heinous actions to someone else who was long dead and unable to defend himself. This is one of the earliest examples, that I am aware of, of the blame game.

∞

Charles Phillipe and Marie celebrated their fiftieth wedding anniversary in Fort Good Hope in 1908. In the pictures of the event, you can see evidence of the travels of Charles Phillipe to the South. It is rather doubtful that the clothing that the family is wearing would have been available in Fort Good Hope at that time.

Agnes Deans Cameron, a Canadian teacher and travel writer, travelled North on the *SS Mackenzie River* in 1908, and subsequently wrote about her travels in *The New North*. The *SS Mackenzie River* was new then and could, in addition to freight and crew, carry fifty passengers.

Charles Phillipe and Marie Gaudet, and some of the family, celebrating their fiftieth wedding anniversary in Fort Good Hope in 1908. Charles Phillipe is holding his grandson, Freddy. Credit: Montreal Gaudet Family.

PART I
31

Charles Phillipe and Marie Gaudet in Fort Good Hope c. 1907. Credit: Montreal Gaudet Family.

The Big House in Fort Good Hope. Charles Phillipe and Marie Gaudet with two of their daughters, c. 1907. Credit: Montreal Gaudet Family.

Inside the *SS Distributor* in 1937 to illustrate what steamboat travel on the Mackenzie River was like. The gentleman in the striped coat is Richard Bonnycastle Sr., whose diaries were a great help in reconstructing travel by the Gaudet boys to go to school in Saint Boniface. Credit: *Life Magazine* (Margaret Bourke-White).

When Agnes Deans Cameron arrived in Fort Good Hope, she spent a considerable amount of time visiting and interviewing residents. One of the first persons she saw when the *SS Mackenzie River* docked was my great-grandfather. She wrote:

Down the steps came a stately figure, Mr. C.P. Gaudet, the head and brains of Fort Good Hope. Of the two thousand servants of the Hudson's Bay Company, this is the man who has the greatest number of years of active service to his credit.

Agnes Deans Cameron also visited my great-grandmother and wrote:

We meet Mrs. Gaudet, a dear old lady with a black cap, the pinkest of pink cheeks, and the kind of smile that brings a choky feeling into your throat and makes you think of your mother. She gives us home-made wine and galettes, and we smell the mignonette flowering in the window ledge and look around the walls of the 'homey' room we wonder if this really can be the "Arctic Circle . . .".

Mrs. Gaudet thinks people rush very much nowadays. "We get mail every year without fail, and sometimes there is a second mail".

Marie died in Fort Good Hope in 1914. She is buried in a prominent location in the Roman Catholic Church cemetery there.

Agnes Deans Cameron also included a story to show the Gaudets' dedication to the HBC. She wrote about one of the daughters who had studied the Scriptures and was asked in church on a Sunday, "And how did God punish Adam and Eve for their disobedience?" The girl's answer came quickly: "They had to leave the company's service."

Charles Phillipe, Marie, and their children became active supporters of the Catholic Church after they settled in Fort Good Hope. The girls of the family provided assistance in the creation of the paintings in the church there. Emile Petitot, the now-notorious Catholic priest and explorer, is mostly credited for the paintings. The church is now a national historic site. As a result of allowing Petitot to travel with him, Charles Phillipe's name was put forward in 1871 to name two geographic sites along the Mackenzie River: Mount Gaudet and Gaudet Island. Additionally, there is a Gaudet Bay, near Fort Resolution, named for the family. Finally, there is Isabella Lake, named for Isabella Gaudet by J. M. Bell. Isabella, also known as Bella, was the oldest Gaudet child from that generation and lived a long life. She never married.

Rick Hardy at Marie (Fisher) Gaudet's grave in Fort Good Hope in 1998. Credit: Maryann Hardy.

Although Marie died three years earlier, Charles Philippe remained in Fort Good Hope until 1917, when he decided to leave to retire to his original home in Montreal. I am sure this was a difficult decision for him, as I think that he had hoped to be buried beside his beloved Marie. However, his son, Frederic, had retired on June 1, 1916, as the clerk in Fort Good Hope, and he and Bella were the only two children left in Fort Good Hope, along with Grandson Freddy. I would imagine that they encouraged the old man to leave, so he could be close to doctors and hospitals, and they could live more comfortably. It would have been a sad day when they left, leaving behind four loved ones in the graveyard.

Aunt Jane, who would have been three at the time, told me that she remembered when the steamboat that Charles Phillipe and the family was travelling on stopped at Fort Providence on its way south. She said that the nuns who were looking after them in the convent took all of them to the boat to say goodbye to their grandfather. Aunt Bella, Uncle Fred, and Mama would have been there. As for Aunt Jane, it is possible that she was there and did remember the visit. However, it is more likely that she was telling me the story based on a manufactured memory resulting from the stories told to her by her older siblings, including Mama.

Unfortunately, Charles Phillipe suffered a stroke during a stop in Winnipeg. He died there in late September 1917, with his two oldest children, Frederic and Bella, and his grandson, Freddy, at his side. He is buried in St. Norbert, which is now part of Winnipeg, beside one of his daughters, Christine Gaudet, who died on October 14, 1909. Christine, who was anemic, had been brought to Winnipeg for medical treatment earlier that year by her brother, Joseph Leon. Whatever the treatment was, it did not work. According to Payment, the family did not learn about her death until a year later when mail arrived in Fort Good Hope.

The last trip in 1917. While Frederic, Isabelle, and Freddy Gaudet were mixing with the other passengers, Charles Phillipe Gaudet was resting in his cabin. Credit: HBC Archives.

Freddy, whose full name was Frederic Alexander Gaudet, was the son of John Peter Gaudet and his wife, Margeurite St. Germaine. John Peter was the second son of Charles Phillipe and Marie. He was born on June 26, 1869, in Fort Good Hope and was raised there. John Peter and the oldest brother in the family, Frederic Charles, attended Saint Boniface College in 1881/1882 and 1882/1883. I don't know what they did in 1883/1884. All of the records of Saint Boniface College prior to 1922 were lost in a fire. What I have are copies of some yearbooks that the college salvaged, which they generously sent copies of to me. Unfortunately, there are none for the missing years. I do know that Frederic Charles started with the company as an apprentice clerk in Fort Providence in 1884. It is likely that he would have started school at Saint Boniface before John Peter did as Frederic was four and a half years older than him.

Graves in St. Norbert.
Credit: Montreal Gaudet Family.

Near the end. Charles Phillipe Gaudet in the hospital in Winnipeg with Isabelle, Frederic, and Freddy Gaudet in 1917. Credit: Montreal Gaudet Family.

Until I learn more, I will assume that Frederic and John Peter attended Saint Boniface in 1883/1884, after which Frederic returned north, and John Peter stayed on to continue studying in 1884/1885. The pattern for students attending Saint Boniface College and those attending St. John's, the Anglican College in Winnipeg, was that they would not return home to the North until their education was complete. Based on the yearbooks that the college provided, John Peter was in attendance for the 1885/1886 and the 1886/1887 school years. He also received many awards for the academics offered, including an Excellence Award for Spelling, Correspondence, English, Arithmetic, and Writing in the Commercial Course in 1887. This was reported in the *Manitoba Free Press* on June 18, 1887.

The only two Gaudets listed as students for 1887/1888 are Charles and Leon. So, where was John Peter for the 1887/1888 year? I assume he went home for that year. His father had travelled to Winnipeg in September 1887 for a meeting of the officers of the company, and John Peter was still there, as shown in a photograph of him with his two brothers.

L to R: John Peter, Charles Timothy, and Joseph Leon Gaudet at Saint Boniface College in 1887. Credit: Hardy Family Collection.

Based on his service record, we know that John Peter joined the company in June 1888 as an apprentice clerk in Peace River. So, it is logical to suggest that he travelled home to Fort Good Hope with his father in the fall of 1887 and visited his mother and sisters and then returned south to start work on June 1, 1888, in Peace River. He retired from the company on July 31, 1904.

∞

When John Peter joined the HBC, he was an apprentice clerk in Peace River and then a clerk in Athabasca. A clerk working

PART I

for the HBC was an employee one step below the partners. Three of his brothers—Frederic Charles, Charles Timothy, and Joseph Leon—also served the company as clerks or post managers. As employees of the HBC, they were all entitled to retire and receive a pension after thirty years of service. The father and the four sons accumulated 180 years of pensionable time. Those who earned full pensions also continued to serve the company in various capacities until their deaths. (These capacities are described earlier in this chapter.)

John Peter married Marguerite St. Germaine on September 18, 1900. They had ten children. I have tried my best to piece together the story from there, but there is still a lot of information that needs to be garnered. Subject to some conjecture, I think I may have found some answers in *The New North*.

Because the Gaudets were known for their excessive loyalty to the HBC, I wondered why John Peter left the company before he had earned his pension. Based on my research, I think the answer is simple: economic opportunity. The Peace River country was opening up, and he took a homestead and started some businesses in town. I also found out that his wife, Marguerite, took land scrip in 1909 for 160 acres. I have wondered if there was bad blood between him and his parents because he quit the HBC.

As described earlier, Agnes Deans Cameron described the trip that she and her niece took down and back up the Mackenzie River in 1908. That was the same year that Charles Phillipe and Marie celebrated their fiftieth wedding anniversary in Fort Good Hope. We are fortunate to have quite a few pictures of the Gaudets from that era, and many are from the anniversary celebration. I understand that the youngest son, Joseph Leon, was the family photographer. Two of the children of Charles Phillipe and Marie, John Peter and Charles Timothy, do not appear in the pictures. I wonder if Granddad and his family had been banished because of the decision to enter into a mixed marriage?

However, there is a young child in the arms of Charles Phillipe in a group photo. We have been able to determine that the child is Freddy Gaudet. I have often wondered how he got there. Based on some church records that Christine Frey, John Peter's daughter, obtained in 1995, we can see that Freddy was born in early 1907. So, he would have been one year old in the pictures.

Cameron and her niece went north through Athabasca to Fort Chipewyan and then down the Slave River and to the Mackenzie River and Fort Good Hope. On the way back, in late summer, they went west from Fort Chipewyan to Peace River. What struck me while reading the book was that she met "Mr. and Mrs. John Gaudet" when Cameron and her niece embarked at Fort Chipewyan to go west. Mr. and Mrs. Gaudet were returning to Lesser Slave Lake after a visit to Fort Good Hope, and they had two of their children with them.

Cameron uses their nicknames, "Char-lee" and "Se-li-nah." They would be Charles Phillipe, who was born on May 13, 1902, and Celina, who was born on February 6, 1905. I think it is likely that Mr. and Mrs. John Gaudet took those two children, as well as Freddy, with them to Fort Good Hope for the fiftieth wedding anniversary celebration. They would have left Freddy there in the care of his grandparents. I also assume that they gave him to them. This was not an unusual practice in 1908. Since then, the practice has been codified in the NWT as custom adoptions.

When they met Cameron, Char-lee would have been six years old, and Se-li-nah would have been three years old. There was also another child, Robert Jean, who was in between Char-lee and Se-li-nah, born on February 12, 1904. I am assuming that this child died before the trip to Fort Good Hope in 1908.

Cameron writes that when she shot a moose near Vermillion on the Peace, Se-li-nah asked for marrow in Cree.

Freddy was the fifth child born to John Peter and Marguerite. Their first child, Johny Jr., died shortly after his birth in June 1901. Freddy remained with his grandparents in Fort Good Hope after 1908. When Charles Phillipe died, Frederic Charles and Isabelle, who were brother and sister and Freddy's uncle and aunt, took him to Montreal and raised him there. One of our Montreal cousins, Isabelle Gaudet (the second), told me that Freddy refused to acknowledge that he was part Indigenous and insisted that he was French.

I still wonder why Freddy was "given" to his grandparents and then to his aunt and uncle. Was he a fiftieth wedding anniversary present? I suppose that in the grand scheme of things, being given is still better than being thrown away, which will be dealt with in chapter six.

Cousin Isabelle related another story to me that was told to her by her father, Julien Gaudet. He told his children about sneaking downstairs at night to listen to the adults in the parlour speaking a strange language. The adults were Frederic Charles, Isabelle (the first), Joseph Leon, and possibly Freddy. The strange language was Slavey, which they had learned in their youth in Fort Good Hope.

∞

Of the ten children born to John Peter and Marguerite, six are in a family photo that was likely taken around 1920. Three had died by then, and Freddy was being raised by his uncle and his aunt in Montreal. Christine also went to Montreal, where she spent time with the family. Celina followed her, entered a convent, became a nun, and spent many years at "different northern points where she taught school and singing classes." I vaguely recollect a Sister Gaudet at Grollier Hall. I knew she was our cousin, but I thought she was a nurse.

John Gaudet and family in Peace River. Date unknown.
Credit: *Peace River Remembers: Peace River, Alberta and Adjacent Districts.*

For the last thirty-three years of his employment by the HBC, from 1878 to 1911, Charles Phillipe was the chief trader in charge of the territory from Fort Wrigley north to the Beaufort Sea. His headquarters were in Fort Good Hope. However, in outfits 1884/1885 and 1885/1886, the chief factor in charge of the entire Mackenzie River District, Julian Camsell, took a furlough. In an article published in a 1935 edition of *The Beaver*, written by his son, Joseph Leon, Charles Phillipe was said to have "had temporary charge of the Mackenzie River District during the furlough." Camsell had his headquarters in Fort Simpson. I have pondered the question of whether Charles

Phillipe moved his family there for the two years that he was in charge of the district. After considering various facts, I have come down on the side of his family staying in Fort Good Hope for the two years. Charles Phillipe normally spent the summer travelling from post to post and to Athabasca and Edmonton to make and check on orders. He could easily carry out these duties as well as others from Fort Good Hope without having to put Marie and the daughters through a difficult move just to end up among strangers, with Charles Phillipe being away most of the time. Besides that, Elise and Francois Hoole [sic], Marie's parents, were likely still running their fish camp up the river from Fort Good Hope. Francois' service record indicates that he died on December 1, 1885. He would have been eighty-seven years old. Elise would have been about seventy. I don't know when she died, so I have assumed that she was still alive in 1885 and staying with her daughter in Fort Good Hope.

∞

As mentioned in chapter one, I recently learned that Elise had an older daughter, Elizabeth, who was born at Dease Lake near the Liard River in 1840. Elizabeth's father was Francois Houle. Interestingly, the records show Elizabeth as being the recipient of Land Scrip Notes A4558 and A5569 for 160 and 80 acres respectively. Her first husband's name was Baptise Bourchier, and her second husband was James Hyslop. I would assume that James was part of the Hyslop Nagle fur trading company, which had various posts that were in competition with the HBC.

∞

Charles Phillipe would have completed his two-year assignment in June 1886 upon the return of Julian Camsell. In 1887, Charles travelled to Winnipeg to attend a meeting of the officers of the HBC and to visit the three sons who were attending Saint Boniface College. I would like to thank James Gorton, the archivist at the Hudson's Bay Company Archives in Winnipeg, for all of his help in finding a lot of this information, particularly during the COVID-19 lockdowns, when he had to work online.

Charles Phillipe, Marie, and Isabelle Gaudet in the front and Christine and Frederic Gaudet in the back, wearing new clothing that Charles Phillipe likely purchased while in Winnipeg for the officers' meeting in 1887. Credit: Montreal Gaudet Family.

∞

When Granddad was buried in Fort Norman in 1952, a large number of Gaudets, which I enumerated earlier, were still living there. Aunt Cecilia married Joe Hall in Fort Simpson in 1928, and they had two daughters. Mama married Daddy in Fort Norman in 1934, and they had five children. Aunt Christine married Ray Overvold in 1939, and they had five children. Uncle George married Phoebe Lennie in 1952, and they were just starting their family. Uncle Fred married Mary Lennie in 1937, and they had a daughter. Aunt Jane remained a spinster.

As I wrote earlier, Aunt Bella married Ted Trindell, and they had two daughters, Florence and Alice, and lived in Fort Simpson. Later in life, Bella and Ted adopted one of our second cousins, Sylvia Browning. Sylvia's father, Jake Browning, was killed in an airplane crash at the Blackwater River.

Sylvia Scow and Alice Trindell. Credit: Sylvia Scow.

Florence (Trindell) Tosh (on the right) on a visit to Fort Norman c. 1950. Credit: Florence Tosh.

L to R: Raymond King, Doris (King) Erasmus, Pete King, and Trudy King. Credit: Trudy King.

Margaret (Overvold) Powder and Edna (Overvold) Larocque. Credit: Margaret Powder.

Edna and Shirley Overvold with cousin, Dorothy (McSwain) Beaulieu, shortly after the family moved to Fort Resolution. Credit: Trudy King.

While working on this book, the sad and terrible stories of the unmarked graves at locations where old residential schools were located came to the public's attention. It caused me to reflect on where our deceased family members might be resting.

What I found out was not good news. I wrote up the results of my research and sent this to some of my extended family members. The first paragraph is a reference to the first note that I had circulated.

LOST GAUDET GRAVES

The red highlighting is information that I have been provided with since sending the note around.

Charles Timothy Gaudet and Sarah Jane Hardisty were married in Fort Norman on July 15, 1899. They had thirteen children between then and 1921. I have been doing research on our family for some time and the recent news about the unmarked graves at residential schools has crystallized that issue for me. I wonder where the thirteen are buried?

The first child, George Alexander, was born in Fort Norman on June 21, 1900. He was baptised on August 3, 1900, in the Anglican Church. He died and was buried on August 6, 1900. Granddad was the Post Manager in Fort Norman then. We could assume that George is buried in Fort Norman. But where? I do not think that he is in the old Anglican graveyard. He could be in the Catholic graveyard. It is also possible that he is in an unmarked grave on the slope below the R.D. Clement Building (Band Office).

I pulled the information, that I am using, together from Granny's Bible, Granddad's HBC Biographical Sheet, Granddad's Scrip Application which is dated July 15, 1921 in Fort Norman and the receipts for scrip payments which were signed on June 29, 1924 in Fort Wrigley. In the Scrip Application Granddad states that three children had died before then and nine were alive. Uncle Georgie was not yet born on that day so he would be number thirteen.

The second child was John who was born in 1901 in Fort Norman. I don't know when John died or where he is buried. I think it is possible that he is buried in Fort Norman in the same circumstances as George. Granddad and Granny stayed in Fort Norman until 1904 when he was transferred to Fort Wrigley. They stayed there until 1909.

The third child was Mary and she was born in 1903 in Fort Norman. Mary married Ted Trindell in 1929 and died two or three years later in childbirth. I assume that she is buried in Fort Simpson but I have never seen her grave.

The fourth Child was Cecilia and she was born on February 9, 1904 in Fort Wrigley. Cecilia married Joe Hall in 1928 and died

PART I

in Edmonton in the spring of 1968 and is buried in the Roman Catholic Cemetery in Saint Albert.

The fifth Child was Rosie and she was born on January 6, 1906 in Fort Wrigley. All I know about Rosie was that she attended St. Peter's Anglican Indian Residential School in Hay River. I would assume that she was Anglican. She was alive on June 29, 1924 when she signed her receipt for her scrip payment in Fort Wrigley. I don't know when and where she died or where she is buried.

The sixth child was Bella who was born on October 28, 1907 in Fort Wrigley. Bella married Ted Trindell after Mary died. Bella died in 1995 in Fort Simpson. She is buried in Fort Simpson in the Catholic graveyard. I know where she is as I was a pall bearer.

The seventh child was Frederick who was born on November 14, 1909 in Fort Norman. Frederick married Mary Lennie on July 30, 1937 and died on September 14, 1993 and is buried in the old Anglican graveyard in Fort Norman.

The eighth child was Alice who was born on January 23, 1912 in Fort Wrigley. The family had moved back to Fort Wrigley in 1911 and stayed there until 1914. Alice married Jack Hardy in July of 1934. Alice died on December 29, 1984 and is buried in the old Anglican graveyard in Fort Norman.

The ninth child was Jane who was born on November 11, 1914 in Fort Norman. Jane never married. Jane died on August 12, 1992 and is buried in the old Anglican graveyard in Fort Norman.

The tenth child was Leon who was born in Fort Norman on October 14, 1915. If we assume that Leon died young and we know that the family stayed in Fort Norman until 1921 it is likely that Leon died there and was buried there. But where? Is he on the slope or in the Catholic graveyard?

The eleventh child was Charlie who was born on September 3, 1917 at Fort Norman. He was still alive on June 29, 1924. Mama told me that he died helping Granddad build a house or, more likely, adding the second story to the house in Fort Norman. Apparently, the blocking slipped and he was crushed when the house came down on him. This would have been around 1930. Or, it could have been in Fort Wrigley when Granddad was building the house there in 1924. I don't know when or where Charlie died and don't know where he is buried.

The twelfth child was Christine who was born in 1919 in Fort Norman. Christine married Ray Overvold on July 13, 1939 in Fort Norman and then Pete King on August 22, 1957 in Fort Resolution. Christine died on August 23, 1996 and she is buried in Fort Resolution.

The thirteenth child was George who was born on August 10, 1921 in Fort Norman. George attended the St. Peter's Anglican Indian Residential School in Hay River. George married Phoebe Lennie in June, 1952 in Fort Norman. George died on December 31, 1992 and is buried in the old Anglican graveyard in Fort Norman.

I have highlighted the names of those whose graves I don't know the whereabouts of. Once the Covid-19 restrictions are lifted I will be travelling to Winnipeg to do research at the HBC Archives. I don't expect to find much there, with regards to graves, but I do recall some graves behind the outhouse that was beside the old HBC store. That store wasn't built until around 1928 so the area of the graves would have been back in the bush at the time of the deaths of the Gaudet's. There is no sign of those graves these days. Whether these were Gaudet graves or not somebody ought to do something about marking and identifying them.

I will then travel to Edmonton to work in the Anglican Church Archives. There should be a lot of information there about births and deaths in Fort Norman, Fort Wrigley and Fort Simpson. I would also like to try to find out which of the children were Anglicans, besides Uncle Georgie.

Someone, other than me, will have to attend at the appropriate Catholic Church Archives. This someone should have at least a basic understanding of French as most of their records will be in that language. I expect that I will be banned and excommunicated from the Catholic Church once my book is published so I better not go there.

I have also left a number of blanks in the above information. Will whoever has that information please let me know so I can fill in the blanks.

Hopefully, once we are done, we will have a permanent record of where all of our Gaudet ancestors, from that generation, are resting, peacefully, I hope. A photo record would be great. Also, it may be necessary, if they are on the slope, to arrange for moving them.

In memorious. Rick Hardy, June 25, 2021.

PART I

47

I have been provided with additional information since the date of the memo and have entered those items as well. One new item was of particular interest to me. It is the information about George Alexander that I obtained from Anglican Archives for the Mackenzie River Diocese, in Edmonton. That information indicated two things to me. Our grandparents started out married life with the intention of being an Anglican family. The second item made me think even harder about where George Alexander might be buried. In order to properly imagine what might have happened we need to take ourselves back to Fort Norman in 1900 and understand what was there then. We need to block what we saw and lived with as we were growing up in order to get a better picture in our mind's eye.

The only buildings in the area then would be the Anglican mission compound and the original HBC compound. The Gaudet house was a single-story building then. There was open space on the slope between the Anglican church compound and the Gaudet house. We know that there are unmarked graves on this slope. I can easily imagine this area being the original Anglican church graveyard. We need to remember that the Anglican mission in Fort Norman was established in 1858. So, where did they bury their dead before what we now call the old Anglican graveyard was established?

It is likely that there are more graves on the slope then we previously understood. A lot of this information should be in the Anglican Archives for the Mackenzie River Diocese in Edmonton. This is a project for someone else to finish.

The Fort Norman that those of my generation remember was not built until the late 1920's and after that. At that time a new and large HBC compound (the one that is now thought of as old), the RCMP compound, the RCCS compound, the Indian Agency, the Mining Recorders office, the hospital and the first schools were built. Most of those buildings are now gone.

∞

The funeral mass for Granddad was held in the Saint Teresa of Avila Roman Catholic Church, but the burial was in what we now call the old Anglican graveyard. Granny was Anglican, and he was Roman Catholic. This, very sadly, led to many conflicts during their lives, as it did for Charles Phillipe and Marie. Because Granny died first, she was buried in the old Anglican graveyard. If Granddad wanted to rest beside her eternally, he had to go there as well. I guess she won in the end. The Catholic/Anglican conflict continued on to the next generation with the mixed marriages of Aunt Cecilia and Uncle George.

In my immediate family, my sister, Diane, married an Anglican, Larry Gordon. The marriage took place in the chapel in Stringer Hall on April 24, 1971, and was performed by Reverend Holman. Mama and Daddy travelled to Inuvik for the wedding, and there have been no disputes over religion that I am aware of.

The new conflicts seem to arise from mixed marriages that are raced based. Religion does not seem to matter any more. Diane was Métis, and Larry was Inuvialuit. Sadly, they are both deceased. They left four children: Stewart, Aaron, Michael, and Meaghen, and four grandchildren. The conflict that I am referring to is which Indigenous group should the children and grandchildren be part of? In Diane's case, she was a member of the Fort Norman Métis Community, but all of her children are registered as Inuvialuit. Another good example is my youngest grandchild, Peter James Hardy. His father, my son James, is a member of the Fort Norman Métis Community. His mother is Tli Cho. Where should Peter be registered?

∞

Diane (Hardy) Gordon, on the right, and Bertha Lennie, with the Saint Teresa of Avila Church in the background, c. 1958. Credit: Hardy Family Collection.

What I do remember about Granddad's funeral is that Mama was holding Diana, who was three months old then, and I was sitting beside them in the church. Mama could not stop crying, so she took me by the hand and left the church with Diana in her arms and me straggling along. I remember sitting on the top of the church steps, which looked huge to my five-year-old eyes. I was crying my eyes out with her. We waited there for the service to end. I remember the men of the community carrying the coffin out of the church, down the high steps, and starting the long walk to the old Anglican graveyard. Granddad's death ended a fantastic era in our family history as well as in the North.

Granddad was the only grandparent who was alive during my life, albeit only for a short time—five years that I barely remember. I often wonder how my life would have been different had there been grandparents in it. Aunt Jane Gaudet, who was a spinster, filled that role to some extent. Sometimes we thought of her as our second mother.

Aunt Jane Gaudet. Credit: Hardy Family Collection.

Charles Phillipe came north in 1851 during the height of the fur trade. His son, Charles Timothy, died 101 years later as the decline in the fur trade began in earnest. Between the two of them, they could claim 102 continuous years of service, including the years of "assistance" to the company that was Here Before Christ and Here Before Canada. John Peter passed in 1941, Joseph Leon passed in 1943, and Frederic and Isabelle both passed in 1955. The total years of dedication to the HBC by the whole family, including Aunt Jane's thirty or so years, exceeds 200 years.

PART I

especially

French Names used in Slavey in Fort Good Hope.

latä = table (la table)	ligardü = bullet (la cartouche)
laleni = wool (la laine)	ligar = playing cards (les cartes)
larmi = mass (la Messe)	ligariyde = carriole (la cariole of sled)
lasuvi = silk (la soie)	ligoda = cotton (le coton)
lebeli = broom (le balai)	ligosha = pig (le cochon)
lebis = shovel (la bêche)	lishale = shawl (le châle)
lebil = frying pan (la poêle)	lishari = wheelbarrow (la charette)
ledi = tea (le té)	limardü = hammer (le marteau)
liguavi = cover (le couvercle)	lisaldä = policeman (le soldat)
ledlu = nail key (le clou)	lisawä = uncivilized (le sauvage)
lejuyi = spoon	lisima = face towel (l'essui-main)
lri = rice (le riz)	le fili = thread (le fil)
leruba = ribbon (le ruban)	legulü = bells (les grelots)
lesuzü = scissors (les ciseaux)	libala = curé (le prélat)
lesil = salt (le sel)	lifari = flour (la farine)
leshé = chair (la chaise)	ligami = rope (le ligament)
leshekolé = chocolate (le chocolat)	lishabü = hat (le chapeau)
lésuvri = chimney (la cheminée)	mahsi = thank-you (merci)
libä = socks (le bas)	ligahrisi = panties (les caleçons)
libábigo = flag (le papillon)	dosho = towel (torchon)
liba dü = scow-boat (le bateau)	legabedeu = boat captain (Capitaine)
lipap = Pope (le Pape)	limahshi = étranger (le marté)
libari = barrel (le baril)	
lilro = cup (le pot)	
librü = mile	
libu dei = bottle (la bouteille)	
li ch'a fi = cache-stage (l'échafaud)	
lidzaye = onion (les oignons)	
li finil = flannel (la flanelle)	
ligafi = coffee (le café)	
li fushi = fork (la fourchette)	
ligamari = kettle (le canari)	isgi = Yeast (Yeast Cake)
ligarakine = rifle (la carabine)	

List of French words introduced into the Slavey Language by Charles Phillipe Gaudet. Credit: Henri Posset, OMI.

A lasting legacy of Charles Phillipe Gaudet is the introduction of over fifty French words into the Slavey language. The list of these words was compiled by Father Henri Posset, who spent many years in Fort Simpson and Fort Norman. Most of the words were used in trading. They included such simple everyday items like tea, coffee, flour, and salt. Interestingly, Father Posset also included "thank you," which is *merci* in French and *máhsı* in Slavey. I noticed that chocolate was included on the list but not sugar. The French say *sucre* while the Slavey say *súgah*. Maybe we can give that one to old CP as well.

In addition to Henry Posset's contribution to the legacy of the Gaudets, a former oblate priest named Bernard Brown also seemed to be a fan. Brown wrote extensively of his time in the North. One of his books is *Arctic Journal*, in which he writes about his time in Fort Norman and meeting Charles Timothy:

> *Some of the most noteworthy characters have worked for the Hudson Bay Company. Among these were the three Gaudet brothers whose combined service among the Hareskins spanned a century. Now only Tim survived and he was spending his retirement years at Fort Norman. Tall, but slightly stooped, with a handlebar moustache drooping under a strawberry nose and with a heavy gold watch chain swinging from his vest, Tim represented the stereotypical HBC veteran.*
>
> *Besides possessing the skills needed by a successful trader, Tim was also skilled in the arts of bush life, like snowshoe-making . . . Tim guided me through all phases of construction, from the proper selection of a white birch sapling, through the splitting, cutting and bending stages, to the final insertion of the babiche (webbing).*

Brown also wrote *End of the Earth People*. Chapter four of that book is titled "Language Complexities and Challenges," where he credits Charles Phillipe Gaudet with providing French names to some of the Dene families. These names include: *Tobac* (tobacco), *San-Couteau* (no knife), *Grandjamb* (long legs), and *Kochon* (pig). My apologies to the Kochon family, on behalf of my great-grandfather.

Because service in the HBC was almost like religion to the Gaudets, Granddad was asked what his last thought was in a near-death experience when he fell through the ice and almost drowned. "Well, I thought, anyway, I am not in debt to the Hudson's Bay Company," he replied. The quote was in an article written by Joseph Hodgson and published in *The Beaver* in June 1924.

Last trip north. Frederic Charles and Isabelle Gaudet travelled from Montreal to Fort Norman to visit Charles Timothy Gaudet. They spent time in Winnipeg, either coming or going, to place the headstones on their father and sister's graves, c. 1925. Credit: Montreal Gaudet Family.

CHAPTER FIVE

THE GAUDET BOYS GO TO SCHOOL

This brings me to a fascinating story about how I think two of the "boys," Charles Timothy and Joseph Leon, got to Saint Boniface, Manitoba, to go to school in 1885. Part of the story was imparted to me by Mama. To my everlasting shame, I did not pay the attention I should have and was dismissive of the story. She told me the story in the 1970s while I was president of the Métis Association of the Northwest Territories. She said to me, "Your grandfather and his brother were in Batoche during the battle between the Métis and the Canadian army." Being the smartass that I was, and maybe still am, I retorted to the effect that this could not be, as Granddad was born in Fort Good Hope in 1872, so how would he have gotten to Batoche thirteen years later when the family was still living in Fort Good Hope? I advised her not to make up stories just to make us more Métis. My grandfather at the Battle of Batoche? Impossible!

As I said, I carry my shame to this day, as she was telling me a true story. I had no comprehension of the mobility of the family members during that time. I simply assumed that they were permanently in Fort Good Hope. She told me that her dad, my grandfather, told her about him and his brother hiding in a grain bin with broken glass falling on them from the bullets being fired by the Canadians. I remained skeptical for years until I told the story to Payment, who was writing about Marie Fisher at the time. I did not know that she is a published author on the history of Batoche, among other topics.

Payment told me that it was possibly a true story, as the boys' mother, Marie, was related to the Fishers of Batoche. The Fishers of Batoche were descendants of Henry Munro Fisher (the second), who was Alexander Munro Fisher's older brother. The Fishers were a large family in the Batoche area, and the boys likely stopped to visit their relatives on their way to school in Saint Boniface. Okay, but how did they get there before or during the time of the battle, which was between May 9 and 11 in 1885? Bearing in mind that they might have travelled all the way from Fort Good Hope, starting in the dead of winter. The length of the trip would have been somewhere near 3,000 miles. It is possible that the trip was made from Fort Simpson if the family did move there for the two years that Charles Phillipe had charge of the entire district. In that case the length of the trip would have been about 2,000 miles. Another possibility

PART I

is that the boys simply went with their father on the last York Boat trip south, from Fort Good Hope in 1884 and stayed with him in Fort Simpson until they departed to Saint Boniface in the early months of 1885.

The 1885/1886 and 1886/1887 yearbooks for Saint Boniface College both show the addresses for the three boys as being Fort Simpson. The third boy was John Peter, who was already attending Saint Boniface College. At first the addresses perplexed both the archivist for Saint Boniface University, Carole Pelchat, and me. I was satisfied that the Gaudet family did move to Fort Simpson while Charles Phillipe relieved Camsell during the two years that the Camsells were on leave in Fort Garry. However, after giving it considerable thought, I surmised that as Charles Phillipe was pretty well constantly on the move, he simply used Fort Simpson as a convenient mailing address for those two years. In either case, I am assuming that the trip started in the winter before the rivers broke up, in 1885. Otherwise, they would have had to leave with the first York boat brigade out, which would not have crossed Great Slave Lake until the end of June. If they went with the first brigade, as the Camsells did in 1884, they would not have been able to get to Batoche in time for the battle.

∞

Prior to starting studies at the College of Law at the University of Saskatchewan, I attended the University of Regina, where I worked on a BA, leaning toward majoring in history. Sometimes I wish I would have completed that line of study, so I would have the skills to do research properly. I do the best I can, but I have not delved deeply into any archives. It is possible that more details about the "trip" can be found in the HBC Archives. However, those archives and others are simply not completely available while I am writing this because of the COVID-19 pandemic.

∞

Payment and I have speculated on how the trip would have taken place. I have also read other accounts that are helpful in recreating the trip. Payment reminded me to bear in mind that Charles Phillipe was an officer of the company, and this would open the doors of every post to his sons. In fact, he was acting chief factor for the entire Mackenzie River District at the time of the trip. Did he send letters to those posts on the last mail out on the river in 1884, if they travelled from Fort Good Hope? Maybe the boys carried letters of introduction with them. One should also remember that in 1884/1885, people did not simply email applications for enrolment to schools. A lot of planning involving the Catholic Church would have been required over a lengthy period of time.

The cost of the boys attending Saint Boniface College was not gratuitous, and Charles Phillipe would have paid a considerable sum of money for the privilege. The 1885/1886 yearbook for Saint Boniface College lists the "Terms" as: Board and Tuition $130; Bedding - $10; Washing - $16; Music Lessons - $30; and, Use of Piano - $5. You can multiply that by three for the three boys for the two years that all three attended together, which would amount to $573 per year, in 1885 dollars, plus the cost of travel there and the cost of boarding for the summer.

It seems to me that the Gaudet family, under the leadership of Charles Phillipe, were quite well to do. When the family left the North in 1917, Isabelle donated most of the family's belongings to the Catholic Church and established a bursary of $2,000 for training priests for the North. That $2,000 would, with the effect of inflation, be worth close to $34,000 in 2021. While inflation rates are not available for the 1880s, I would venture a multiplication rate of thirty, making the attendance fee for the three boys in the $17,000 range per year for the years they were in attendance.

I have, from Mama, the original of Grandad's certificate of communion and confirmation issued by Saint Boniface Cathedral, stating that he was confirmed on June 3, 1885. So, we know he was definitely in Saint Boniface shortly after the Battle of Batoche. Again, the date of his confirmation shows that the boys could not have gotten there then if they travelled with the brigade that year.

But the question still remains—how did they get there? I am thankful to Richard Bonnycastle and Heather Robertson for describing a similar trip from Fort Good Hope to Fort McMurray, made by Bonnycastle between November 15, 1928, and March 16, 1929. After reaching Fort McMurray, he and his companions caught a train south to Edmonton. They describe the trip in *A Gentleman Adventurer – The Arctic Diaries of Richard Bonnycastle*, edited and compiled by Heather Robertson.

Bonnycastle and his companions took over 120 days to make it to Fort McMurray from Fort Good Hope. I think that if the boys and their companions had taken the same route from Fort Good Hope to Fort McMurray, it is likely they would have taken considerably less time. Bonnycastle and one of his companions, Hugh Conn, were senior employees of the HBC when they made the trip. In fact, Bonnycastle worked for Conn. Consequently, they spent many days at each post carrying out inventories and checking the books and other related tasks.

Tim Gaudet's communion and confirmation certificate from Saint Boniface College, 1885. Credit: Hardy Family Collection.

Based on Bonnycastle's diaries, I can see that they spent nine days at Hay River, nine days at Fort Resolution, seventeen days at Fort Smith, and thirteen days at Fort Chipewyan. Bonnycastle does not record enough detail for the other posts—such as Fort Norman, Fort Wrigley, Fort Simpson, and Fort Providence—to see how long his party spent in those posts.

However, based on the contents of the diaries and my own knowledge gained while growing up, I am reasonably comfortable working with the assumption that the boys could have made the same trip from Fort Good Hope to Fort McMurray in seventy days, more or less. They would likely have wanted to reach Fort McMurray before the end of the winter travelling season. I think the last date that they would have been able to travel by dog team would have been in late March or early April 1885. The rivers broke on April 9 of that year in Fort McMurray, which is still the earliest recorded date for a breakup there. Working backwards from April 1 would mean them leaving Fort Good Hope in mid-January 1885. If the boys were still at home with their parents in Fort Good Hope, they would most likely have stayed there for Christmas 1884, especially because of their adherence to the Roman Catholic religion.

They would have had longer travelling days than the Bonnycastle party because the days would have started getting much longer in mid-January with the returning sun. It took Bonnycastle a week to travel from Fort Good Hope to Fort Norman during the dark period at the end of November 1928. Bonnycastle left Fort Good Hope with Conn and another HBC employee, a Métis guide, and an Indian guide. The Métis guide was Victor Lafferty, and the Indian guide was Old Chinna. Bonnycastle tells us that Old Chinna returned to Fort Good Hope the day after they left, as had been arranged. He does not tell us when Victor left them, but my guess would be that he left them at Fort Providence, which was where, I believe, he was from.

Whether the boys started the trip from Fort Good Hope or Fort Simpson, I don't imagine that Charles Phillipe would have let them go in 1885 without a guide. It is possible that he may have even travelled with the boys himself. As he was in charge of the entire district at that time, he may have taken them all the way to Fort McMurray or even farther. Charles Phillipe did travel extensively in the winters by dog team, checking on the posts and trading furs directly with the Métis and Indian trappers in the bush.

If the trip started in Fort Simpson, it is likely that it would have taken them about forty days to reach Fort McMurray, which means they would have left Fort Simpson in mid-February 1885. They would have had long travelling days with the returning sun but would have had stops at each post along the way.

If either of these scenarios was the way that the boys travelled to get to Saint Boniface, it would be likely they would have stopped in Fort Providence for a visit. The oldest brother, Frederic Charles, was spending his first outfit of service, 1884/1885, there.

Bonnycastle left an excellent record of his trip. He recorded the following in his diary on November 21, 1928:

By daylight we had been travelling three hours. Conn is in good form and we had a bit of fun at the last fire camp taking snaps. Then we crossed the river, passed by Bear Rock and Bear River, crossed again opposite the fort, climbed the bank, and we were in Fort Norman. What a relief to arrive here. My feet are in absolute agony. Distance today about 31 miles.

Unfortunately, Bonnycastle did not record any comments on the stay in Fort Norman or the length of it. One of the boys, my grandfather, was the assistant post manager at Fort Norman at the time.

However, Bonnycastle's editor, Heather Robertson, does provide the following:

In the next six weeks, as Bonnycastle and Hugh Conn continued to leapfrog upriver from Fort Norman to Fort Wrigley, Fort Simpson, and Fort Providence, Bonnycastle's illusions about the romance of travelling by dog team evaporated into the reality of running 30 miles a day over rough ice, making camp at 40[degrees]F below zero, and the incessant strain of Hugh Conn's savage, unpredictable temper. Arriving at a post footsore and exhausted, he was put to work immediately on the books, while Conn started taking inventory with barely a pause for tea.

Whether their departure was from Fort Good Hope or Fort Simpson, the boys should have reached Fort McMurray in early April 1885. As there were no trains travelling to that area then, they would have had to find another way from there to Saint Boniface via Batoche.

So, most likely, they would have continued on by swinging east on the Clearwater River from Fort McMurray by York boat. This meant waiting for open water, which would have been near the middle of April that year. That would have left the boys and their retinue, if they had one, about three weeks to get to Batoche.

The description of the rest of the trip is based on conjecture by me after reading chapter three of *Son of the North* by Charles Camsell. The Camsell family all travelled together to bring young Charles to Winnipeg, where he attended Saint John's College for eleven years. They left Fort Simpson as soon as the water was open to travel on June 10, 1884. They travelled with the York boat brigade to Fort Smith. From there they took the portage to Fort Fitzgerald where they boarded the *Grahame*, one of the first steamboats introduced to the area. Then they travelled to Fort McMurray and transferred back to York boats to head east on the Clearwater River.

Son of the North should be required reading in the Northwest Territories school system to help young people better understand what life was like in that part of the North 150 years ago. Chapters three, four, and five of the book describe the trip to get to Winnipeg, eleven years of attending Saint John's College with two older brothers who were already there, without going home until his return in 1894.

Granddad essentially followed the same pattern, making the trip to school with his brother in 1885, meeting the third brother at Saint Boniface, attending school for nine years, and returning home in 1894. However, Granddad and his brothers attended Saint Boniface College, which was the Catholic school, and they were French Half-Breeds. I wonder if this is why Camsell never mentions them in his book. Granddad joined the HBC as an apprentice clerk in 1895 to 1898 in Fort Norman. These were the years that Camsell taught school there. Again, he fails to mention Granddad. This makes me wonder, what was the problem? I guess the *anglaise* actually did consider themselves to be superior. That may be an unfair criticism, as the Gaudets did not write any books where I might see if they mentioned the Camsells.

There was a time when I would have said that the *anglaise* actually did consider themselves to be superior. However, while that may be true, I must face the reality that the French Catholics were just as bad, if not worse. While Charles Phillipe was flexible in terms of religions, Marie was rabidly Catholic. As a result of this, the boys likely strongly believed that the Camsell boys, not being Catholic, were going to burn in hell. It is fine for a person who feels affronted to complain, but he or she ought to take a long, hard look in the mirror to find out what the other person is seeing.

There is no question that their fathers, Julian Camsell and Charles Phillipe Gaudet, knew each other and that they both attended the September 1887 meeting of the Officers Council of the HBC in Winnipeg. Surely, the three Camsell boys attending Saint John's College in Winnipeg and the three Gaudet boys attending Saint Boniface College, whose fathers were both officers of the HBC, living and working together in the Mackenzie River District, would have at least associated a bit with each other.

Later on, I will discuss the early relationships between the Anglican students in Stringer Hall and the Catholic students in Grollier Hall when those residences opened in 1959. While those relationships were acrimonious, we need to understand

PART I

59

where the attitudes in play back then came from. It is wrong for me, a descendant of French Catholic Half-Breeds, to disparage anyone who is not exactly like me even though that was what the priests preached to us in church. This is likely what my great-grandmother believed and taught to her children.

Charles Camsells father, Julian Camsell, was an Englishman who was born in Ceylon and went into the army at an early age. He was part of a troop that was sent to Red River in June 1857 to protect the settlers from the Indians. One can only imagine what attitudes he carried when he left the army to join the HBC. Charles Camsell writes in *Son of the North*, that Julian was married to Sarah Foulds, and emphasizes her English background. Charles Camsell also wrote "I lived at Fort Liard until I was six years old. My family and the missionary were the only white people in the place; the rest were Indians or half-breeds, employees of the Company." Since reading the foregoing I have seen an application for Mackenzie River District Half-Breed Scrip by one of Julian and Sarah's sons, Frank Ernest Camsell. Frank's answer to question eight in the application is that his mother was a "Half-Breed." I communicated with Terry Camsell, a very well-known northerner and a descendant of Julian and Sarah, and learned that the family was always aware that Sarah was Métis and that other siblings of Frank Ernest had applied for and received scrip as well.

After leaving Fort McMurray in 1884, the Camsells went as far as the Long Portage, which is also known as the Methye Portage. They crossed the portage in oxcarts and then worked their way south to Qu'Appelle, where they caught the train to Winnipeg.

The Gaudet boys would have followed the same route a year later, in 1885, except they would have stopped at Batoche to visit the Fisher family and, coincidentally, in time for the battle. After the battle and their visit with the Fishers, they would have then travelled to Qu'Appelle and taken the train to Saint Boniface where they, or at least Granddad, were confirmed into the Catholic Church. When they arrived in Saint Boniface, John Peter would have just turned sixteen, Granddad would have just turned thirteen, and Joseph Leon would turn ten years old that fall. It is also likely that the Gaudet girls were going to school at Île-à-la-Crosse at that time, and the boys may have stopped to visit them as well. That community is now in Saskatchewan, but the province did not exist at the time of the trip.

What an adventure for two young boys, or perhaps more appropriately, young men. I would like to thank Blair Jean for providing the detail for the Clearwater River from Fort McMurray to the Methye Portage in his excellent book, *Clearwater River Fort McMurray to Methye Portage*. His descriptions helped me imagine what that part of the trip would have been like.

∞

It would be negligent of me not to mention that the daughters of Charles Phillipe and Marie were also educated. I am just as guilty as the men of my great-grandparents' time in ignoring the women. The education of the daughters is set out clearly by Payment in *Contours of a People.* She describes the conflict that almost drove the family apart in 1870. The conflict was over education: Marie wanted a French/Catholic education versus Charles Phillipe, who wanted an English/Anglican education. Payment also states that Marie actually took the children in 1870 and went to Île-à-la-Crosse, where she pleaded with the leaders of the Catholic Church to assist her. The upshot was that the daughters were allowed to attend school at Île-à-la-Crosse College in the 1870s and 1880s. While there the daughters were "taught English, music and painting by Sister Sara Riel (sister of Louis Riel)." The youngest of the daughters, Dora, attended the residential school in Fort Providence in the 1890s. I have no doubt in my mind that Charles Philippe also paid a pretty sum for educating the daughters. Payment also writes that Bella and Christine "worked with their brothers at various posts doing journals and processing accounts, as they were better book-keepers."

∞

Following the deaths of Marie (1914) and Charles Phillipe (1917), all but one of their children moved to southern Canada. I deliberately do not use the word "returned," as they were not from the South. All of them were born and raised in the Mackenzie River District. They, along with the Camsells, were likely the first immigrants of European descent going in that direction. There are no Gaudets in Fort Good Hope today despite the large number of children that Marie and Charles Phillipe raised there.

The one child who remained in the North was Granddad. He married and settled in Fort Norman with Sarah Jane, where they raised a large family. There are no Gaudets in Fort Norman today. They also spent a number of interim years in Fort Wrigley, where a number of the children, including Mama, were born. There are no Gaudets in old Fort Wrigley or Wrigley today. However, it is likely that—like Fort Good Hope and Fort Norman—there are a number of Gaudet graves at old Fort Wrigley. The task of finding them is one that my cousin, Arnold Gaudet, has started working on.

PART I
61

Tim and Sarah Gaudet with Alice (Gaudet) Hardy, Mary (Lennie) Gaudet, Leo Hardy and Rod Hardy on a spring hunt in 1939. Credit: Hardy Family Collection.

Tim and Sarah Gaudet at another spring hunt camp. Credit: Hardy Family Collection.

Joe Bourque, Jack Hardy, and Red Anders dropping the picnickers off on Windy Island, 1935. Credit: Hardy Family Collection.

The picnickers (L to R): Christine Gaudet, Celestine (Clement) Doctor, Sarah Jane (Hardisty) Gaudet, Leo Hardy, and Alice (Gaudet) Hardy, 1935. Credit: Hardy Family Collection.

George Gaudet and his family after the funeral for Aunt Jane Gaudet in August 1992 in what used to be the Hardy front yard. Credit: Hardy Family Collection.

CHAPTER SIX

THE HARDISTYS

I was born on May 13, 1947, at 12:20 p.m. at home in Fort Norman, Northwest Territories. These details are from the *Story of Our Baby* book, which I found in Mama's trunk while I was cleaning up the family property during the summer of 2020. I cleaned up the property to sell it to the Parks Canada Agency, which wanted it to build the head office and a visitor's centre for the Naats'ihch'oh National Park Reserve of Canada. I was glad that Parks Canada was taking over the property, as it would be well looked after and would maintain a lot of its character. I also appreciated the juxtaposition of this development to my life, as I had played a pivotal role in establishing the park. (I will tell that story later.) The sale of the property, completed in September 2020, marked the end of my family's 140-plus years of continuous involvement with Fort Norman.

The first of my ancestors to permanently live in Fort Norman were my matrilineal great-grandparents, Allan and Mary Hardisty. Allan was born in 1851 and Mary in 1861, if the Canadian Census records of 1891 are correct. They were married on June 29, 1877 and moved to Fort Norman shortly after that. I have seen a reference where Allan is called "Métis Lenoir [Allen] Hardisty." Mary's full name was Mary Ann Koketa. Allan was described by Charles Camsell, in his autobiography, *Son of the North*, as "an Indian lay reader at the mission and a protégé of Bishop Bompas who had received some education in Winnipeg." This was in 1895 when Camsell was teaching school at the Anglican Mission in Fort Norman.

∞

Great-grandfather Hardisty built what we now call the Old Anglican Church, in 1880, in Fort Norman. When he built the church, it was named the Holy Trinity Anglican Church. It is now the oldest standing church in the Northwest Territories and is designated as a historical site. One of Allan and Mary's daughters, Sarah Jane Hardisty, married my grandfather, Charles Timothy Gaudet, on July 15, 1899, in the Holy Trinity Anglican Church.

Anglican Mission in Fort Norman in 1932 with the Gaudet house, up the hill, on the right. Credit: Anglican Church of Canada, General Synod Archives (Bessie Quirt photo albums).

The following inscription is found in Sarah Jane's Bible: "February 13th 1918 my poor dear Father departed from this world, he died very happy." However, we knew nothing more about his death. I was very fortunate to have the assistance of Laurel Parson, the archivist for the General Synod Archives for the Anglican Church of Canada. She was able to locate the information that we needed to confirm and determine the dates of death for Allan and Mary, as well as the location of their graves. Laurel confirmed that Allan did die on February 13, 1918, and Mary died on October 25, 1919. They both died and are buried at a location called the "Head of Line." The location is south of Jean Marie River on the west side of the Mackenzie River. Arnold Gaudet is committed to visiting the location soon and determining what is there. The area is called Head of the Line because that is where the trackers were able to set down the lines that they used to pull the York boats through the swifter water of the Mackenzie River. If they were heading south, oars and a sail could be used from that point onwards to propel the boat.

Sarah Jane's Bible also lists all thirteen of the children of Allan and Mary. There are only two sons listed who survived into adulthood: Arthur and W. Lucas. As far as I know, Arthur made his home in Fort Wrigley. I don't know where W. Lucas lived. There is also a list of some of the grandchildren. Interestingly, this list only includes grandchildren from the daughters and not the sons.

I have been given a copy of a family tree started by my cousin, Florence (Trindell) Tosh, and her husband, Allan. They lived in Fort Simpson for quite a few years and knew many of the Hardistys. The tree they started shows five children of Allan and Mary: Arthur, Sarah Jane, Mary Patsy, Dora Isaiah, and Cecilia.

That tree shows four children of Arthur and his wife, Jessie McSwain. Those children are Frank, Edward, William, and Percy. The tree shows Mary as having three children: Julian, William, and Fred. Dora is shown as having four children: Stanley, Eva, Charlie, and Celena. There are no children shown for Cecilia. Arthur would have been Mama's uncle and his

Allan and Florence Tosh. Credit: Doug MacIntosh.

children, and the children of Mary and Dora would have been her first cousins. I look forward to the day when we can get a complete and up-to-date family tree for Allan and Mary's progeny.

Although, I was able to find many pictures in the Anglican Church archives, there were none of Allan or Mary.

Arthur and Jesse Hardisty, "in front of their house at Fort Wrigley (1963)."
Credit: NWT Archives (Native Press Fonds).

PART I
67

"Ft. Wrigley Build by Tim Gaudet 1923 H.B. Co Res." – the caption on the back of the photo in Alice Hardy's handwriting. Credit: Hardy Family Collection.

Edward, Albert, and William Hardisty, attending Saint Peter's Anglican Residential School in Hay River in 1929. Credit: Anglican Church of Canada, General Synod Archives (Diocese of the Arctic Fonds).

The large lad at the right of the picture is George Gaudet. The picture was taken in June 1935 of the confirmation class at St. Peter's Anglican Residential School in Hay River. George was thirteen at the time. Credit: Anglican Church of Canada, General Synod Archives (Diocese of the Arctic Fonds).

Rosie Gaudet (left, back row), at St. Peters. The picture was taken in July 1918 when she was thirteen years old. Credit: Anglican Church of Canada, General Synod Archives (Diocese of the Arctic Fonds).

I have always been curious about the Hardisty side of our family. What we knew was that our grandmother, Sarah Jane Hardisty, was one of the daughters of Allan and Mary, and who her siblings were. We also knew that Mama and her siblings had many first cousins in the Dehcho Region of the NWT. They would have visits in the summertime, by boat, from people such as Julian Hardisty from Fort Simpson and Edward Hardisty from Fort Wrigley. Visitors like Julian and Edward would stay with Uncle Fred as he was more likely to have a fresh brew pot on than my parents would. Of course, they would always come to visit once the party was over.

Mama also spoke about other relatives, through the Hardistys, in the Isaiah, Browning, and Squirrel families. She also spoke

PART I

69

fondly, from time to time, of Arthur and Jesse Hardisty. During the days that I was actively involved in the NWT Métis activities, I came to know some Hardistys in Wrigley, such as Edward, Gabe, and Henry. I knew we were cousins but was never quite sure how. These Hardistys were very active supporters of the Dene Nation. I also learned that we were related to the McSwain's through Jesse Hardisty, who was a McSwain. Recently, I finally realized that some of Edward Hardisty's children went by the last name of Moses. No doubt, the seeds of Allan and Mary Hardisty have been spread far and wide.

Still, I wondered. I was sure that Allan was Dene and was educated, having taught school in Fort Norman in the 1880s and 1890s. This seemed like an anomaly, as few Dene, if any, from that generation had a formal education. However, what really piqued my curiosity was how he came to have a name like Hardisty, which is obviously Scottish. So, I kept looking and recently came across Project Canterbury on the Internet. One of the compilations published by the project includes excerpts from the diaries of Charlotte Selina Bompas, the wife of Bishop William Bompas. Here I found the answers that I had been looking for.

Allan Hardisty's birth father was "Baptiste le Noir, an Indian hunter," who "threw away" his two oldest boys when he married for the second time. One of the boys, Allan, "was received by Mr. Hardisty, the Hudson's Bay Officer at Fort Simpson, and named him after him." The other boy was taken by the Bompas family and was named "William" after the bishop. While searching through the Anglican Church Archives, I found a picture of a student at St. Peter's Anglican Residential School in Hay River named Alice Bompas. I also found a picture of her grave marker. The grave marker indicates that she was born on May 28, 1919, and died on June 6, 1933. Census records indicate that William, who was "thrown away," took on the full name of the bishop, "William Bompas," and started a family with that name. The records also indicate that William married and had one child, David, and was then widowed. Alice could likely have been his granddaughter. The census records also indicate that David was widowed and had only one child. This seems to be the end of the adopted Bompas name in the NWT. While the Hardisty name flourishes, there are no more people named Bompas that I know of. However, there is much more research to be done in the archives once the world reopens after COVID-19.

Alice Bompas (age ten) on the left. Credit: Anglican Church of Canada, General Synod Archives (Diocese of the Arctic Fonds).

The HBC officer who "received" Allan was named William Lucas Hardisty. One question that I am left with is this: who is my great-great-grandfather? Is it Baptise le Noir or is it William Lucas Hardisty? If Allan Hardisty was deciding, I think he would go with Hardisty, as he named a daughter, Mary, the same name as William Hardisty's wife, and he named a son William Lucas. There are no progeny named Baptiste that I am aware of. It would make sense to say that, by nature, it would be le Noir, but by nurture, it would be Hardisty.

Grave marker of Alice Bompas.
Credit: St. Peter's Anglican Church (Hay River NWT) (Ted Wickson Fonds).

William Lucas Hardisty came to the Mackenzie River District in 1842 as the apprentice in charge of Fort Halkett. That post was located on the Liard River in what is now called British Columbia. At the time of Hardisty's arrival, it was part of the Mackenzie River District in Rupert's Land. In 1849, Hardisty became the clerk in charge at Fort Norman. He eventually rose through the ranks to become the chief trader in charge of the district in 1862 and then chief factor in charge of the district in 1868, at Fort Simpson. Hardisty would have been Charles Phillipe Gaudet's superior officer from the time Charles Phillipe arrived in 1851 until Hardisty retired and left the district in 1879. It is likely that Hardisty attended his "son" Allan's wedding in 1877.

∞

That, of course, raises the larger philosophical question of the relationship between adopting parents and the adopted children and their progeny. Along with that question, we also have to consider the "nature" versus "nurture" issue. Can a full-blooded

Dene person, as a result of nurturing by non-Dene parents, become something other than a Dene person? Part of the answer lies with the age of the child when adopted. Nurturing a newborn would have a much different outcome than nurturing a child from age twelve. I do not believe that there are any hard and fast rules to resolve the issue. By nature, I am 28.125 percent Dene, but by nurture, I am fully European. This is a result, in my view, of continuous European education and upbringing over at least five generations before me. My mother, by nature, was 50 percent-plus Dene but was, by nurture, fully European.

This truth dawned on me while I was doing the clean-up of the family property in 2020. I held a number of sales of the family's personal property, and these became informative visiting events. One of the Dene elders, who has been a long-time friend of our family, visited one day. As we were reminiscing, she said something that surprised me at the time. She said, and I am paraphrasing, "Your mother, you know, even if she was a White woman, could really speak good Slavey." That remark answered my question about who we were, at least from a Dene perspective. We were seen as being Whites or, from a deeper perspective, Europeans. My grandmother, Sarah Jane, was, by nature, completely Dene, but by nurture was mostly White. She was educated, having attended the Anglican residential schools in Fort Resolution and Hay River in the 1890s, raised in the Anglican Church, and married a man who was, by nurture, European.

Sadly, we have not maintained close ties with the Hardistys. The generations that included Edward Hardisty and my mother and her siblings did maintain close relations, but the generations after that have not. One factor certainly is that the generations of Edward and my mother and their siblings were all fluent Dene Kedee (Slavey) speakers. The next generation of Hardistys continued that fluency, but the descendants of the Gaudets, in my generation, with few exceptions, did not. This was largely a result of the decisions taken by our parents' generation to focus on education and professional training. My three older brothers were educated formally and, on the land, while my sister and I received only formal education. As a result, our older brothers had some fluency with Slavey, but I did not. They eventually lost what fluency they had as English became the predominant language of our country.

Starting in the 1970s, the two families were also at odds politically, with the Hardistys being strong supporters of the Dene Nation while the large majority of the descendants of the Gaudets, just as strongly, supported the Métis Nation. Perhaps my children and grandchildren will be able to make the repairs that are needed. The fundamental difference was based on competing views of what the future would look like. The Dene Nation was promoting ideas that were very socialist, even communistic, while the Métis Nation was much more interested in individualism and free enterprise. The Dene generally opposed any sort of development of the land while the Métis supported projects such as mines, pipelines, and oil-and-gas development.

Fred Gaudet and his wife, Mary (Lennie) Gaudet, and their daughter, Violet Gaudet.
Credit: Fort Norman Métis Community.

PART II

GROWING UP IN FORT NORMAN

L to R: – "Rod Hardy Bobby Overvold Ricky Hardy Walter Hardy Charlie Overvold Ft. Norman 1950" in Alice Hardy's handwriting. Credit: Hardy Family Collection.

CHAPTER SEVEN

MY EARLY LIFE

The *Story* also reveals that the "doctor" at my delivery was "Cecilia & Barbara," and the "Nurse" was "Barbara." These individuals, neither of whom was a doctor, would have been my aunt, Cecilia Hall, who was my mother's second-oldest sister, and Barbara Sherwood, who became my godmother. Barbara was a daughter of a local pioneer family and was a nurse. She eventually left the community and spent the remainder of her career working at the Charles Camsell Hospital in Edmonton.

I was baptized on May 18, 1947, as "Richard Irving Timothy Hardy." My godparents were Barbara Sherwood and Sammy Campbell. Sammy was a free trader in Fort Norman at the time and was renting the Northern Traders' compound. I have been told that Sammy was an alcoholic. I was also told that he was so drunk at my baptism that he pissed himself. Barbara maintained a lifelong connection with me on my birthday and at Christmas. Sadly, I never reciprocated the love that Barbara extended to me over all those years as often as I should have. This was despite the urgings from Mama to write letters and send cards to her. I never heard from Sammy. He eventually left Fort Norman, most likely in 1949.

Ricky Hardy's baptism (L to R): Father Jean Denis, Barbara Sherwood, and Sammy Campbell. Walter and Rod Hardy in the front.
Credit: Hardy Family Collection.

Although my formal name is Richard, most people call me Rick, and some who are close to me, like Mama, Diane, and a few school friends, called me, and still do, Ricky. "Irving" was one of my dad's brothers, and "Timothy" was my mother's father, Charles Timothy Gaudet. I still find it hard to believe, but my parents named me for a hit tune in 1947 called "Open the Door, Richard." I find it hard to believe because I don't recall them as being the type who would follow the hit parade. However, I do know that we all change as we grow older.

The *Story* also tells me that my first visitors were Mabel Hall (likely after struggling to town through a blizzard), Father J. Denis, Mrs. Botten, Sarah Hall, and Mrs. Mackinnon. Mabel and Sarah were sisters and were our older cousins. Mabel used to love telling me, in our later years, how she trudged through a snowstorm, so she could get back to town, from the trapline, so she could help at my birth. Father J. Denis was the priest who baptized me into the Roman Catholic Church. Father Denis remained a friend of our family for the rest of his life. He would remind me, from time to time, that as the person who baptized me, he held a lifelong responsibility for my spiritual well-being.

Ricky Hardy, at about ten months, in front of the family home. Credit: Hardy Family Collection.

Ricky Hardy holding up Hib McCauley. Credit: Hardy Family Collection.

Father Denis was a kind and generous person. He should not be grouped with all the bad characters that the Roman Catholic Church sent to our communities over the centuries.

The *Story* tells me that my playmates, when I was very young, were Bobby Overvold and Hib McCauley. It also tells me that I got a toy dog and a toy duck for my first Christmas. On my first birthday, I got presents from Aunt Cecilia and Mrs. Botten. On one of my birthdays, I got a gun from Granddad Tim Gaudet. I assume it was a toy! Yes, it was likely the one I am using in the picture where Hib McCauley is "Hands Up."

One other event of note is related to my birth. Our parents transplanted a birch sapling to the front of our house to mark my coming into the world. It has grown into a large, sturdy birch tree and is still there. Daddy and Mama also planted one for Diana after she was born five years later. I went through a very emotional time while deciding to sell the property, and a lot of that was related to those trees. My parents were looking forward to a future different from the one that happened.

PART II

The birch trees in 1999. Both trees are still there as well as others that were planted in later years. Credit: Maryann Hardy.

Peter James Hardy in front of the birch trees eating a wild raspberry, in 2020. Credit: Author.

Peter James Hardy and Tianna Hardy Mainville, down the hill from what used to be the Hardy property, in 2020. Credit: Joel Walton.

CHAPTER EIGHT

THE BELT

As I grew up, I seldom felt impoverished. However, with the benefit of hindsight, I now know that all things are relative to one's immediate surroundings and circumstances. Even though we had very little, it appeared to others that we had plenty. My late brother, Rod, had a knack for turning a blunt phrase. When he was accused of having more than anybody else in Fort Norman, he would respond with, "What's the matter with you, you silly bugger? Just because we had three hungry dogs and you only had two doesn't mean we were any better off than you."

Having said that, I do recall a time when we had no food in our house, and I was hungry. More importantly, I remember the anger and frustration felt and expressed by Mama. That incident marked me for life. On the one hand, I am frugal, and on the other, I can be very generous. The time that we had no food was in the spring of 1956. Diane and I were home with Mama while Daddy, Rod, and Walter were out spring hunting. I would have been nine years old, and Diane would have been four. Leo was living in Edmonton, after being discharged from the Charles Camsell Hospital, having been cured of tuberculosis. He had begun a new life in the city.

Mama was waiting for Daddy and the two boys to come home with the beaver and muskrat pelts, which would be sold to either the HBC or a free trader. Then we would have money to buy groceries, at least the little bit that was left in the stores at that time of the year. They would also be bringing beaver meat and ducks and geese. Maybe they might even bring a few local delicacies, rat tails. No one in the community would have let us go hungry for long if they had food to share.

Even though we had no food, I remember having one of the best meals ever during that time. When a person is hungry and is given food, the event stands out in their memory. Most families who lived in Fort Norman at that time would move out to the bush for the spring hunt. Spring hunting was a serious business then and not the holiday, by helicopter, that it has turned into. Because of Mama's insistence on me being formally educated, I never did go on a spring hunt while growing up.

Some individuals on the hunt would walk in and out town from time to time to pick up additional supplies. On this particular occasion, Noel Gladu, the foster dad of my friend, Mike, walked across the ice on the Mackenzie River, which was a very dangerous thing to do in May. He brought some fish to the community, including a large jackfish. He gave that jackfish to Old Lady Karkagie, who was too old to go spring hunting anymore and stayed home in her tiny little house next door to Dan Lennie's house. Her house was much like a hobbit house. It was small and made up of one room, of, I would guess, 150 square feet with 6-foot walls and no ceiling. Her bed was in one corner across from a small table and her two chairs. In the centre was a barrel stove, which had an oven built into the stovepipe. The place where the ceiling would have been had poles strung across it and held various items, such as towels and items of clothing. These poles would be used to hang meat to dry when moose meat was available. Most houses had the aroma of moose meat or tanned moose hide. When I breathe those aromas now, I am reminded of a time when life was much simpler and easy going.

The "hobbit" house beside Dan Lennie's house. Taken in the mid-1960s. Credit: NWT Archives/Bart Hawkins Photographic Collection.

In both good and bad times, Mama used to take Diane and me to visit those who had stayed in town. When we got to the old woman's house, she was just getting ready to cook that jackfish. She asked us if we wanted some, and, of course, Mama said yes. The old woman, who was bent over and moved slowly, cleaned the fish, getting most of the bones out. At the same time, she was stoking the wood fire in the stove. She fried that fish to perfection in an old cast-iron frying pan with lard. The smell was mouth-watering, and the taste of the fish was absolutely delicious. The old woman also made tea for Mama and gave each of us a small piece of bannock. The old woman and Mama took the two chairs at the table, and Diane and I sat on the floor while the old woman and Mama talked to each other in Slavey. We ate out of tin plates. That was the best fish and bannock that I ever ate. I will never forget the old lady's kindness.

PART II

A year or so after that jackfish meal, our schoolteacher decided we would hike to Plane Lake and back and have a picnic lunch out there. We were again low on food and did not have anything to prepare a picnic lunch from. Mama was angry and frustrated. The Gaudets were a prideful family and frequently quarrelled among themselves. Mama could have easily asked Uncle Fred or Aunt Jane for some help, but she didn't because of a quarrel. She found some loose change somewhere and gave it to me. She told me to run to the store and buy something before we left on the hike. I bought a package of Glosette raisins. I was a bit embarrassed at the picnic, but, hey, the raisins tasted great.

∞

That year was also the spring that "Duke" disappeared. Duke was a Black man who worked for the Northern Transportation Company Limited at the Bear River Camp. Duke and the other southern workers would fly up from Edmonton on a DC-3, early in the spring and open up the camp for the summer season. A part of the Bear River facility was an airstrip, called Bennett Field, which could accommodate planes the size of DC-3s. That particular year, Duke wandered off into the bush shortly after arriving. He did not return, and the RCMP were notified. A search was organized, and the two communities nearby, Fort Norman and Fort Franklin, were advised. Panic set in. Most Indians in those days still followed their own beliefs, notwithstanding what the Christian churches might have to say about it. Some still do. One of the major beliefs that they have is in "Náhgáneh," the bushman or bogeyman of their belief system.

The situation was complicated further because Duke was a Black man. Some of the Indians had seen Black men before when the American Army came north during World War II to build the Canol Pipeline in the 1940s. The Indians called them "Black White men" in their own language. However, none of those Black White men wandered off and got lost, as far as we know.

So, the likely conclusion reached by the Indians was that Duke had been taken by Náhgáneh and was now one of them. I guess a Black Náhgáneh, was double peril. The RCMP did not know about Náhgáneh, but they did ask everyone to keep an eye out in case Duke found his way to Fort Norman, which was about forty miles away from the Bear River Camp. They didn't have to ask, but everyone locked their doors and windows. Mama swore that Duke had come to town because she saw him looking through the window of her and Daddy's bedroom. Hmmmm? Duke was never found, so he is probably still out there, gallivanting around with the other Náhgáneh, looking to carry off beautiful women or bad children who didn't listen to their parents. I understand that Náhgáneh are like bears and sleep all winter.

One good thing came out of the search for Duke, for us. The RCMP, or perhaps Northern Transportation Company Limited, hired a helicopter that was in the area to help in the search. The helicopter stopped at most hunting camps, including Daddy's, to put the word out. Daddy asked the helicopter pilot to take some of his spring hunt furs to Fort Norman for us, so we could get some cash sooner rather than later. So ended that period of no food.

∞

Daddy was a self-taught musician who came from Antigonish, Nova Scotia. He used to play the fiddle for the community dances, at least until I started getting older. By then Mama had stopped going to dances and other social activities in the community. His fiddling style was from his Maritime roots, but he adapted to the Métis style, which is much livelier. He also played the guitar and the accordion. Mama was also quite musical and played the organ for church services and loved to hum tunes. I have heard stories of Daddy being known as the crooked-armed fiddler during the years that he spent in northern Alberta. He had broken his arm, after being thrown from a horse, earlier in life, and it never healed properly. One of my pleasant childhood memories is of Daddy sitting on a chair in our backyard playing plaintive old Scottish tunes on his fiddle in the evening.

Daddy had the story of his life written for our family in booklet form. He led a fascinating life. His life started out in a somewhat Dickensian fashion. The booklet is titled *From East to West: Drifting with The Wind – The Story of Jack Hardy.* Daddy had, at best, a grade one education, and he could barely read or write. In the first part of his life in Fort Norman, Mama did all of the reading and writing for him. After Mama took sick, I became the one who filled that role, at least when I was home.

Daddy was involved in many memorable events in Fort Norman. One of those that he seemed to relish in his storytelling was to do with a visit by Governor General Georges Vanier and Madame Vanier to Fort Norman in June 1961. I was not there, as I was in school in Inuvik. The governor general was touring the Northwest Territories. How Fort Norman was chosen as a stop is not known to me. It may have been a last-minute decision, as there was a bit of a panic in the community about what to do with the vice-regal couple. The only way they could get in and out of Fort Norman, at that time, was by floatplane. The problem with that was that both of the Vaniers were elderly and would not be able to walk up the wet slopes that were the "roads" at the time. So, Daddy swung into action and built railings, of a sort, on his farm wagon, "borrowed" Mama's couch, and put it on the wagon for the Vaniers to sit on. Then he hooked his Caterpillar D2 tractor up to the "vice-regal carriage" and headed down to the beach of the Mackenzie River to wait for the airplane.

Fortunately, NTCL had already started operations for the summer and had a tug and barge handy in the Bear River. This provided for one event—a ride on the tug to and from Bear River. However, the Vaniers still needed to have a tour of the community. The barge came in handy this time as it was used as a dock for the floatplane. This made it much easier for the Vaniers to disembark. Otherwise, they would have had to climb down a narrow set of stairs, get off the plane onto the floats, somehow find their way to the shore, and then into the muck that covered the beach. The ice from the annual breakup had only recently thawed. Instead, they were on a large, sturdy barge with a large, sturdy gangplank to the shore. Daddy backed the vice-regal carriage into the water right beside the gangplank, and the Vaniers were easily able to make the transition from the barge.

Jack Hardy hauling Governor General Vanier (standing) and Madame Vanier (sitting on the couch) up from the beach in Fort Norman in 1961. Credit: NWT Archives/G-1979-011:0053.

The next step in the transportation saga was to get the vice-regal carriage and the vice-regal couple up the first hill to the first bench and then up a second hill to the second bench where the transient rulers of the community were waiting. Some in the vice-regal party, other than the Vaniers themselves, had their doubts about the contraption being able to do the job. However, there was little to worry about as Daddy had hauled many much heavier loads of freight up those hills with the same equipment. As you can see from the photo, it was quite an experience for everyone. Daddy used to love finishing the story with, "Well, the old governor was a pretty good guy. He got quite a kick out of the whole trip."

∞

Because I wanted to find out more about Daddy's family, I made two trips to Nova Scotia to find Hardy family members and learn more about Daddy. The first trip was with, my first wife, Bea and the children. We found his sister, Grace, and some of her children. I was shocked at how similar their looks were. Grace referred to him as Joseph or Joe, which was his childhood name. The second trip was with, my second wife, Maryann. Unfortunately, Grace had passed away by that time. Maryann and I spent a lot of time in the archives of Saint Francis Xavier University in Antigonish and learned quite a bit. We also visited graveyards and parish offices. During one visit, I asked one of the kind ladies who maintained the church records if it was possible that Daddy was part Mikmaugh. The answer was not definitive but left the door open. She indicated it wouldn't be surprising because of the many intermarriages over the centuries, after the coming of the Scots. The reason I asked is because, a few years before his death, in 1997, Daddy started claiming that he was part Mikmaugh through his mother, Catherine MacDonald.

We learned that I was from the clan Solomon MacDonald, and they had come to Nova Scotia in the late 1700s. Needless to say, we could not find confirmation of Daddy's claim of being part Mikmaugh. However, while on this this trip I was reminded that Daddy could still speak Gaelic even after being away from his roots for many decades. This knowledge came as a great surprise to us and, I think, to him when we found out. Finding this out took place sometime in the late 1960's after the Northwest Territories was finally linked to the rest of Canada by long distance telephone service. Daddy decided to try the new service out so called the long-distance operator to connect him to his sister Grace in Glace Bay, Nova Scotia. They had not seen or heard each other for over forty years but she began speaking Gaelic to him almost immediately. To his and our great surprise he responded in the same language.

∞

As I explained earlier, I have no original memories of my first few years in this world. The early memories that I do have come from stories told to me by Mama and other relatives, especially my aunt, Jane Gaudet. Of course, traumatic and other significant events also lead to the creation of memories.

The first such significant event in my life was a few days after the birth of my sister, Diana, in April 1952. I was still four years old at the time but would turn five about a month after that. These memories were formed by a combination of stories told to me many, many times by my mother, and actual recall by myself. Mama gave birth to Diana at the community nursing station. I don't recall this, but it is likely that I was at home with Daddy and one of my older brothers, Walter George Benjamin Hardy. Rod and Leo were both away in hospitals with tuberculosis. Walter was six years older than me. He was the third child in the family, and I was the fourth. Of course, Diana was the fifth. I recently found the origin of the name Walter. Or, more accurately, my wife, Maryann, found it for me. Daddy had a brother named Walter, who was two years older than him. I do know that "George" was for our matrilineal uncle, George Gaudet, and "Benjamin" was for a patrilineal uncle, Benjamin Hardy, the oldest of Daddy's siblings. Walter was born in June 1941, and he died in a tragic boating accident on June 14, 1965.

These memories have Walter bringing me to the nursing station to see our new sibling, the first girl in the family. Mama was in a hospital bed, and Diana was in one of those old steel-railing-sided cribs. It rattled when the rail was touched. Mama told Walter to lift me up, so I could see our new sister. Walter, unusually, did what he was told to do. Up I went and leaned over the railing to see what the fuss was all about. Apparently, my reaction was, "What's that?" Mama replied, "That's your new sister." I didn't know what a sister was, and whatever it was, I was not happy! I squirmed and fussed and managed to get myself taken home. Looked like competition to me!

The part of the story that is my actual memory is the hospital bed, the crib, and Walter lifting me to the edge of the railing while it rattled. I don't know if I actually recall the rest of the story. I don't remember going to the nursing station or returning home. However, as I was told the story so many times, it is now embedded as part of my memory.

Another very important event in my life is tied to the birth of Diana. I got my first haircut. I have been told many times, mostly by Aunt Jane, that even though Mama's first four children were boys, she was determined to have a fifth—a girl. My mother was a very determined person. She was forty-one years old when Diana was born. That is old for a woman having children, or

PART II

Diane, Ricky, and Alice Hardy. "They won't call me a girl anymore." Credit: Hardy Family Collection.

so I am told. Mama was born on January 11, 1911, in Fort Wrigley. Her name at birth was Alice Louise Gaudet. Diana was born on April 3, 1952, in Fort Norman and was baptized as Diana Alice Hardy.

You can see the smile on my face because of the haircut in the picture in which Mama is holding Diana up for a photo. Because Mama was determined to have a girl, and I was the youngest son, I was not given a haircut until the decree was fulfilled! You can see the beautiful curly locks that I had up until that time in the pictures taken by Mama. My *Story* says that my remarks after my first haircut were, "They won't call me a girl anymore."

∞

Interestingly, as Diana grew older, I became the older brother who loved her dearly and looked out for her. She became my ally, as you can see in the picture of both of us pouting. She had nothing to pout about but was giving her support to me in the crisis at hand. This picture was likely taken in the summer of 1956 when I was nine and Diana was four.

The crisis arose from the way in which we got new clothes in those days. Many items that we wanted were too expensive, because of the bulk or the weight, to be shipped by our monthly mail, which came by ski or floatplane. So, these items were shipped by barge on the Mackenzie River in the summertime. The orders were placed by mail to Simpson's, Eaton's, or Woodward's in March or April of each year and usually came cash on delivery (COD) on the first barge near the end of June. We didn't know what credit cards were in those days. Simpsons, Eaton's, or Woodward's would package up the orders, and they would be shipped by rail from Edmonton to Waterways.

The shipments would all be marked "Via Waterways." Years after the shipping route changed to "Via Hay River," there were still packing crates lying around Fort Norman (and other communities being served the same way) with the words "Via Waterways" written on them. You could always tell who the newcomers to the community were as they couldn't figure out what "Via Waterways" meant. It didn't help them that the name "Waterways" was slipping into the annals of northern history. Interestingly, the three stores mentioned—Simpson's, Eaton's, and Woodward's—have also faded into the annals of history. Waterways was, in essence, part of Fort McMurray, which, of course, exists today. Fort McMurray started its existence, as did Fort Norman, as a fur trading post.

When the shipments arrived by train in Fort McMurray, they were transferred to one of the barging companies operating on the Athabasca and Mackenzie River system—usually Northern Transportation Company Limited. They would then be carried by barge, starting in Waterways, down the Clearwater River to the Athabasca River to Lake Athabasca and across it and then down the Slave River to Fort Fitzgerald, Alberta. The goods were then portaged by trucks (originally by oxen and then horses) through Fort Smith to Bell Rock. Then they were loaded onto another barge and hauled down the remainder of the Slave River to Fort Resolution and then across Great Slave Lake to Hay River and then to the mouth of the Mackenzie River. Then they would be on their way to the children of Fort Norman and in all the other communities along the river who were also waiting for their new clothes. Of course, a lot more important freight was on the barges as well.

The barge would have to land and unload in Fort Providence, Fort Simpson, and Fort Wrigley before it got to Fort Norman. After Fort Norman, the barge would continue on to Norman Wells, Fort Good Hope, Arctic Red River, Fort McPherson (via the Peel River), Aklavik, and, sometimes, Tuktoyaktuk. Yes, it was a bit like Christmas, but the children who lived closest to the North Pole had to wait the longest.

∞

Daddy must have had a good winter cutting wood and trapping that year, as Mama was able to order new clothes for all three of the children who were still at home. My order included a new shirt with all kinds of fancy little cowboy and Indian logos on it, a new pair of jeans, and, above all else, a new belt with a fancy buckle. My Lord, would I show my cousin Bobby who should be the leader of the cowboys now!

A word of caution here for younger readers, like my children and grandchildren: as difficult as it is to imagine, in the Internet age, Mama had to order months in advance by mail. We also had to wait months until the order arrived to see if everything we wanted had been shipped. So, there was always a bit of anxiety waiting to see if everything would arrive.

I was an ardent Roman Catholic altar boy then, so I expect, like the boy in Roch Carrier's *The Hockey Sweater*, that I likely slipped in a few prayers for Mr. Simpson, Mr. Eaton, or Mr. Woodward to fill my order completely, especially the belt.

So, the days of waiting and anxiety ended. I don't recall all the details of the barge arriving, but it would have been surrounded by the usual excitement in the community, as it was the first barge of the year—yeah—apples, bananas, and other goodies. Other goodies would include chocolate bars, as the HBC store had long sold out of the previous year's supply. Maybe that was the year when they first brought soda pop to the community. Whether it was that year or another, I remember my first taste of Orange Crush from a bottle. Heavenly. Those magical barges.

As our order, like most in those days, was sent COD, Mama would have had to dig out the cash from her trunk, count it out to Daddy, and he would go to find the purser who was responsible for getting the money for the COD before the parcels would be released.

Sometimes people would order their goods and supplies COD, hoping they would have the money ready when the barge arrived. Getting the money after placing the order usually meant a good spring hunt and reasonable prices for muskrat and beaver pelts that year. Sometimes they didn't have a good hunt, or the prices were not as high as hoped for. Then the goods would stay on the barge and go north to the end of the line in Aklavik or Tuktoyaktuk. The barge would then stop on the way back, loaded with goods being shipped south as well as the unpaid for CODs. If the purchaser had the money by then, the COD would be released. If not, the goods simply went back to Mr. Simpson, Mr. Eaton, or Mr. Woodward.

Could that happen to us? Absolutely not! Mama was the daughter of three generations of HBC traders, including two chief traders, for the northern area of the Mackenzie River District, and she would not, under any circumstances, countenance embarrassment of any sort, especially being known as someone who would order from Mr. Simpson, Mr. Eaton, or Mr. Woodward and not be able to pay for the goods when they arrived. It was bad enough that we were not buying these goods and supplies from the HBC. The ancestors would not have approved.

A few years later, Mama and Daddy were appointed as the agents for the Northern Transportation Company Limited in Fort Norman. They provided a small shed in which the CODs could be kept until the customers had the money. However, if the money was not forthcoming by the time the last barge was going south in September, the goods were hauled down the hill to the barge and shipped back to Mr. Simpson, Mr. Eaton, or Mr. Woodward. Being a small community, everyone knew everyone else's business in Fort Norman. Not much has changed in that regard in what is now called Tulıt'a. I do recall feeling a lot of empathy for those families who had to face the embarrassment of having their CODs returned. At the time I didn't know what empathy was, but I felt that what was happening was wrong.

Of course, our parcels arrived. Mama and Daddy had the money, which was paid to the NTCL purser. Daddy was given the parcels, and he brought them home when he had time. I don't recall him being around for the rest of this story. I guess he knew what was coming down! Actually, he was likely busy hauling freight up the hill for the HBC and other businesses with one of his tractors and a farm wagon and had come home for what we called dinner. Nowadays, that meal is called lunch.

Mama opened the parcels and inspected the contents and checked them off while Diana and I waited outside to be called in to enter the world of new clothes. Walter got to stay inside to "help." When Diana and I were called in, I caught a glimpse of my new belt. Before I could put my hands on it, Mama announced that not everyone's order had been completely filled. What did I care? Mr. Eaton or one of the other guys could keep my shirt and pants, as my precious belt was there. Glory be.

Then my world crumbled. Mama announced that the only item that had not been shipped was Walter's new belt—one of those factory-beaded fake leather belts meant to look like Indian handicraft. My reaction, of course, was, "So what?" The "so what," unfortunately for me, was that because Walter was older than me, he needed a new belt more than I did. At least, that was what I was told.

All my bad emotions, guided by the green monster, began to rise in me as Mama announced that Walter would get my belt, and I would get his old one, as a hand-me-down!

Arrrrgggghhh! Walter's belt was practically worn out, and I was certain that he had used it as part of his dog harness, as needed, from time to time. I cried and bellowed, to no avail. Walter was probably sitting right there smirking at me.

Comrades in arms - Ricky and Diane Hardy.
Credit: Hardy Family Collection.

Mama let me have my outburst for a limited period of time. Then she said, "Okay, Ricky and Diane, get into your new clothes, so I can take a picture."

"I don't want my picture taken with that stinky old belt," I retorted.

I should have realized I was on very thin ice. "I said get into your new clothes." I knew the gig was up, but I could be as determined as Mama.

"I will put my new pants and shirt on but not with that stinky belt."

"Put the belt on!" By this time Mama's "raised in the convent voice" had taken over. This was the voice that the nuns had used while she was in residential school in Fort Providence. It was a distinctly unpleasant voice. It was now "flight or fight" time for me.

I guess a weak fight was my response. I put the stinky belt on with my new pants and shirt and continued to sob. Diana and I were then ordered outside for the picture. Of course, the "raised in the convent voice" ordered us to smile. By God, Diana and I refused to comply, and we won the point! As you can see from the picture, we stuck with our "I hate you" looks for the picture. Diana had no skin in the game, but she stood by me. There was certainly no need for those feelings of jealousy that I had when I first saw her in the crib, four years earlier.

Of course, Diane—the name she came to use—and I did not hate Mama. We loved her dearly to her dying day. Mama had spent ten years in the residential school in Fort Providence from the age of six years. The residential schools in those days were commonly referred to as convents. The convents were run by the Roman Catholic Church, and they always hoped to capture young girls who had "vocations."

Mama hated the nuns because she wanted to be a schoolteacher, but the Church would not allow any further education for her unless she would agree to become a nun. She did not want to become a nun. As I said earlier, she was a determined person. Mama spent ten years in the convent and achieved the highest level of education offered there: grade four. She told us that she spent a lot of time scrubbing floors, doing laundry, and working in the kitchen.

Ricky and Diane Hardy in the Halloween costumes made by Alice Hardy, probably in 1958. Credit: Hardy Family Collection.

Mama and her contemporaries who attended this convent used to facetiously call it *"l'universitie de providence."* Her brother-in-law, Ted Trindell, also went to school there. In his memoir,

Ted Trindell Métis Witness to the North, he writes, "Went to school in Providence, and came out in 1914, with my university degree—Providence, grade two." Ted had spent five years there.

Mama was, unfortunately, born left-handed. The nuns and, most likely, the Roman Catholic Church believed that being left-handed was a sign of the devil. This allowed them, not that they needed any allowance, to beat her left hand with rulers and other instruments of torture. Another student who attended the same convent as Mama around the same time, Bridget Harris Volden, tells her story in *If Only the Rod Had Been Round*. The "rod" she is referring to is the one the nuns used to smash her left wrist, so she could never use her left hand again. While I read this part of her book, I cried, not only for Bridget but also for my mother, who had been tortured in the same way.

Volden's book was given to me by Mike and Lorna Cooper when I came to the Cooper Barging office in Fort Simpson to pick up my truck in September 2020. It was a surprise that materialized after I told them about the book that I was writing. The book that they gave me was truly a gift as I was reading a firsthand account of how miserable life in the "convents" really was. The book corroborated many of the stories that Mama told me. I thank Mike and Lorna Cooper for this gift. More importantly, I thank Bridget Harris Volden and her co-author, Ruth Thiekle, for writing the book, which will be a real reference point for the evil that was committed on so many children by the Roman Catholic Church.

Ironically, Mama's father had to pay for all of his children to attend these so-called schools because they were not Indians, and he was not destitute. Interestingly, my first wife, Bea Bloomstrand, attended a similar school in Fort Chipewyan, and her father, Peter Bloomstrand, had to pay for his children to attend there. What particularly incensed Bea was that her father would send them tins of butter and other food that they would not get at that convent. She and her siblings never got any of the food, as it was given to the priests and the nuns. I recall Mama telling us that the same thing happened to them in Fort Providence.

Mama did not have any happy memories of the convent that I ever heard of. She left us quite a collection of pictures when she died. Included in the collection was a photo of the convent and related buildings, taken in 1924. She scribbled in a side note: "Ft. Providence where I went to school run by nuns. We used to eat fish 3 times a day, hung fish too." Hung fish was usually used for dog feed. The fish were caught in nets in various lakes in the area. They were then hauled back to the community and were "split" in order to be hung on poles to dry. They usually spoiled in the process. Notwithstanding this, the spoiled fish would freeze and would be good enough for the dogs.

∞

Walter and Diana were the two siblings on either side of me, age wise. We had two other older brothers. The oldest was Leon Charles William Hardy, who was born on May 21, 1935. He was named for his matrilineal granduncle, Joseph Leon Gaudet, his matrilineal grandfather and great-grandfather, Charles Timothy and Charles Phillipe Gaudet, and finally his patrilineal grandfather, William Hardy.

The second child in the family was Roderick Allen Hardy, who was born on June 10, 1938. To tell you the truth, I don't know why the name Roderick was given to him, but I do know that Allen was a patrilineal uncle, Allen Hardy, and, of course, our great-grandfather, Allan Hardisty. Rod died of a massive coronary on April 17, 2008.

I do not recall much about Leo or Rod during my young years. This was a result, at least in part, of them having been infected with tuberculosis and being sent away from home to different hospitals. Another reason was that the children in our family had fairly large age differences. Leo is twelve years older than me; Rod was nine years older, and Walter was six years older. I am five years older than Diane. Additionally, the three older siblings were raised mostly under the influence of Daddy while Diane and I were more influenced by Mama. Fortunately, Mama did not lose any children in childbirth or while they were still young, as happened so often with her mother and grandmothers.

∞

The fact that we were mostly raised by Mama likely contributed to Diane and I being pushed to complete our formal education. Leo, Rod, and Walter completed their first few grades by correspondence courses, as there was no school in Fort Norman at that time. Mama saved the materials and assignments from the correspondence courses, and I found them in her trunk while cleaning up the family property.

Mama and Daddy were among the parents who battled with the government to get a government school established in Fort Norman. Mama told me that one of the major moving forces for the establishment of that school was Chief Colin Campbell. The first school building was the old mining recorder's office, which had been built in Fort Norman during the Fort Norman Oil Wells oil staking rush. Apparently, it was the first government building built in the Northwest Territories.

After a few years of using that building, the community was blessed with a brand-new school. It had two classrooms with large folding doors that could be opened to create a large

PART II

95

community space. This was used for the annual Christmas concert. The space was also used as a gymnasium. The school also had separate indoor bathrooms for boys and girls, including flush toilets. There was also a three-bedroom apartment on top of the mechanical room for use by the principal and his family. The flush toilets did not work when the weather got really cold, and the septic system would freeze up. The contingency plan was the building of two outhouses behind the school, one for the boys and men and one for the girls and women.

Initially, the school was named the Fort Norman Federal Day School. A few years later, after people began to realize that they had some political power, the school was renamed as the Colin Campbell Federal Day School to recognize the work that he did to get the school established. Alas, the school building ended its useful days and was replaced by a new, much larger school. For reasons that I don't know, the new school was also given a new name.

I describe the Colin Campbell school as if it was the first in Fort Norman. However, the first school was run by the Anglican Church as part of its mission to Fort Norman starting in 1859.

∞

I have some memories of attending the early grades at the Fort Norman Federal Day School. During the winter when there would be a blizzard, we could have stayed home. But, no, Mama would not allow us to miss a day of school unless absolutely necessary. Walter and Rod would have been old and big enough to walk through the blowing snow as the wind, which would come off Bear Rock, would be at their back while walking to school in the morning. But I was young and small and might have gotten blown away or lost. So, Mama would make Walter hitch the dog team up, bundle me up in the cariole, and drive me to school. Walter loved driving his dogs, so I guess that was not such a chore for him.

The other memory is manufactured as a result of Rod telling the story so many times, especially in social settings. The story was that when he and Walter had to walk me to school, they would be constantly irritated by me because I would go too slow for them. So, they complained to Mama, thinking I would be told to keep up with them. To their chagrin, Mama told them that I was thinking and should be left to take my time. She also told them that they ought to take some time themselves to do some thinking, like I was doing.

∞

As for the barging system, it too has slipped into the annals of history. During the years that I was growing up, the barges were an integral part of life along the Mackenzie River. A number of companies were part of the industry from approximately the mid-1880s until the late 1960s. By that time only the Northern Transportation Company Limited offered full service to all of the communities. The need for the barges dissipated as highways were extended north.

First, the Mackenzie Highway was extended, and Fort Smith, Fort Resolution, Hay River, Fort Providence, Fort Rae, and Yellowknife no longer had much need for the barges. Then the Dempster Highway was finished, and Fort McPherson, Arctic Red River, and Inuvik started getting most of their goods by road. The third highway to be built into the North was the Liard Highway, which meant no more barges were needed to ship goods to Fort Liard and Fort Simpson. The Mackenzie Highway was then extended to Fort Wrigley, so the only communities that remained dependent on the barges were Fort Norman, Norman Wells, Fort Good Hope, Colville Lake, Fort Franklin, Aklavik and Tuktoyaktuk. The Dempster Highway was recently completed to Tuktoyaktuk, so only the five communities in the Sahtu and Aklavik continue to depend on the barges. That dependence has been reduced considerably with the construction of the winter road system to those communities.

Another reduction in the need for the barges to these communities has been the increase in wealth, which enables the people who live there to pay high costs for food, which is now flown in on a year-round basis. It baffles me the amount of soda pop and potato chips that are flown to these communities and are bought at exorbitant prices. Yet, people complain bitterly about the high cost of living. If they would just stop buying what are, essentially, luxury items, they would have more money in their pockets, and their health would be much better. Progress?

The history of the steamboats that plied the northern river routes until the mid-1950s is the subject of a new book that will soon be available from Blair Jean. The title of the book is *Steamboats on Northern Waters*. I understand that this book will be followed by one about the tugboats that replaced them.

Barges still work the Mackenzie River to move heavy loads of building supplies and equipment as well as petroleum products. There is also one company left that still moves general goods into some of the Sahtu communities. That company is Cooper Barging, and it runs the service out of Fort Simpson. Cooper Barging has been in business for seventy-five or more years, and the owners have many personal relationships with residents of the communities that they serve. Eventually, the Mackenzie Highway will continue its crawl north, and the need for barges to supply the communities will, sadly, become a thing of the past.

PART II

CHAPTER NINE

GROWING UP

Following Granddad's death, my life became a period of mostly childhood happiness and bliss. I had entered the time of actually having memories of my own. The largest exception to this period of happiness was the death of Uncle Ray Overvold. Uncle Ray had come to Canada from the state of Washington and eventually settled in Fort Norman, marrying Aunt Christine Gaudet, the youngest daughter of my grandparents. The Overvold and Hardy children were roughly the same ages and lived the same lifestyle and were, of course, first cousins. Uncle Ray, Uncle Joe, Daddy, and others, such as Bill McNeely in Fort Good Hope, Hib Hodgson in Norman Wells, Bert Furlong in Fort Good Hope and Fort Norman, Jim McCauley in Fort Norman, Oscar Granath of Norman Wells, George Douglas of Fort Norman, Red Anders, the McGurran family and Bill Boland on Great Bear Lake were what some would call White settlers. They all, except Red Anders, married women from the country and were very versatile with their hands and their brains. They formed the first nucleus of a permanent White presence and a small business community. There were also some White families, such as the Sherwoods and the Matsons.

The people that I speak of in the previous paragraph would not be "transients" which is a term that I use a number of times throughout the book. The transients that I refer to would be those that were sent to the community by governments, government agencies, the HBC and the Catholic Church. None of the transients sent to the community were meant to be there for a lengthy period of time. Additionally, they were all provided with good furnished housing which had forced air furnaces and hot and cold running water.

The White settlers would run sawmills, cut wood for the steamboats, prospect, run fishnets in summer and winter, grow truck gardens, bake and sell bread and pastries, run scows on the rivers, lay cable to move tugs through rapids, haul water and ice to the houses of the transients, haul wood for the locals, trap and hunt, and do anything else that would bring in a few extra dollars to provide for their families. When our family ran a sawmill, we even bagged and sold the sawdust to Imperial Oil in Norman Wells, where it was used to berm the large oil storage tanks. I spent two summers doing this bagging and was paid twenty-five cents a bag for my labour by Daddy. Locally, shavings from the planer mills were used for wall insulation.

Uncle Joe, Uncle Ray, Bert Furlong, Bill McNeely, Oscar Granath, and Bill Boland were also free traders, in addition to their other activities. A free trader was anyone who had a trading licence to buy wild furs, issued by the GNWT, which was headquartered in Ottawa at that time. That is, anyone other than the HBC, which was the dominant force in the fur industry. Being "free" meant not being the HBC. There were also a number of other free traders, but they did not leave as much of a permanent mark as those mentioned.

These people, along with Daddy, were likely the ones Gabriel Cho had in mind when he would sneer at me as I passed his house, which had been built by a free trader. The sneer would be accompanied by a gruff-voiced "Mǫlazha". This happened a number of times and was not intended to be friendly or a tease. It was an expression of hatred aimed at a child. Mǫlazha means child of a White man. When it is spit out, you know it is not friendly.

I recently learned that I was not singled out for this treatment. My cousin, Margaret (Overvold) Powder, wrote to me that she remembers the kids calling her that name when she was in school in Fort Norman.

To be fair, most Dene who lived in Fort Norman at that time were friendly. Paul Macaulay and his family lived across the road from Gabriel Cho. Paul, like Gabriel, was a unilingual Dene. Paul was a happy man. He would speak to me in Dene, and I didn't really understand what he was saying, but his smile and his body language always imparted good feelings to me. I will always remember Paul and his wife, Celine, for their kindness in sending fresh meat to my parents whenever they had a successful hunt. Paul and Celine were representative of the majority view of the Dene to our family.

∞

Being a free trader meant being in opposition to the HBC, which I mentioned earlier was managed by many of our family members with religious zeal. Aunt Cecilia had married Joe Hall, who was not only a free trader but extremely anti-Catholic, being an Irishman of that persuasion. I wonder if he ever accompanied his wife, Aunt Cecilia, when she visited her father, Charles Timothy, who was the leading Catholic in the community and employed by the HBC. The collection of family photographs from Mama doesn't include Joe Hall in any photos with Charles Timothy. I wonder if Charles Timothy even went to the wedding.

I mentioned Hib Hodgson, who became Daddy's best friend after Daddy came to the country in 1930. "The country" is the term that we use to describe the part of the North that we live in. "Came to the country" was a term that was used by one of the so-called elders from Fort Norman in front of Judge Berger in 1976 during his inquiry into the proposed Arctic Gas Pipeline. This elder was talking about my grandfather. The elder, I am told, said that he remembered when my grandfather "came to the country." That is not a complimentary thing to say about someone. The problem, in this case, was that my grandfather was born and raised in the country, long before this particular elder was born. I think this is just another example of manufactured memories. Being an elder is not solely related to age. It also means being wise and thinking before running off at the mouth.

The Hall family (L to R): Sarah, Mabel, Cecilia, and Joe Hall on the north shore of Great Bear Lake, ready to go trapping. Credit: Hardy Family Collection.

Grandad did attend the wedding of Aunt Christine and Uncle Ray, even if it was carried out by the local Anglican minister. We have the picture!

Ray Overvold and Christine Gaudet (second and third from right), getting married in Fort Norman. Credit: Hardy Family Collection.

Prior to Daddy coming to the country, Hib Hodgson, along with Charles Timothy and other local residents, joined the rush to stake for oil around the Fort Norman Oil Wells in 1920 and 1921. The name of the community that was eventually established in the area was shortened to Norman Oil Wells and, finally, to Norman Wells. Hib Hodgson staked the area south of Sucker Creek up to the Mackenzie River. Charles Timothy staked the area around Prohibition Creek, on the other side of the Mackenzie River.

Hib Hodgson, Charles Timothy, and the others had visions of getting rich with their claims. At least, that is the story that Mama told me. The hope of the oil-and-gas prospectors was to sell their claims to large companies like Imperial Oil. Mama told me that Charles Timothy, being the loyal servant that he was, sold to the HBC at a low price. He might have been one of a handful of locals who managed to turn a dollar on the staking rush. This was the first of the cycles of booms and busts for the oil-and-gas industry in our part of the world, that continued for 100 years.

Another family member who made some money off the oil boom was Uncle Ted Trindell. The authors of his life story, Jean Morisset and Rose-Marie Pelletier, wrote his spoken words:

1920, Fort Nelson to Norman Wells, staking a claim. But it cost twelve hundred dollars to stake a claim and we didn't have that kind of money. So Imperial Oil hired ten of us young guys at ten dollars a day. They deducted us one day and staked the claims in our name, and gave us six hundred dollars on that. So, for ten days work we made six hundred and ninety dollars.

I assume that the "six hundred and ninety dollars" was for each of the ten young guys. That amount of money would be worth $10,165 in 2021.

I think that when Uncle Ted says that "they," meaning Imperial Oil, "staked the claims," he likely means "registered the claims." The mining recorder's office was in Fort Norman. There was a limit to the number of claims that an entity or an individual could register. Nowadays, oil-and-gas rights are granted in the form of exploration licences through an open bidding process based on work commitments over a period of years. In 1920, oil-and-gas rights were issued in the same way as other mineral claims in the mining recorder's office. The one difference was that a gold claim was limited to 40 acres while an oil-and-gas claim could include as much as 2,250 acres (four square miles). Four-foot rights of way had to be cut to mark the claim.

The late Dick Hill used to own a bookshop in Inuvik that specialized in old books dealing with northern history. I would

PART II

101

always try to stop by when I was in Inuvik to try to find something to add to my collection. During one stop, Dick called me over and said he had something that he thought I would be really interested in. I don't know if it could be called a book, as it was printed on eight-and-a-half-by-eleven paper, and it was a self-published story. It was called *Way . . . Way . . . Down North*, and it was written by William G. Ogilvie. It is about the attempt by Ogilvie and his companions to cash in on the oil-and-gas boom. It is a fascinating account of the boom, how they got to Fort Norman Oil Wells with a small boat from Peace River, and the way in which they staked their claims. There were four of them, so they were able to stake sixteen square miles. One of the interesting things in the "book" was the reproduction of a map showing some of the claims that were staked.

I couldn't believe it; the map showed the claim staked by my grandfather at Prohibition Creek. Suddenly, the stories came alive. Mr. Ogilvie and his companions staked part of their claims abutting Granddad's.

Mr. Ogilvie wrote about how one of his companions first caught the bug. The companion had been up North in 1920 and was returning home to Toronto in the fall:

> *Fantastic rumours dogged their voyage back to Peace River before entraining for Edmonton and points east. Imperial Oil, Dutch Shell and other mighty oil corporations were said to be offering unbelievable prices for claims to add to their slim holdings—twenty, thirty and even up to fifty thousand dollars were being offered.*

So, Mr. Ogilvie and twenty others formed a syndicate, called the W. S. Dyer Syndicate, and raised enough money to send an expedition to the oil field to, hopefully, make a fortune. They got there on June 18, 1921, and completed the staking on July 17. By the time they got back to Toronto in early August, Mr. Ogilvie wrote in his journal: "the bottom had dropped out of the market so far as selling any of the claims we had so tediously staked." It seems that the large companies had decided to simply wait out the claimholders.

∞

The discovery of oil at Norman Wells, as it is now called, has been a source of a long-running disagreement in Fort Norman between the Blondins and others. The disagreement is about who "discovered" the oil. On June 26, 1975, John Blondin and his sister, Elizabeth Yakeleya, swore oaths to tell the truth to Judge Thomas Berger at a hearing held at Brackett (Willow) Lake. John Blondin said:

> *About the oil, who found the oil? What year was it found in? 1916. What was the name of the man that found the oil, it was our own father, Francis Nineye, the first guy that found oil there. When he found the oil, what did he do with the sample of oil. He took a little bit and he put it in a lard pail and he brought it to Fort Norman.*

Mr. Blondin went on to testify:

> *He took a sample of that oil in a lard kettle and brought it into Fort Norman. He gave it to Gene Gaudet, the Hudson's Bay manager and he sent it out on the boat. . .and we never heard of that oil again and we never got the lard kettle back.*

Mrs. Yakeleya then testified: "I said this because my brother, John Blondin, has been talking about the Wells, because my dad found that oil in 1916 . . ."

Both Mr. Blondin and Mrs. Yakeleya testified that their father died in an accident after he brought the lard pail/kettle in. The reference to "Gene" Gaudet is obviously wrong and is most likely a mispronunciation of "Tim." There has never been a Gene Gaudet in the area. It is likely that the court reporter simply misunderstood the pronunciation. Tim Gaudet was my grandfather, and he was the post manager in Fort Norman for many years, including the period of 1914 to 1921.

This dispute had been going on for some years before Judge Berger appeared on the scene. Mama told me that her dad, Tim Gaudet, had told her that it was Tatsie Wright who had brought an oil sample in to him in a lard pail. He also told her that he had shipped it out on the boat. Nothing was ever mentioned about the Blondins or Francis Nineye. At that time, other fur traders were operating in Fort Norman. Perhaps Francis Nineye gave his lard pail to one of them.

Even if he did give the lard pail to someone else, it wouldn't have mattered, as the Fort Norman Oil Wells were already being staked by then, and plans were underway to begin drilling. The lard pail that the Blondins claim to have belonged to their father, in 1916, would not have played a role in anyone's decision to stake. Rene Fumoleau, OMI, in his landmark history of the time, *As Long As This Land Shall Last,* wrote:

> *Alexander Mackenzie had seen it oozing from the ground there in 1789, as he passed enroute to the Arctic Ocean; geological surveys had established the existence of an immense oil field within the Mackenzie Basin in the late 1880s; and amid considerable excitement, red-brown crude had been collected from the surface near Fort Norman and brought to Athabasca Landing in 1912. The location of the first test well was chosen in 1914.*

PART II

103

Fumoleau provided footnotes for his statements, and I followed up on two of them in the *Edmonton Bulletin* on August 30, 1912, and September 5, 1912. The *Bulletin* reported, on August 30, that:

> *The parties who arrived from the Mackenzie River on Tuesday and Wednesday last brought with them the absolute evidence of the existence of illuminating oil in the far north. At a point in the Mackenzie River, near its easterly bank, about twenty-five miles below Fort Norman, which is at the mouth of the Great Bear River, Joseph Hudson, a former employee of the Hudson's Bay Company, and for the past two years a resident there, secured a quantity of the oil last winter and samples have been brought to us by Campbell Young manager of the Northern Trading company and . . .*

The reference to Joseph "Hudson" should be to Joseph "Hodgson," who spent a number of years in the employ of the HBC in Fort Norman as well as with the Anglican Church. He was known as a raconteur and is rumoured to have fathered a child in the area, who, in turn, left many descendants. In the context of the disagreement in Fort Norman and the preceding evidence, it might be fair to say that the oil was "discovered" by Joe Hodgson in 1911 or 1912, and he gave it to the manager of the Northern Traders' store in Fort Norman.

The first gusher at Norman Wells came in 1920. Joe Blondin, who was born in 1914, two years after Joseph Hodgson "secured a quantity of the oil," is quoted in *We Remember the Coming of the Whiteman* as if he was there in the late 1910s. Memories are a tricky thing, especially when they are manufactured. In any event, I hope I have cleared up the alleged involvement of my grandfather, Tim Gaudet, with the Blondins. If John Blondin was still alive, I would be happy to tell him that he was barking up the wrong tree for his father's lard pail. The more important issue is this: what else did he and his sister misremember in front of Berger?

The one loose end that I want to do further research on is Tim Gaudet's statement to my mother that it was old Tatsie who brought him a lard pail with oil in it. If that is correct, I would like to know what year it happened. If it did get shipped out, what happened to it? If she did give her lard pail to my grandfather it would have been between "ca. 1914 – 1921" during which time he was the post master in Fort Norman, as evidenced by his biographical sheet in the HBCA. That being the case her lard pail would also have been of no significance to the decision to drill the first well.

∞

Uncle Ray and Uncle Joe were operating a sawmill in Fort Norman in the early 1950s. Being as far north as Fort Norman, good timber was is not easy to come by. Uncle Ray would log on the west side of the Mackenzie River and haul the logs into town with a Caterpillar D2 tractor and logging sleighs. This was normal for anyone operating a sawmill in the area. It was either the western bank or the islands abutting the western bank.

Of course, Uncle Ray, like all the other operators in the area, had to wait for the river to freeze over before he could cross with his equipment and begin hauling logs to town, where the sawmill was located. He was doing this early in 1954 when a tragic accident took his life. The circumstances of the accident remain cloudy to this day. As everyone who was involved that day is now dead, it is unlikely that there will be a satisfactory resolution to the issues, for those that question what really happened that day.

The practice in those days was for visitations to be made to the bereaved family to view the deceased in the home. There were no undertakers then. My mother brought me up to the Overvold house to comfort Aunt Christine and do what we could to help our grieving relatives. Uncle Ray's body was laid out on his and Aunt Christine's bed, just off the living room. I do not remember seeing Granddad's body, so Uncle Ray was the first dead person I remember seeing.

I had to kiss him goodbye. I was frightened, but I was also very sad because our two families were so close. I can still see him to this day. He had been hit on the head by a falling log, and both of his eyes were badly blackened.

$$\infty$$

I was very fortunate to have been born when I was. I got to experience what life must have been like for my ancestors. Like them, we lived with the four seasons. Each season had its own uniqueness, and when blended together, they provided for continuity, year after year. In the spring there would be the spring hunt and fresh meat from ducks, geese, and beavers. The lakes would melt, and the ice on the rivers would melt and move. When the Mackenzie River froze over in the fall, it was not unusual for the ice to be eight feet thick in places. It was and still is a spectacular force of nature to watch the ice break up in the spring. There would be chunks as large as small houses being flung in the air and crashing down with a thunderous grinding noise. An exclamation point for the arrival of spring!

When summer came, Daddy would plow the ground and prepare it for planting. We would plant root vegetables, mostly. However, we would also have lettuce, peas, and radishes for summer eating. We also had raspberry bushes, and wild berries were plentiful in the fall. Fishnets were strung in the rivers in the summertime, and fish were put up for the coming winter to feed the dogs as well as the humans. Firewood from large drift logs was cut up on the shores and packed up the hills to the houses that would need to be heated in the coming winter.

Ricky Hardy, Walter Hardy, and Hib McCauley in the garden.

Alice, Leo, Rod, and Walter Hardy with part of the flower garden.

Leo Hardy riding the horse while Jack Hardy steadies the hiller.

Rod Hardy in the garden, in front of the house.

Alice, Walter, Rod, and Leo Hardy harvesting potatoes. Credits: Hardy Family Collection.

Fall would arrive, and we would take the gardens out and store the vegetables in our root cellar, below the house. I sometimes joke that I still have dirt under my fingernails from digging potatoes up. Then it was time for the fall moose hunt as well as the sheep hunt up the gravel river. Enough meat had to be brought in to feed us over the winter. We would be ready with our vegetables in the root cellar along with jarred berries, meat, and dried fish in the warehouse and plenty of wood in the yard.

Soon the dogs would be struggling with their chains in their desire to get going, as there was now snow on the ground. Trapping season was upon us. Fishnets had to be run under the ice in nearby lakes. The fish that were caught would mostly be to feed the dogs, but some of them found their way onto our table—the fish, that is. Winter was also the time to hunt caribou and moose. We would work our way to spring and start the cycle over again. This was all very serious business, as our lives depended on it.

∞

I doubt there were many, if any, hunters who could bring a moose down like Granddad did in the late 1890s. The story was written by Joseph Hodgson and was published in the June 1924 edition of *The Beaver* magazine. The story was titled: "An H.B.C. Hercules" and was made up of a number of feats of strength and daring do by Granddad. Hodgson was Granddad's immediate supervisor at the time, and he writes about the killing of the moose by Granddad, as follows:

Jack and Walter Hardy after a successful fall hunt. Credit: Hardy Family Collection.

> *That winter, I sent him and an Indian with a dog team to carry the mail to Fort Simpson—a three-hundred-mile journey. The Indian, on attaining the top of a bank, suddenly called to Tim, 'Moose, moose!' The animal tried to get away, but the snow was very deep there. It got about thirty yards, when it stopped. 'Let us kill him' said Tim. 'But we have no gun,' replied the Indian. 'That's nothing; we have a knife and an axe, haven't we?' 'Bad medicine kill a moose that way,' the Indian answered. 'Not for White man' said Tim. 'Besides I hear that there is not much dog feed at Wrigley.' Tim tied his scalping knife to a pole and walked up to the moose. It charged. He jumped to one side and drove the blade into its head below the ear. His spear handle broke near the knife and the animal rushed on for a space with the knife handle sticking out of the side of its head. The hunter approached it in the rear with an axe, intending to hamstring it. By this time the knife had done its work, for the animal fell on its wounded side and drove the knife into its brain.*

∞

Granddad's legacy to us, in addition to being a great hunter and the strongest man around, included the fact that he applied for scrip payments in 1921 instead of becoming an adherent to Treaty Number 11, or colloquially, a Treaty Indian. We have had copies of all of his scrip documents for many years, and they were central to my major paper in law school. Mama also told me about what transpired, as told to her by her dad. Mama told me that they knew that the treaty party was coming, and Granddad corresponded with his brothers about what he should do. The brothers would have been Frederic Charles, in Montreal, and John Peter, in Peace River. Frederic Charles was one of the witnesses to the signing of Treaty Number 8 in Fort Resolution in 1900, and John Peter took scrip in 1899 from the Athabasca Half-Breed Commission, which was part of the Treaty Number 8 party.

As a result of this exposure to Treaty Number 8, Frederic and John advised Granddad not to become an adherent to Treaty Number 11, primarily because it would lead to a loss of freedom. Not only did they know what was in Treaty 11 because it was basically the same as Treaty 8, they also knew how Treaty Number 8 was being implemented. They knew what it would mean to live on a reserve. Mama also told me that Granddad was pressured by Bishop Breynant and H. A. Conroy, the Treaty 11 commissioner, to adhere to the treaty. He refused.

I have often thought about it and am confident that Granddad would have shared the information that his brothers sent to him, with the Indians of Fort Norman. The Chief, at the time, was Albert Wright and he had received some formal schooling so he could read and write. From what I understand the Indians chose to believe what the Catholic Bishop Breynant told them about the treaty being good for them. It is very unfortunate that there was no transcript of the deliberations taken.

CHAPTER TEN

MÉTIS SETTLERS

My cousin, Bob Overvold and I were quite close as children. We called him Bobby. I have a lot of good memories of being with him and the Overvold family. One of those memories involved one of the local Catholic priests, Jean Grias. With a last name like that, you can imagine what two young boys could do with it. Aunt Cecilia and Uncle Joe Hall lived next door to the Overvolds. Both of their children, Mabel and Sarah, were adults by this time and had left the community. So, we were occasionally "volunteered" to do chores for Aunt Cecilia. She was the oldest of the living Gaudet siblings and was, shall I say, somewhat strict and very Catholic. This was so, even after marrying an anti-Catholic Irishman, as mentioned earlier.

Of course, Bobby and I were oblivious to practically everything except our own immediate little world. On this particular occasion, we were "volunteered" to fill Aunt Cecilia's kitchen wood box from the pile of cut and split wood in the yard. I don't remember how it started—probably by Bobby! I think I said something about Father Grias, and Bob responded with something about "Father Green Ass." Oh boy, the chance to use the "ass" word. I responded with something about "Father Pink Ass," and on it went until we had used up the basic colour chart, and Aunt Cecilia caught on to what we were laughing so hard about.

Aunt Cecilia had studied to become a nun and was very strong in her Catholic beliefs. She did not think our little game was very humorous at all. I don't remember her hitting us, but if she had, that would not have been unusual. Maybe we got a good whack on the back of the head. This kind of punishment was learned by all the daughters of our grandparents who attended the Catholic residential school in Fort Providence. We did get a good lecture, during which we were told, in no uncertain terms, to never ever make fun of a priest (even if he was a pervert). I don't think we were ever "volunteered" to do her chores again.

To the best of my knowledge, Grias was not involved in the residential schools. If he was, the boys would have been safe, as he liked young girls just going into puberty. I mention in the next chapter that we would go to the mission house to warm up while sliding on Mission Hill. We, boys and girls, would also spend a lot of other time there, such as when we went for the French-language newspapers. The chapel area of the mission house also served as a large public area where people could go just to visit and talk. We, the youngsters, would go there, and Grias would encourage roughhousing and wrestling, which would inevitably result in him on top of the young girls with their legs spread. Many of those girls still complain about that today. This is the priest who used to get all boiled up about us playing moose-skin ball, which I will come to in a later chapter.

∞

In those days we did not have many toys, so we made swords, slingshots, and bows and arrows and played Robin Hood, Cowboys and Indians, War, and other rough games. These ideas came from the movies that were put on once or twice a week by the Community Club. Even the Indians cheered for the cowboys when a western was shown. Most of the kids in town would join in these roughhousing games, and we would battle from one end of town to the other, into the muskeg behind the community and up the cliffs on the way to Bear River. Of course, we had to split into teams, just like for shinny or scrub baseball. Bobby, being a bit older than me and quite a bit bigger, was always one of the captains. He always made sure he was the leader of the cowboys and that I was relegated to the Indians.

Sometimes the games got out of hand, and kids ran home crying after being shot with an arrow or a pebble from a slingshot. When I was cleaning up the family property, I found one of those arrows. We used 30-30 or similarly sized shell casings as arrowheads. I guess that would hurt if it hit you in a soft spot.

∞

To my great regret, and for reasons that I had no way of understanding, Aunt Christine and all of the children moved away after Uncle Ray died. Bob was sent to join Charlie at the All Saints Anglican residential school in Aklavik. I think Charlie was already there, as he had been in the hospital run by the Anglican Church there. I believe he was there because he had tuberculosis. Aunt Christine and the two younger girls, Carrie (Edna) and Shirley, moved to Fort Resolution, where she got a job working in the Catholic hospital. The oldest child, Margaret, had already moved to Fort Smith to go to school. They all ended up in Fort Resolution about two years later when Aunt Christine remarried and started a second family. Her new husband's name was Pete King. I remember him always being kind to us the few times that we saw him. That marriage produced three more first cousins for me: Doris, Ray and Trudy King.

Life is always full of "what ifs," and I often wonder how differently our lives might have turned out if Uncle Ray had not met with that tragic accident.

After Margaret left Fort Norman, she sent Aunt Jane or Mama a picture of herself in front of the grotto in Fort Smith. They jumped to the conclusion, or at least speculated, that Margaret was going to become a nun, based on the picture. I think Margaret might have been staying at the convent in Fort Smith, which likely also fuelled the fire of hope. I told Margaret about this years later, and she was not amused.

Margaret, Bobby, and Charlie Overvold, in Fort Norman. c. 1946. Credit: Hardy Family Collection.

Before leaving Fort Norman, Margaret spent one spring staying with us. It was the year that another tragic accident occurred. A young child from the transient community was mauled to death by the RCMP dogs that made up their dog teams.

There were few roads to speak of in Fort Norman in those days. The two leading up to the school on the second bench were Hudson's Bay Hill and George Doctor's Hill. The spring melt had flooded the bottom of George Doctor's Hill that year. That was the path that Margaret and I would normally take to school in the morning. So, we took the longer path around and up Hudson's Bay Hill. When we got to the top of that hill, the dogs were on the poor child, and pandemonium had broken out. The dogs would normally be kept in a large corral. On this occasion, they got out somehow, pack instinct set in, and they attacked the first moving creature they saw, the poor unfortunate child. I recently learned that the dogs had broken out of the corral on their own initiative by throwing themselves against the gate.

I often wonder if that might have been me if George Doctor's Hill had not flooded that spring. The attack took place right on our normal path to school. Of course, all of the dogs were destroyed shortly after the tragedy. The child is buried in the old Anglican graveyard in a very solidly constructed grave. As far as I know, his family has never returned to the community.

∞

After they left Fort Norman, I lost touch with my Overvold cousins for a number of years. Eventually, we all found each other again as adults. I stayed in Fort Norman and attended the Fort Norman Federal Day School from grades one to six and the second half of the year to complete grade seven. The grade seven situation was a result of the start of the blackest period in my life—Grollier Hall.

Life went on in Fort Norman. I did very well in school, I was an altar boy and a Boy Scout, I played hockey, I drove dogs, I fished for chubs and swam in the Mackenzie River, I went on river trips with Daddy, and I did many other things that formed happy memories for me. I also focused on old and new friends.

Michael Gladu became my best friend. He and Bob Overvold are still my best friends to this day. Mike was not born in Fort Norman. He was adopted and raised by Noel and Harriet Gladu. His mother, Rachel Gladu, was not married when Mike was born, so as would happen more often than not in those days, she "gave" him to a family member who did not have children of their own. In this case, it was her uncle, Noel Gladu. Mike was born in Fort Smith and came to Fort Norman on an airplane as a very young child.

Noel Gladu was an interesting character. Earlier, I mentioned the coming of the White settlers who gave rise to our family. At the same time, many southern Métis were emigrating north from northern Alberta and the Fort Smith area, in the NWT. These included the Ernie McDonalds, the Jim McDonalds, the Cadieux's, Joe Bourque, the Lennies, the Tourangeaus, the Rivetts, and others, including Noel Gladu. They all lived in the Fort Norman area, and a lot of them, along with some local Métis, eventually moved north to Aklavik in the 1940s during the muskrat boom. This boom was caused by a strong demand for muskrat coats and parkas worldwide.

Noel Gladu came to Fort Norman to work for the RC mission as a labourer, cutting and hauling wood, driving dogs, running fishnets, working in the gardens, and doing similar tasks. He might not have remained in Fort Norman for the rest of his life, but he met a widow who also did not have children. Her maiden name was Harriet Horassi, and she had married Albert

PART II

Wright, who, as I mentioned earlier, was the chief of the Fort Norman Dene at the signing of Treaty 11 in 1921. Harriet and Albert were Shúhta Got'ıne, Anglican, and had some formal education. Consequently, they were good friends with Granny, who attended services faithfully at the Holy Trinity Anglican Church with them. The church was just down the hill from Granny and Granddad's house.

Two of my older brothers, Leo and Rod, remembered going to services with Granny in that church. Sunday mornings at my grandparents' house must have been a bit strange. This would have been especially so in light of the oppressing role that religion played in the lives of people in those days. Perhaps this is why we have no pictures of Granny with a smile on her face. Or perhaps the dour look developed from giving birth thirteen times. Or perhaps it was having a tyrant for a husband. Most likely, a combination of all those things would be the answer.

So, there you have it. I have one great-grandfather who was an Anglican missionary and another who became staunchly Catholic and a fur trader working for what was effectively the government of the country at the time, the HBC. Their children, one Catholic and one Anglican, married and thus extended the Catholic/Anglican struggle for souls in the Mackenzie River District. The company had a great deal of influence over which church could try to harvest souls in which community, and they preferred the Anglicans. This religious dichotomy has affected our family through four or five generations. The dichotomy has essentially dissipated with the loss of power and influence by both churches, on one hand, and the HBC, on the other.

CHAPTER ELEVEN
END OF CHILDHOOD

I was talking about my friend, Mike Gladu, who was raised by Noel and Harriet Gladu. Neither Noel nor Harriet had children of their own and had both been to residential schools—Noel to a Catholic one and Harriet to an Anglican one. Life was not easy for Mike. Because he was Noel's relative, he was slotted into the Catholic stream. This might have also been because, by that point in time, the Catholics had essentially won the tug of war for the hearts and souls of the Fort Norman Dene. The Anglicans had abandoned the field sometime in the 1940s after Granny died, and the hospital that the Anglican Church had built for the community burned to the ground. The hospital was not rebuilt and was replaced by a nursing station, which was run by the federal government.

The Anglican hospital. Credit: Hardy Family Collection.

The Anglican hospital burning in 1946. Credit: Hardy Family Collection.

Noel, in particular, thought that the way he had been raised, in a residential school, was the proper way to raise children—discipline and hard work. Consequently, Michael had a curfew that everyone in town knew about. At 9:00 every night, Noel stepped out of their house and would yell, "Michael, time to come home!" If Michael did not immediately appear, Noel would cut a willow switch and start looking for poor Mike. More often than not, Mike's evening ended with a thrashing. In addition to the thrashings, Mike also suffered from the continual embarrassment of being hollered for.

Despite this, Mike and I had a lot of fun times. In those days there were no street lamps in Fort Norman, and only the very privileged transients had electricity. Our homes were illuminated with gasoline lanterns in the dark days of fall and winter, and outside light was provided by battery-powered flashlights. Those who could not afford flashlights would use a candle in a lard pail. The lard pail would be about a gallon in size. Part of the side would be cut open with a knife, and a candle would be placed in the centre of the contraption and lit. The inside of the lard pail would provide a bit of a reflection, and the sides of the pail would provide protection from the wind. The lard pail's handle would remain intact, and that was how we held it up. We had not heard of Diogenes at that stage of our young lives.

Mike and I were not looking for the proverbial honest man but would use the lard pail lights to visit around town. We used to visit old Tatsi Wright quite often, and she and other elders were very adamant that we were not to disturb the northern lights by whistling when the lights were out. If we did, the northern lights would swoop down and take us away. Guess what Mike and I used to do? Of course, we would run around town with our lard pail lights, whistling as best as we could. Old Tatsi and the other elders would get absolutely incensed at us. Mike spoke and understood Slavey, so he knew what they were saying. I, not so much. Of course, Mama would tell me not to believe that nonsense!

Old Tatsi was the mother of Chief Albert Wright and the mother-in-law of Harriet. She and the Gladus lived in the first "duplex" in Fort Norman. Tatsi lived in what I think was the original house, which was a large one-room log building with an upstairs, which had been Harriet and Albert's home. The Gladus lived in an extension that had been built on to the original house. There was no adjoining door, thus the idea of a duplex.

I guess we were such poor whistlers that we were never swooped away. Of course, we had great imaginations and could see the lights curling and forming in readiness to get us. Fortunately for us, it never happened. The lights were especially beautiful on cold nights, which would result in clear skies. There would be the lights, swirling like paintbrushes, spreading colour across the skies, which were filled with bright stars that glittered like diamonds.

This activity, of course, happened in winter, as by March of each year, the northern lights disappeared until October or November, and the fun would start again, at least until we got too old and sophisticated for such childish foolishness. But it was fun while it lasted.

Another wintertime night activity was sliding, especially down Mission Hill. Fort Norman is located on two benches, one being nearer the river and the other just above that one. Four paths led from the first bench to the second, which were called hills. They were Hudson's Bay Hill, George Doctor's Hill, Mission Hill and an unnamed hill by our house. The Hudson's Bay Hill was probably the best for sliding, but it was much too dangerous because of the steep drop at the end of the run. So, Mission Hill was the site for much winter fun. Of course, we could also slip into the mission house to warm up once in a while on really cold nights. George Doctor's Hill was called that because George Doctor and his family lived right beside it, at the bottom.

If someone had a really good sled, he or she could make it right down to the frozen ice on the river. This did not happen often. The most fun would be when the McDonald children would bring their dad's big cariole to the hill. As many children as possible would pile in, and off they would go. Of course, most of them would disappear when it came time to pull that big cariole back up the hill. So, the pulling would be left to the older, stronger children. If the northern lights were out, that simply increased the fun. We used to slide right by Granny Clément's house, whooping and hollering.

Granny Clément's House, Mission Hill, and Church. Credit: Unknown. The picture was published in the *News of the North* on April 12, 1978. Unfortunately, the paper described it as being in Fort Good Hope and not Fort Norman.

We would all begin to drift off at a reasonable hour, so we could be up bright and early for school the next day. The only traffic we had to worry about while sliding was the occasional dog team making a late return to the community. As I said earlier, there were very few moving vehicles in Fort Norman at that time.

∞

Most homes in the community did not have electricity or indoor plumbing. All of these homes were heated by burning wood. Some of the occupants of the homes used their dog teams to haul the wood into town. Others were provided for, at a price, by Daddy hauling the wood in with his horses and later with his Fordson tractor and wood sleighs.

Jack Hardy crossing the frozen Mackenzie River with a load of wood, likely from Windy Island. Credit: Hardy Family Collection.

Of course, it was a bit more complicated than that. He would have to identify which stand he wanted to harvest in a particular winter, and he would hire a family that was trapping in the area to do the cutting and piling and to help him load the wood onto the sleighs when he got there. If I remember correctly, he could haul four cords at a time. He got to this amount by having the wood cut in sixteen-foot lengths. I would make an occasional trip with him. However, my role in life at that time was to go to school and get good marks, which I did.

Jack Hardy driving the Fordson Tractor. Credit: Hardy Family Collection.

Having that role in life did not let me completely off the hook for other work. Our house needed to be heated by wood, but a sixteen-foot tree would not fit into the stove! Most homes had what were called sawhorses, which were simple cradles with two ends made of two boards or larger branches each, nailed together in an X, with the two X's joined together by slats about two or three feet long. Then we would put the sixteen-foot log in the cradle and go at it with a Swede saw. If we had a very large tree, we would probably use a crosscut saw. We would cut the tree into stove-length blocks, and then we would split the blocks with an axe, so they would fit in the stove and burn more easily.

Daddy had a buzzsaw and a power drive on the old Fordson, so cutting wood was easier for us than at most houses in Fort Norman. However, we had not yet acquired a mechanical splitter. Guess who got to do a lot of manual splitting? Actually, we never did get a mechanical splitter. Why? Most likely because we moved to using heating oil to heat the house and propane for the cookstove. Of course, this happened after I left for residential school.

Rod Hardy chucking wood from the buzzsaw with Jack Hardy. Credit: Hardy Family Collection.

Leo and Ricky Hardy on top of the woodpile. Credit: Hardy Family Collection.

Then there was the daily chore of filling the wood boxes and getting the "shavings" ready for lighting the fire in the morning. We had two wood boxes. One was for the big old kitchen stove, which was used for cooking and heating water. The other was the heater, which was in the living room and was the main source of heat after the kitchen stove went out. Shavings, these days, are called kindling. They would be cut from dry wood with a smaller axe or a large, sharp knife. On a good morning, there would be embers from the previous night's fire available to get the fire going again. This would happen on what we would consider a relatively warm night—minus 20°C or so. On cold nights—minus 40°C or colder—there would be no embers left unless, of course, someone got up during the night to load the stove.

Whoever had the job of getting up and getting the fires going, usually Daddy, had to get up around 5:00 a.m., get the heater going, and put some ice in a bucket on that stove. They would go back to bed for about an hour and then get up again and see if the ice had melted, which meant there was water for coffee or tea. He or she would make the coffee or tea and get the fire going in the kitchen stove, so breakfast could be cooked for everyone. If it was Daddy, he always brought a cup of coffee or tea to Mama. As I got older, these tasks sometimes fell to me. We wore what were called union suits for underwear in the winter. You know the ones that were one piece, with the buttoned flaps in the rear? I swear to God, I can still feel the cold on my rear end when I forgot to close the flap and rushed downstairs to get the fire going.

No, I did not make coffee or tea or breakfast. I got the fire going and then crawled back upstairs and into my feather robe. If someone wanted me to go to school, they had to get up and do the rest. At the time I had no idea how spoiled I was.

I mention the cookstove being used to heat water and the heater being used to melt ice. There was no indoor plumbing, and no one delivered water to us in the winter. Consequently, no flush toilet and no taps for the basin or a bathtub. One of my jobs was to keep the water barrels in the porch filled with ice or snow. We melted the ice and used the water for drinking and cooking. The snow water was used for washing our bodies, brushing our teeth, and doing laundry and cooking dog feed. By dogs, I mean the dog teams, which were a crucial part of making a living in those days.

Daddy used to cut and haul ice to the ice houses of the transients, who would use the ice to keep things cool in the summertime—imagine that! They would use sawdust from the local sawmill to keep the ice from thawing too quickly in the summer. Daddy would take advantage of being geared up to do that work and would bring ice home for us as well. It would be later in the winter before he could get out on the frozen river to do this work safely. Until then we used to gather large shards of ice, broken off during freeze-up, and pull them up the hill on small sleds or by dog team, so we could have potable water until Daddy could get the big blocks to us.

Laundry or bath day would be another big day that happened about once a month. More water would be needed than what would be in the snow barrel, so both stoves would be kept full of wood, and tubs of snow would be placed on each stove to melt and provide more water. Melted snow does not provide as much water as one might think. So, we were kept busy packing in more snow from outside and dumping it into the tubs as the other snow turned to water. I never kept track of how much snow it took to make a full barrel of water, but it was lots.

We all bathed on one day, and laundry was done the next day. Yes, we bathed once per month. We used face cloths on the other days to wipe ourselves down and washed our hands and faces in a washbasin every day. By the time I was ten years old, laundry was no longer done with a scrub board. The world had produced the gas engine laundry washing machine. This washing machine was used outside to avoid the fumes, which would likely have killed us. Laundry was done on warmer days. Still, everything would freeze stiff after being hung on the clothesline. I learned that clothes do dry when they are frozen.

Yes, we had to go to the toilet too. Minus 40°C, and we had to go! If nothing else, whatever we had to do was done quickly. If it had to be number two, it was usually accompanied by my bitter mumblings aimed at Walter. Why? Because he had, again, peed on the edge of the toilet hole, and at minus 40°C, it had frozen instantly. There I was with my bare bum sitting on a block of frozen pee, trying to poop. Oh, the good old days!

∞

I was ten years old when Father Biname, the local members of the RCMP, and the local members of the Royal Canadian Corps of Signals organized a Boy Scout troop. Normally, the youngest one could be to join a Boy Scout troop was twelve, but because there were not many boys in Fort Norman, they allowed ten-year-olds in. I was in.

Because my parents' focus for me was a formal education, I did not have the same skills that most of the other boys in the community had with regard to being in the bush. However, I was a good student and could read and understand instructions and written ideas much better than most of the older boys. Boy Scouting has a lot of emphasis on merit badges. Some leeway is granted for practical hands-on skills, but earning some badges required some formal education and memorizing. Meetings took place once a week in the Scout Hall, which was built out of logs by the local residents, near the RCMP barracks. We got assignments—make a wooden cup with a knife and so forth. Mama treated these assignments as homework and made sure I always had my assignments done. As a result of my efforts and Mama's, I emerged as the first Troop Leader of the First Fort Norman Boy Scout Troop.

As Scouts, we all had to make our own staffs. They had to be exactly five foot six inches long with the feet marked properly for the five feet and the inches marked properly for the six inches. So, the owner ended up with not only a good walking staff but also a good measuring stick. The staff had to be a certain diameter and had to be cut from a sapling in the bush.

One outing with the Scouts that I remember is when Constable Bob Gilholme walked us across the river to Windy

Ricky Hardy - "Be Prepared". Credit: Hardy Family Collection.

Island to a logging camp that Daddy had set up with Walter and Alfred Lennie and Alfred's family. I had never walked that far out on the frozen river before and found climbing over the frozen ice piles that had been created by the freeze-up to be very challenging.

Walter and Alfred were keeping their dog teams at the camp. When we got to the camp, we saw that Walter's bitch, Daisy, had just had a litter. I was shocked when we were told that Daisy had eaten most of her newborn pups before anyone could get them away from her. Later, I learned that was not unusual, as the bitch would confuse the newborns with the afterbirth, which she would normally eat. We learned that it was very important to keep a close watch on the bitch when she was giving birth.

∞

Even though our family had dog teams, they never were very fast. Our teams were working dogs, meant to pull heavy loads. If we wanted to drive a really good, fast team, we would borrow dogs from our next-door neighbours, the McDonald family. They always had the best and the fastest dogs in town. I vividly recall one day when they let me use five of their dogs with a cariole just to go for a ride. It was magnificent. It must have been February or March, as the sun was shining brightly and the snow was slick, and the temperature was crisp. Many dog team trails were cut in the bush leading to and away from the community. The trails were only wide enough for one team at a time—no passing lanes. I headed toward Martin River. After a couple of hours, I stopped to rest and decided to head back home. Once they were turned around, the dogs knew they were heading home, and we flew like the wind. It was great.

When I got home, I found out that my face had frozen while flying like the wind. I also found out that a willow had gashed my face. I found this out after I got into the house, and blood started running down the side of my face after the thawing started. When your face is frozen, you don't feel things like gashes when they happen. Mama rushed me out of the house and made me rub snow on the frozen parts of my face and continue until the part of my face that had been frozen was thawed out. It was not a very serious freeze or gash.

∞

That was the idyllic, at least in my eyes, world that we lived in. But change was coming. I remember standing on the Hudson's Bay bank—riverbank, that is—with Uncle Fred and others from the community and him saying to me: "Look, look, Richard,

PART II

there's the Sputnik crossing over the Mackenzie Mountains." At that time, Uncle Fred was retired from being a special constable with the RCMP and was now the school janitor. He also did some trapping and hunting on his own time. Consequently, he was relatively well off and could afford subscriptions to periodicals such as *Life* and *Time* magazine. That generation of Whites and Métis, from the country, all thirsted after knowledge. This was likely because they had received some education, and reading materials were more readily available to them. Uncle Fred's magazines were circulated to the other homes as each home finished with them, with Uncle Fred being first, of course.

We had mail by plane once a month then, so the circulation of the magazines could start afresh every mail day. Another source of monthly news was at the RC mission, which received piles of daily French-language newspapers from Montreal on mail days. Once the priests had finished reading them, they would let us have them. Of course, we were not proficient in French, but that didn't matter, as all the boys in my age group were interested in was the sport section—*les Canadiens*! I have remained a lifelong fan of the Canadiens and have passed that "value" on to my children. Those were the glory years of the Canadiens—Maurice "Rocket" Richard, Henri "Pocket Rocket" Richard, Bernie "Boom Boom" Geoffrion, Jacques Plante, Doug Harvey, Tom Thompson, and my favourite, Dickie Moore. I would cut the pictures out of the papers and keep them in a notebook. I wonder what became of that notebook.

During that time the community built a skating rink at the school, and the Red Cross sent in a few boxes of skates and other hockey equipment. We were in our glory. When winter was starting, the big muskeg would freeze before the skating rink was ready, and we would head there after school almost every day. The muskeg was, maybe, a mile or two long, so we had lots of room to skate. Sometimes we would break through the ice, but the water was only a few inches deep in most places, so no real harm happened to us. Once the adults had finished making the ice on the skating rink, it fell to us to keep it shovelled and clean. We did not complain and were happy to do it. We were on skates while we did the shovelling, so, I expect, that contributed to the lack of complaining!

During this time period, I was the victim of an incident in school. I suppose it may have been something that could have been simply brushed aside as a result of children playing together. That might have happened had it not been for the other things that happened to me later in my teenage years, as described in the coming chapters. What happened to me later simply cemented the incident that I am talking about.

I was, to be blunt about it, a favourite of the adults that I interacted with—school, Boy Scouts, church, and so forth. This likely made some of my peers jealous. The revenge came in the form of a gang of older girls in the school. They would lie in wait for me as the students arrived for the start of the school day. The teachers were normally not yet in the classroom. I can still hear the gang leader yelling, "Here he comes. Let's get him." I would be swarmed by a number of girls who were all bigger than me. They would drag me into the girls' bathroom, pull my pants down, and grab at my penis and balls. I was too embarrassed to complain to anyone. This happened more than once. If I remember correctly, I was ten or eleven years old at the time.

As I said, this would have all been swept aside but for what happened to me when I left Fort Norman to go to school in Inuvik.

As I have experienced life over my many years, I have come to learn that children and young adults living in the same house as older adults tend to reflect the views that are expressed by those older adults. When I was eleven turning twelve, we were in a time of stress in the community. It may be that the gang that attacked me were simply acting out on words that they had heard in their homes.

∞

Canada had established the Nelson Commission in 1959 to investigate why the Indians would not take the reserves provided for in Treaty 11. I remember the members of the commission coming to Fort Norman and meeting with Chief Paul Baton and some of his people. Chief Baton was also, coincidentally, the handyman and guide for the Indian Agency. As a result, he had a nice big house that had a parlour that was enclosed by French doors. The meeting was held in that parlour and the adjoining living room. I don't remember why I was there, but I was sitting on the floor beside Chief Baton, who was sitting in an armchair. Chief Baptise Cazon from Fort Simpson was also there, as he was a member of the commission. It is likely that Chief Cazon did the interpreting.

Apparently, something was said at the meeting that was either misinterpreted or taken out of context. I believe the words were deliberately picked up by agitators for their own purposes. From the best of my recollection, the words had to do with certain surveyed lots in Fort Norman. These lots were held by the Crown for the benefit of the Indians. I think the discussion was around the question of whether or not these lots were reserves.

PART II

Naturally, the Indians did not want to live on those lots if doing so could be construed as them accepting reserves.

The agitators picked up on this later and claimed that all lands that had been surveyed in Fort Norman were set aside for the Indians. Then they extrapolated this wrong idea into a position that all White and Métis settlers should be "run out of town" and their lands taken away from them. As I said, it was a tense time. I recall talk about keeping the guns ready in our house.

At the time, Daddy was in the process of acquiring the remaining portions of one of those surveyed lots, lot 9 and the buildings on it, through the proper legal processes. This meant that the neighbours who were renting the buildings on lot 9 would have to leave. The titles were finally issued, and shortly after that Daddy knocked four of the buildings down with his bulldozer. Northern Traders had held the first title issued for the lot and had had constructed five buildings on the lot. When the HBC had purchased all of the shares of Northern Traders the property was sold to someone that I only ever heard of as "Old Law" who continued the fur trading operation for some time. I assume that he eventually turned the fur trading operation into a property rental business. The four buildings had been occupied by three families who moved to other communities, two to Norman Wells and one to Fort Franklin.

Two other buildings were not immediately knocked down. The first was owned by Alfred Lennie, who had purchased it from Paul Baton, who, in turn, had purchased it from the original owner, Jim McCauley. The second building was one of the original Northern Traders buildings and was occupied by Uncle Georgie and his family. After Uncle Georgie became permanently employed by the Government of Canada in Fort Franklin as the maintenance man, he moved his family there. At that point, Daddy knocked that building down as well. As for Alfred Lennie's house, Daddy helped Alfred move it to the northern end of the upper bench with a great view of the Mackenzie River and Bear Rock. The entire process might have led to some of the tensions that were in the air. It has always befuddled me why most people simply refused to acknowledge the coming of the common law. This was particularly so with regard to the ownership of lands and buildings. Ownership or simple occupation of a building does not necessarily carry ownership of the land on which it sits. The days of squatters' rights had ended.

CHAPTER TWELVE

SPORTS DAY AND YELLOWCAKE

My goodness, you would think that all we had was winter. We did have wonderful summers and all sorts of summer activities. In addition to the "war games" that I mentioned earlier, we also played scrub baseball, usually, on the road in front of the McDonalds' house. The community had a larger ball diamond, which was in the RCCS compound. This diamond was used only on special occasions, like the first of July, which is now called Canada Day. Back then it was called Dominion Day.

On that day the men from the NTCL camp at Bear River Rapids would come to town to play a baseball game against the local men. This was a big event for everyone and was run by the Community Club. One year the Community Club, for reasons that I don't remember, could not get the usual concession stand organized for the baseball game. So, another friend, Randy Stowell, and I, with the permission of our parents, decided to run it. It was all very last minute, but we managed to get credit, with the help of our parents, from the HBC for pop, chocolate bars, and hot dogs, which we bought and then sold at the concession stand. Randy and I were exhausted by the end of the day, but we cleared a tidy sum as a profit. I guess I had the old Gaudet trading instincts! I felt so proud of myself when I gave my share of the profit to Mama.

Randy and I became good friends, and we would camp on our own in the bush near town. This would usually be above the high cliffs near Bear River. Randy's father, Ken Stowell, was the Indian agent. The main agency for our area was located in Aklavik, and Fort Norman had the sub-agency. Ken was a WWII veteran and had a number of souvenirs, including a German Luger pistol, a German helmet, and a German bayonet. Randy and I were fascinated with these items, and Mr. Stowell actually let us fire the Luger once or twice.

One thing that was different between Randy and the other boys in the community was that he liked to read, as did I. We were quite into Tom Sawyer and Huck Finn during the Stowell's' last year in Fort Norman. The books were introduced to us by Maurice Cloughley, our teacher that year. Randy and I were so into it that we plotted to steal a canoe and run away from home by paddling to Fort Good Hope. I don't know whose canoe we were going to steal, and I don't think we knew exactly where Fort Good Hope was other than downstream from us.

PART II

I suppose we thought we would find a "Jim" on an island, and he would do all the work for us. Oh, the imaginations of eleven-year-old boys.

The Stowell's, like most if not all of the government families, were transients and only stayed in Fort Norman for a few years.

∞

Another large transient family, the Eliasons, lived in Fort Norman around this time, from 1957 to 1962. Mr. Eliason was the game warden, and he was married to a Métis woman named Marge Olson, who was related to the McKay's from Lac la Ronge, Saskatchewan. At that time, we did not know that Mrs. Eliason was Métis. After all, she lived among the privileged transients. If I remember correctly, they had six children, five girls and a boy. The girls were mostly tomboys, and they willingly joined in all of our activities.

∞

As kids, one of our favourite activities in the summer was fishing for chubs. It was actually work disguised as fun. The fun part was preparing to fish and catching the fish. The work part was that the fish were too small and bony for human consumption, but they made excellent dog food. So, we would string our catch on long willows and bring them home, beaming with pride. Dog teams were still prevalent in Fort Norman. Even though they did not earn their keep during the summer, they still had to be fed. Our small catches of chubs helped out.

This activity was relatively simple. Mama would get us started by giving us a small cloth bag with dry flour in it. The bag would be tied closed, very tightly. Then it would be tied to a stick about three or four feet long. We would go down to the water and would jam the stick into the gravel and sand as far as we could push it, so the bag would be about three or four feet from shore. The bag with the flour would come in contact with the flowing water, and a flow of fluid flour would start. The chubs loved this fluid. If we could find a small eddy to place the flour bag in, the results would be even better. How did we catch them? We would find an appropriately sized pole on the shore and tie some line to it with a small hook. Mama would make a small can of bait for us, which was simply flour mixed with a bit of water. We would put small balls of this mixture on the hooks and, voila.

In addition to the chubs, we would also catch suckers, which we all pretended to be scared of. "Be careful it doesn't clamp onto your arm" would be the collective warning. Occasionally, we would get lucky and catch a grayling that had wandered too close to shore. If that happened, it would be break time, and we would get a fire going and cook the grayling over an open fire. Grayling—or blue fish, as we called them—don't keep, so they have to be eaten almost right away. One of the boys usually had a box of matches and a salt shaker with him. Our fingers were our forks. Mm mm good. On a really good day, someone would have stuffed some bannock in his pocket before leaving home.

Once the fishing and snacking were done, and the chubs had been delivered home, it was time to go swimming. "Make sure you wait for two hours after eating, or you'll get cramps and drown." That was the warning we always got from the adults. Our response was usually, "Oh, for sure, it's been two hours. C'mon guys, let's go." In mid-July, temperatures in the 30°C range were common in Fort Norman. Down to the river, down to the skivvies and sometimes less, and a great day of fun. We tried to avoid swimming in front of the town and preferred going to the point or down to Gordon's Creek, which was named for Don Gordon, who I mention later. But there would always be some nosey adult going by to check on us. If it was a cooler day, or it was getting close to evening in August, we would build a huge bonfire to stay warm. Once school started in September, that was pretty well the end of swimming for that year.

One side note on the chubs. In the mid to late 1950s, the Pentecostal Church started moving into Fort Norman. The first two missionaries were Robert Schneider and Forrest Cumming, and they lived in a tent near the shore of the river just below the HBC compound. I think they paddled down the river from Fort Simpson. They would attract us children to their camp with singalongs. Schneider would play the accordion, and we would sing Christian songs like "Jesus Loves Me" with them. I still remember most of the words. I would get hell from Mama when I got home and was told to stay away from those "Protestants." Ironic in light of our family's religious background, which, by now, was compounded by Mama "sending" us to church and not going herself.

Whoa, I was going to tell you about the chubs. These Pentecostal missionaries were serious fishers of souls but also of chubs. This was quite a surprise to us as we watched them patiently fishing and filling tubs with chubs and later salting the catch. This was part of their winter food supply.

Of course, Father Grias was incensed at the arrival of these patient competitors, especially since it had been only about ten years since the Anglicans had thrown the cassock in. The Pentecostals persevered. First, they contacted Uncle Joe Hall in Edmonton, where he and Aunt Cecilia had retired, to inquire

PART II

129

about purchasing his property. A deal was struck, and they then had a permanent base and improved it by converting Uncle Joe's old store into a church. Daddy found out that they were experienced sawmill men and mechanics. They had the skills Daddy needed for his business, and they were absolutely dependable. When Robert Schneider worked on the sawmill for Daddy, he would have dinner (lunch) with us, and he would always have to say grace beforehand. This was not something that we ever did, but Daddy always looked solemn about it, and we followed his cue.

Eventually, Robert moved on to Fort Good Hope, where he established a mission, and Forrest moved to Fort Franklin, where he also established a mission. They were replaced by Dan and Grace Priest, who spent many years in the community before moving on to Coppermine, now called Kugluktuk. Dan was a skilled carpenter and furniture maker. When he left, he was replaced by Mr. Cameron who had been a professional welder. Daddy was certainly happy to have all of them living in the community. The initial followers of their church in Fort Norman were mostly members of the Holy Trinity Anglican Church who had lost their own minister. Dan and Grace were respected and loved by the members of the community and are still missed by many.

∞

One summer, Mama was quite ill with heart disease and had to be hospitalized in Edmonton. I don't remember where Diana stayed, but it was most likely with Aunt Jane and a babysitter. A babysitter would be needed, as Aunt Jane had followed the Gaudet family into service with the HBC. Noel and Harriet Gladu took me for a month. They and Michael had already gone to their summer jobs with NTCL at the Bear River Rapids. Harriet was the camp cook, and Noel was a labourer. NTCL ran a barge that started at Port Radium on Great Bear Lake. The barge was towed by the *Radium Gilbert* from there to the start of the Bear River, where the Franklin Camp was located. They were hauling bags of yellowcake, which was a form of uranium. The uranium was mined at Port Radium and had, earlier, been used to build the bombs that had been dropped on two Japanese cities at the end of WWII.

The yellowcake would be offloaded at the Franklin Camp and placed on another barge, which was pushed by another tug to the start of a portage on the Bear River. This barge was then unloaded onto trucks, to be portaged to the foot of the Saint Charles Rapids, which was part of the Bear River. At that point the yellowcake would be transferred from the trucks onto shallow draft Bear River barges, which were pushed by a shallow draft tug like the *George Askew* or the *Radium Prince* to the confluence of the Bear and Mackenzie rivers where the Norman Camp was located. The yellowcake would then be transferred from the Bear River barges to the much larger Mackenzie River barges, which were pushed south by larger tugs like the *Radium Dew* or the *Radium Charles*, eventually reaching the railhead and then to wherever the yellowcake was going.

It is one of the great shames of Canada, the way the yellowcake was handled. There was no such thing as Personal Protective Equipment in those days, and the workers, mostly local Indians and Half-Breeds, were readily exposed to the uranium, which had been pummelled into yellowcake. I saw workers sweeping the yellowcake off the decks of barges into the Bear River. Imagine that happening today!

One season before I was born, the last shipment of yellowcake for that season missed the last Mackenzie River barge going south. Consequently, NTCL hired Daddy and his horses to haul the yellowcake off the barge to a location on the riverbank in Fort Norman, to be stored until the next shipping season. Many years later, when the danger of doing this was finally recognized by the authorities, this site, and others, had to be cleaned up. The clean-up showed serious contamination where the yellowcake had been piled and which a local family had built a house on. Eventually, all the sites were cleaned up, and the contaminants were shipped out to a proper processing location. Of course, like the local and other workers, Daddy did not have any Personal Protective Equipment. This likely led to his cancer in the 1970s.

To be fair, many workers from "outside" were exposed as well. These were the workers who were brought in by airplane at the start of each season from Edmonton. These were mostly the truck drivers, the cat skinners, the mechanics, and such. There was no such thing as two weeks in/two weeks out in those days. Our family was friends with many of the people who worked this shipping route, including Isadore Yukon, Ollie Olson, Andy Brass, and Don Gordon.

Andy was the boss of the system, and he had a fast speedboat as well as a landing barge that he used to go back and forth between the Norman Camp, the Bear River Camp, and the Franklin Camp. Olie was the captain of the *Radium Prince* and Don was the foreman of the Norman Camp and used to walk to town when movies were being played or just to visit. Earlier, I mentioned Gordon Creek. It was named for Don. All of these fine gentlemen lived in Edmonton in the off season and took time to visit patients from Fort Norman and Fort Franklin at the Charles Camseil Hospital. Yes, the same Charles Camsell

I talked about in an earlier chapter. Isadore Yukon was a Dene person who was from Fort Norman originally. He was the best pilot on the Bear River. He was an orphan and had taught himself to read and write. Whenever he had an opportunity, he would drop by to visit Daddy and Mama.

I suppose I got exposed to the yellowcake as well when I was quite young and caught a ride on the *George Askew*, which was the last sternwheeler working on the Bear River. We left the Norman Camp late in the evening. Being late, I should have slept. The *Askew* struggled against the strong current. The noise from the diesel engine indicated it was under a heavy load. The chain-driven paddlewheel had its own loud sloshing noise. Sleep was impossible in my unfamiliar surroundings. We made slow progress against the swift current. At the helm was Captain Bill Marsh.

George Askew. Credit: Maurice R. Cloughley (*Spell of the Midnight Sun*).

At the Bear River camp, some of the local workers who had brought their families with them lived in tents set back from the main camp but nearer to the Bear River. Those workers who did not have families with them stayed in bunkhouses at the main camp. I stayed with Harriet and Noel and Mike in their tent. Because Harriet was the camp cook, their tent was set up close to the cookhouse. When Harriet was done feeding the crew breakfast, she would bring bacon and toast back to the tent for Michael and me. We had a great time that summer.

The NTCL was a significant part of the lives of many people from Fort Norman and Fort Franklin. Among other stations, they kept a camp right next to Fort Norman high on the banks of the Bear River. The work of the employees who stayed at the camp took place mainly at the mouth of the Bear River, which was just below the camp. Cece McCauley was the camp cook for a few seasons. We used to make the hike through the bush to visit her. She would always reward us with some freshly baked pie or pastries and a friendly smile.

Sometimes, the ships' crews would give us short rides on a tug, such as the *Radium Prince* or the *Watson Lake*, from the dock at Fort Norman to the staging area in Bear River to pick up a barge. During one of these short rides, I had my first taste of fresh tomatoes. I knew what canned tomatoes were, but I had no idea of where they came from. It was a wonderful taste, and I still love fresh tomatoes. Mike was there then, and he had already experienced fresh tomatoes. In a superior way, he told me how one should put salt on the tomato before eating it. This was a bit confusing to me as we would put sugar on the canned tomatoes.

As Mike and I got older, our ideal childhood life was coming to an end, but there is one other story from my childhood that I would like to share with you.

∞

A big event in my life that took place every year was the celebration of my birthday. From about the ages of seven to twelve, the party would be a picnic. Being born on May 13 meant that the picnic would be in the spring with the leaves just beginning to come out and all the wonderful smells of spring, such as the sap beginning to rise and the soil being released from winter's grip. Mama would make a layered white cake from scratch. The filling was usually canned raspberry jam. The icing was usually made from icing sugar and other magical ingredients. However, the main course at the picnic was fresh wild goose cooked on an open fire. Thus, the need for a picnic, so we could be in the bush.

Although our people can now hunt freely, killing ducks and geese in the spring in those days was illegal. There were some years when the game wardens and the Mounties were quite strict. Other years, we had sensible administrators of the law. However, it was best to keep a low profile. We only had one native game warden in those days, and he was one of the sensible administrators. His name was Bob Douglas, and he was a close friend of our family. Bob was the son of a manager for Northern Traders in Fort Norman, was born and raised in the area, and had trapped and hunted for a living. He used to like coming into a camp in the spring and make a remark like, "Sure glad to see you enjoying that turkey cooking by the fire!"

Bob Douglas and Walter Hardy with Walter's catch from the Blackwater River area. Credit: Hardy Family Collection.

As I grew older, I spent more time with Bob and learned a lot about him. Bob joined the RCAF during WWII. He had seen action but was not willing to talk about it. He had also started university after the war and stayed at that for a couple of years, studying engineering. However, he decided he liked being in the bush more, so became a game warden, as they were called then. I looked up to him and wanted to become a game warden myself. Bob died after I became a lawyer. I was honoured by his children by being asked to deliver the eulogy at his funeral service, which was held in the Catholic church in Fort Rae, now called Behchoko. I remember saying that Bob had been my hero when I was growing up. He was.

CHAPTER THIRTEEN

FIRST BIG TRIP

Early in 1959, I made the first long trip of my life. I was eleven years old. I had to go to the hospital in Aklavik. Prior to that I had travelled the Bear River to stay with the Gladus, spent a week with Daddy in a fish camp at Twelve Mile Point, and travelled to and from Norman Wells by boat with Daddy. I had also taken my first airplane ride with Bob Hattie. These short trips opened some wonders. When Daddy took me to Norman Wells, I was ten years old. The people there were celebrating Dominion Day. Norman Wells was a company town, owned by Imperial Oil and populated, primarily, by White people from Alberta. They received all of their groceries and household supplies directly from Edmonton in a DC-3 owned by Imperial Oil. The DC-3 would make two or three flights a week. As a result, the people of Norman Wells, at least those employed by Imperial Oil, had a regular supply of fresh fruits and vegetables.

I had never heard of, let alone tasted, watermelon. An Imperial Oil employee named Tex Morgan handed me something that was large and green and red. I looked at it, bewildered. Tex smiled. "You're supposed to eat it," he said. "Take a bite." Not wanting to be embarrassed, I took a tentative nibble from the slice. My goodness, that watermelon tasted wonderful, and it was cool because it was kept in a large tub filled with ice. I started taking larger bites, the juice dribbling down my face, and I thought, *what a wonderful life these people have.*

∞

I digress. I don't recall the examination, but the community nurse decided that I needed to have my tonsils out. The nursing station in Fort Norman was not equipped for such a procedure. I don't know if the hospitals in Aklavik, which were run by the Anglican and Catholic churches, were the closest ones, but they were the easiest to get to. CP Air operated a weekly scheduled service that connected Fort Norman to Aklavik and points in between. I don't know why I was sent to the Catholic hospital instead of the Anglican one.

On the day the flight was to go, my parents brought me to Plane Lake, which, when frozen, was the community's landing strip. We likely went to the lake by dog team or maybe by snowmobile, as these machines were now starting to appear

PART II

135

in the country. The community nurse was also there to see me off. The airplane came from Norman Wells, where CP Air had its base. The pilot was the well-known and grumpy Stew Hill, who had flown that route for many years. After the mail and the freight were unloaded, the nurse said, "Okay, you can get on the airplane now." I must have looked apprehensive, as she said, "Don't worry. Isadore Yukon will be getting on the plane in Franklin, and he will keep an eye on you until you get to Aklavik." I laugh to myself every time I think of this. Eleven years old, and nobody worried about me having an escort. Good God, if anyone tried that today, it would create a political firestorm.

So, off we went, into the sky and on to Fort Franklin, as the community was known in those days. It is now called Deline. Yes, Isadore Yukon was waiting for the plane, and he made sure to tell me that he was watching out for me. The plane landed right in front of the community on Great Bear Lake. As a result, most of the community, at least those not out on the traplines, would greet the airplane and see who was coming and going. In the crowd were a number of eleven- and twelve-year-old girls, including one who had been my "girlfriend" in Fort Norman the previous summer. I certainly felt shy, if not embarrassed, as all of those girls had obviously come to take a look at me. The girls all had bright red lipstick on and wore colourful kerchiefs and were giggling. My "girlfriend" looked starstruck. When we became adults, we used to have quite a laugh about this. Puppy love.

All aboard. Off we went to Fort Good Hope. There were no landing strips in those communities in those days. So, the landing in Fort Good Hope was out on the Mackenzie River, quite a distance from the community. Because of the distance, we were not greeted by a great number of people. It didn't take long to get their mail and some parcels unloaded and to load some more passengers. We were travelling in a single Otter on skis. These planes were not exactly warm, and we all wore good winter clothing: long johns, heavy socks, duffels, mukluks, heavy pants, sweaters, homemade parkas, a scarf, a hat, and, of course, warm mitts.

The next leg was to Fort McPherson, which was fairly lengthy. The landing strip in Fort McPherson was on the Peel River in front of the community, probably about a mile away We landed, and something caused a delay. I think it might have been a problem with a ski that occurred on landing. Anyway, we all got out of the plane and waited for the damage to be assessed. Eventually, Isadore came over to me. "You see those buildings over there?" he said as he pointed to the HBC compound. I could barely make out the buildings in the distance. "You need to go there until we call for you." So, off I went, by myself, over the snowbanks, in strange country, and finally up the hill to the store. I guess I must have just walked in. I was greeted by one of the friendliest people I had met up to that point in my life. That person was Frank Firth, who was working as a clerk in the store. Frank became a lifelong friend.

The Firths, like the Gaudets, were generational servants of the HBC. At the time I did not know that Great-grandfather Charles Phillipe Gaudet had spent a few years managing the post in Fort McPherson before John Firth arrived there. Frank said, "Come in, come in, take your outer clothes off, and have a seat here." The store was well lit and heated, and it felt great.

I don't know how long it was, but Frank eventually said, "Okay, it's time to go." I put all my outer clothing back on, then bounded out the door and down the hill and back to the airplane, all by myself. Then it was off to the final stop—Aklavik. Dusk was setting in as we took off, and it was dark by the time we got to Aklavik. Aklavik was much larger than Fort Norman, and its lights shone brightly as we came in for the landing. Although Aklavik was the business and governmental centre for the region it was just on the verge of becoming smaller because of the impending move of various services to a new community to be called Inuvik. At that time, Inuvik was being built and was called East Three.

Single Otter at Fort Norman in 1967. Northward took over the VFR operations from PWA, which had taken it over from CP Air. Credit: Hardy Family Collection.

My recollection of the rest of that day is a bit hazy. I recall Isadore saying, "Okay, I am going to Peffer's, and I will see you next week." I had no idea what a Peffer was and did not know why he would see me next week. As I got older, I learned that a Peffer was Stan Peffer, who owned a local establishment that included a trading post and a restaurant. Cece Macaulay, who was from our part of the country and a friend of Mama's, worked for Peffer. I think she ran the restaurant and pool-hall. I think that Peffer's establishment was also well known for some high-stakes poker games. That was likely the attraction for Isadore.

I believe I was picked up in a Bombardier and was taken to the hospital. My tonsils were taken out the next day, or maybe it was the day after that.

The nurses were nuns, and they were assisted by some local native women who may have been nurse's aides. Whatever they were, they brought me ice cream after the operation. My goodness, ice cream in the winter. What a great idea. It was delicious. It did not take long for my throat to heal, and I was soon eating dried fish and bannock like the other patients for a nighttime snack. I was on the third floor, and I discovered what I thought was the strangest toilet I had ever seen. It was indoors, and it had a regular toilet seat to sit on, but the pee and the poop would disappear down a gigantic pipe to only God knows where. Quite interesting for a curious eleven-year-old boy.

As I recovered, a short, squat nun came to visit me and introduced herself. She seemed happy to see me. Her name was Sister Hebert. She would play a significant role in my life a few years later. She told me that there were some children from Fort Norman staying in the residential school, which was connected to the hospital by a corridor. She offered to take me to see them the next day. I was happy to be able to see someone my age who I knew. So, the next day I was given my clothes to wear instead of the hospital pyjamas, and off I went with Sister Hebert. I remember meeting George McDonald and Gordon Lennie there. We had a good visit and played a few games.

Then Sister Hebert took me back to my hospital bed. When she was leaving, she said goodbye and something that I did not understand at the time: "I will see you in Inuvik in the fall." What was Inuvik, and what did "in the fall" mean? No one had yet told the people of Fort Norman, as far as I knew, about the calamity that would turn my life, as well as the lives of many of my friends, upside down later in the year.

After the week was over, we took the same plane home, stopping at the same communities in reverse order. Sometimes I wonder how Isadore did at Peffer's.

∞

The trip to and from Aklavik was not my first airplane ride. Bob Hattie, who was from Norman Wells and was a partner with Daddy in the sawmill and contracting business, also owned a small airplane that he would hire out. It was in the early spring of 1958 when I was still ten years old. He had skis on the plane, which meant he could land in deep snow and still take off. He had a contract with NTCL to check the amount of snow on Bennett Field to see if their DC-3 could safely land there, or if there was still too much snow. Our friend, Ed Hodgson, was with him when they landed at Plane Lake. They came into town to see Daddy, and while they were there, Bob asked Daddy if I might want to have a ride with them to Bennett Field and back. It was a beautiful day with clear skies and bright sunlight. We could sense that the spring melt was about to start.

Daddy said sure and told Bob that this would be my first airplane ride. Everyone was in a good mood, and my little adventure added to the good feelings. So, off to Plane Lake we went. When we got there, I noticed that there were only two seats in the small airplane, which would be occupied by Bob and Ed. I was put in the cargo area on the floor and was told to hang on. I hung on for what was a fifteen- to twenty-minute ride, but it seemed to take forever. That forever feeling resulted from me being airsick and having thrown up two or three times in the area where I was sitting. We got to Bennett Field and, after making a few passes, Bob landed the little airplane, and it promptly sank in the deep snow.

With hindsight, I am so thankful that Ed was with us. After Bob made a couple of futile attempts at takeoffs, Ed jumped out of the plane with a snow shovel and went to work. Within an hour he had enough of a runway cleared that the plane was able to take off. Within twenty minutes we were back at Plane Lake without further incident. Everyone had a laugh at me for getting airsick, and so ended the little adventure. Of course, NTCL had to wait a few more weeks before they could get their DC-3 safely into Bennet Field. I have never been airsick since then despite the thousands and thousands of miles that I have flown as a passenger in all kinds of weather.

HBC aircraft at Taylor's Lake, near Fort Norman, in 1938. L to R: Cece (Hodgson) McCauley, Mary (Lennie) Gaudet, Rod Hardy, and Alice (Gaudet) Hardy. Credit: Hardy Family Collection.

PART II

Interestingly, I wrote a report on the trip to and from Aklavik for our school newspaper, the *Norman News*. The report pegs the dates of the trip as January 17 and January 24, 1959. Some of the details are a bit different from what I recalled here. Most importantly, I did not mention the ice cream in my report. Maybe I didn't want to stir up any more jealousy. It also seems that my excursion to the HBC store in Fort McPherson took place on the return trip. Maybe it happened on both legs? The news report also stated that I was escorted back home, from Aklavik, by Judge Phinney, the magistrate who flew from community to community to deal with charges arising from local crime. Judge Phinney became well known for his decisions on Indigenous rights in the Northwest Territories, especially "Re Sikeya." My brother, Walter, was among those that met us on the return home, and he gave Judge Phinney and me a ride to town. I assume that would have been with his dog team.

I am so thankful that Mama saved so many things from my childhood, including a number of issues of the *Norman News*.

I returned home from the adventure to Aklavik enthused and ready for more. I was in grade six, and our teacher was Maurice Cloughley. Yes, the same Maurice Cloughley who moved to Fort Franklin and then to what was called the Eastern Arctic. Eventually, he ended up being sentenced to ten years in prison for the molestation of his students. As difficult as it may be to believe, to the best of my knowledge, Cloughley did not molest any students while he was teaching at the Fort Norman Federal Day School. Mike Gladu and I would most certainly have known about any molestations, as we would have been prime targets. Having said that, there was some talk about Cloughley making a hole in the wall to the girls' bathroom to spy on them. Mike and I took piano lessons from Cloughley for two years, after school. I must admit that I was not much good on the piano or any other musical instrument. On the other hand, Mike turned out to be quite a good musician, artist, and athlete.

Cloughley did leave a written record of his time in our community. The book that he wrote is titled *The Spell of the Midnight Sun*. The first chapter is "A Winter at Fort Norman." I found the chapter to be an excellent read and an accurate portrayal of life there in the late 1950s. There is also a chapter titled "Faith and Pursuit of Sin." I especially enjoyed the part of that chapter where Cloughley describes the activities of Father Jean Grias during his late-night visits to the only female teacher in the community and the reactions of the other transient residents.

In addition to describing the Indians and the Métis, Cloughley also invented a third category of natives: the "not quite Whites."

When I first read it, I thought I was in that group, but after thinking about it, I believe it was a reference to a particular family in the transient community. I didn't mind being among Cloughley's Métis, as he praised the Métis parents for caring about their children's education. He likely came across the term "Métis" when he was writing and not while he was teaching in Fort Norman. In those days we called ourselves "Half-breeds," as in, "I'm a Half-Breed. Wanna do something about it?" I can still hear our friend Alfred Lennie snarling that phrase. I find it interesting that Cloughley did not mention that we were officially "Others" in the school records— "Indians, Whites, and Others."

When I was in grades four and five, our teacher and school principal was Frank Frey. Mr. Frey was from Saskatchewan, and one of his claims to fame was that, while attending university, he had a tryout for the Saskatchewan Roughriders. My memory is a bit hazy on this point, but I think he was offered a spot on the team, which he declined in favour of continuing his education. With the benefit of hindsight, I can see that the story was likely part of his encouragement to us to continue our education. I don't doubt the veracity of the story, as he was an ardent footballer, and he introduced it to us on the school playground. Mrs. Frey was the sister of Fernie Flaman, one of the fiercest defencemen in the NHL at the time. However, he played for the Boston Bruins, the nemesis of *les Canadiens*. The Freys were staunchly Catholic and had five or six children. I remember the oldest two, Linda and Gary. When the Freys left at the end of the 1957/1958 school year, Cloughley became the principal. Being from New Zealand, Cloughley did not have many inspirational "hero" stories about Canadian sports.

∞

When the Freys left Fort Norman, the apartment above the school was taken over by the new female teacher, Mrs. Margaret Bachner, and her young son, George. Mrs. Bachner became the object of the affections of Father Jean Grias. Interestingly, Mrs. Bachner transferred to the new school in Inuvik for the 1959/1960 school year, where she had two students from Fort Norman in her class—Bertha Lennie and Norman Andrew. Father Grias also left Fort Norman and, eventually, the priesthood. He married a woman who already had children, and they lived in Hay River, where Grias was employed as a social worker. A number of years later, when we were active in the Métis Association of the Northwest Territories, we held a board meeting in Hay River at the Legion. Lo and behold, there was Jean Grias selling strip pull tickets at the front door.

I did not recognize him, but Charlie Blondin did. Charlie was not at all shy, and he greeted the former priest effusively. He was rewarded by being ignored. Grias was there for a few more hours, selling tickets, and he would occasionally look our way and glare at us.

But wait, there's more. Frank Frey had also moved to Inuvik for the 1959/1960 school year as the vice principal, responsible for the school's Catholic wing. At first, I was happy to see him. However, I got a cold shoulder as he appeared not to want to have anything to do with his old students from Fort Norman. I and others from Fort Norman found this a bit strange, as we had held him in high regard. I never did understand why he acted the way he did.

I found another surprise when looking through the 1959/1960 yearbook for what was then known as the Inuvik Federal School. There were two Hardisty children in attendance: Sarah Jane Hardisty and Gabriel Hardisty. These were two of my cousins from Fort Wrigley. Sarah Jane was in the same class as Larry Gordon, who married my sister, Diane! Based on the names of the students who were in the same classes that Sarah Jane and Gabriel were in, I would surmise they were in the Anglican residence, Stringer Hall, that year. I did not know they attended school in Inuvik that year. Small world!

∞

One of the things that Cloughley would have been responsible for would have been to advise our parents, as well as the students, that, at the end of the 1958/1959 school year, no grades above grade six would be taught in Fort Norman. Up to that point, there were usually a few students in grades seven, eight, and nine. This meant that students in those grades would have to leave home or take correspondence courses, as my friend, Faye Eliason, did. A large group, including Mike and I and a number of our friends, including Robert Clement, left Fort Norman in September 1959.

I don't think our parents were told of this development until late in the school year. I do know that my parents were unhappy when they learned about it. They did not want to send me away for education until I was older. Daddy was not well educated, and Mama did not have the confidence to guide me through grade seven correspondence course materials. Once they realized there was nothing that could be done, they decided I should go to Edmonton to live with my oldest brother, Leo, and his wife, Liz, and attend public school there. Mama and Daddy assumed this was something I would be happy about. I was not.

All of my friends, not only from Fort Norman but also from Norman Wells and Fort Franklin, were going to a brand-new students' residence and a brand-new public school in Inuvik along with a few hundred other students from other communities in the same situation that we were in. That sounded much more adventurous than going to live with family, who would be like parents. I kicked up an ongoing fuss with my parents, and they eventually agreed that I could go with my friends. None of us foresaw that this decision would have a horribly negative effect on my life for years to come.

Larry Tourangeau and Rick Hardy in front of Semmler's Store in Inuvik in 1962. Credit: Hardy Family Collection.

PART III
STUDENT RESIDENCES AND THE DEVILS OF GROLLIER HALL

Grollier Hall Hockey Team 1960/1961 – Notre Dame Huskies. Back row, L to R: Mike Gladu, Robert Clement, Larry Tourangeau, Norm Hodgson, James Cockney and Rudy Cockney. Front row, L to R: Andy Tardiff, Frank Green, Walter Masazumi, Jerry Ruben and Rick Hardy. Credit: Author.

Rick Hardy in a boat being driven by Father Franche in 1961. This picture was taken by Martin Houston on the way to Reindeer Station. The trip was a reward for the Huskies having won a game earlier that year. Martin Houston had arrived a year earlier to take charge of the senior boys and had already molested Rick. Credit: Author.

PART III

145

CHAPTER FOURTEEN

FIRST STEPS TO HELL

It was early in September 1959. It was a bleak day. I had turned twelve that May and had been promoted to grade seven in June. Coincidentally, that was the same age that my grandfather was when he and his younger brother, Joseph Leon Gaudet, left their home in Fort Good Hope to attend school for nine years in Saint Boniface, Manitoba, before returning to the North.

There were seventeen of us, all children from Fort Norman, loosely assembled on the shore of the Mackenzie River in front of our community, with our parents and other family members and friends. It was a typical fall day. As it was early in the day, the overnight chill was still in the air, and there was a bit of a wind, which caused the muddy water of the river to be choppy, and waves washed up on the shore. We, the children, were all clutching small, cheap suitcases or bags, which held one or two changes of clothes and some personal items. We all had our good clothes on, as if we were about to go to church. I was wearing my faux black leather jacket, my black slacks with the brilliant white snap buttons on the pockets and, of course, my black and polished jet boots.

All of us—the children, the family members, and friends—were waiting for the Pacific Western Airlines de Havilland single Otter airplane, which had just landed on floats, to cough and splutter to the dock and tie up.

At that time, Fort Norman had a population of less than 300 people, and 17 of the children were being taken out of the community for the coming school year. This tragedy was a result of decisions taken by the Government of Canada to concentrate and streamline the education systems in the smaller communities in the Northwest Territories.

∞

William Carpenter Bompas was the Anglican Bishop of what was called the Diocese of Mackenzie River from 1873 to 1891. He issued *Diocese of Mackenzie River* in 1888. He wrote that the first Anglican Missions in the Diocese were established in 1858 starting at Fort Simpson and then Fort Norman. The first school in Fort Norman was established in 1859 and Mr. John Hope and wife, was the school master from 1859 to 1864. John Hope was followed by Mr. Murdoch McLeod from 1866 to 1868, Mr. Jos.

Hodgson and wife from 1873 to 1879 and Miss A. Morris from 1881 to 1883. These teachers were followed by others, including Allan Hardisty and Charles Camsell, until both the Anglican Church and the Roman Catholic Church, with the helping hand of the Government of Canada, established residential schools in centralized locations. As a result, the Anglican Church stopped providing education in Fort Norman and the children of their adherents were sent to Saint Peter's Anglican Indian Residential School in Hay River, which was established in 1894 and continued operating until the 1940s. These students included my Aunt Rosie Gaudet and my uncles Charles and George Gaudet, as well as our Hardisty relatives.

Prior to the establishment of Saint Peters, my grandmother, Sarah Jane (Hardisty) Gaudet and her sister Mary did attend an Anglican School in Fort Resolution in 1892 and 1893. During those years their parents had been transferred to the mission in Fort Wrigley and there was no school there. The mission and the school in Fort Resolution were called Saint James. The school was discontinued with of the opening of Saint Peter's in 1894. I don't know, for sure, how many years Granny attended Saint James but I am assuming that she spent two years there and was then shifted to Saint Peter's. I speculate that she stayed at Saint Peter's until she returned to Fort Norman in 1896 to rejoin her family after they returned there from Fort Wrigley.

∞

The Roman Catholic Church established the Sacred Heart Residential School in Fort Providence in 1867. My mother and my aunts Mary, Cecilia, Bella, and Jane and my Uncle Fred all attended this school.

This went on until the mid to late 1940s when, as a result of petitions from the parents in Fort Norman, the Fort Norman Federal Day School was established. Although some children from Fort Norman did continue to attend the Roman Catholic Sacred Heart Residential School in Fort Providence or the Immaculate Conception Residential School in Aklavik, most then attended school at home in Fort Norman. Others, such as my cousins Charlie and Bobby Overvold, attended the Anglican All Saints Residential School in Aklavik.

Although the demand for higher grades was not great, the Fort Norman Federal Day School did provide courses up to and including grade nine, prior to the switch to Inuvik in 1959.

PART III

147

One of the first classes in the new Fort Norman Federal Day School c. 1946.
Rod and Walter Hardy are wearing striped T-shirts. Credit: Hardy Family Collection.

Another early class from the first federal school. Fred Clement Senior is in the front row to the left of Walter Hardy.
Credit: Hardy Family Collection.

The details of the decision, that was implemented in 1959, to concentrate students in grades seven to twelve from the smaller communities into schools in larger communities are not known to me. However, I do know that the establishment of the Anglican and Catholic residences and the new school in Inuvik was a result of the Government of Canada's decision to move the services that it provided from Aklavik to the brand-new community of Inuvik. The government deemed this necessary because, in its view, Aklavik was sinking into the Mackenzie Delta. While the government could not force people to move, it incentivised individuals and institutions to do so. Both the Anglican and Catholic churches had residential schools and hospitals in Aklavik, funded, at least in part, by the Government of Canada, and the government wanted them moved. So, one can imagine the negotiations that took place. The new residences, one for Anglican students and one for Catholic students, built in Inuvik, were much larger than what was needed to accommodate the number of students that were in residence in Aklavik.

So, where would the additional students come from? The answer, from my perspective, led to the decision to cap the grade level at six for small communities like Fort Norman. Then, anyone wanting further education would have to go to one of the residences in Inuvik and attend the day school there. So, we were fodder for the education machine, which included the two churches that we were turned over to by the Government of Canada. The original plan for the Inuvik institutions was to bring students in from as far south as Fort Norman and as far east as Gjoa Haven. A similar plan was put in place for communities south of Fort Norman, with similar centralized institutions in Fort Simpson and Fort Smith. However, some students from as far south as Fort Smith and all points in between were sent to Inuvik for the 1959/1960 school year, including my cousins Sarah Jane and Gabe Hardisty from Fort Wrigley. I don't know why the students from communities south of Fort Norman were sent to Inuvik for the 1959/1960 school year but they did not return after that year.

Few of the seventeen children from Fort Norman who gathered on the shore on that chilly September morning had much of an understanding why we were being taken away from home and what would be waiting for us when we got to Inuvik. Some of us were scared and confused, and some of us, like me, thought it would be a great adventure. The airplane docked, and the pilot hopped out and tied it securely to the dock. The de Havilland single Otter is built to hold ten passengers, and that was normally the total number of seats available.

PART III

149

This event took place over sixty years ago, and my memories of that day are not as clear as I would like. However, I have had help to reconstruct those memories from my friends who were on the same airplane and who are still alive. I do know that seventeen students from Fort Norman went to Inuvik to go to school that year. I know that there were nowhere near enough seats for all of us. Mostly, we sat on our suitcases. I am sure that the airplane stopped at another community, most likely Fort Good Hope, to pick up more children. I'm also sure that there were more than twenty of us after that stop. Most of the children had never been on an airplane, and between the motion of the airplane, the fumes from the engine, and the loud noise from the engine, most of us got airsick. I remember the awful smell of the puke. That smell made those of us who had some tolerance for airplane rides sick also. Fortunately, I did not succumb to the airsickness, but I did not feel particularly well.

I do not remember the adults or our friends and relatives wishing us bon voyage or anything like that. I expect that the overwhelming emotion was one of sadness, with the mothers openly crying. I do not remember if Mama was on the beach with us.

∞

The system in Inuvik was new and different from the residential schools that preceded it. Previously, the residences and the schools were combined units, usually in one building. For example, the Catholic and Anglican churches ran separate residential schools in Aklavik. My understanding is that there was very little opportunity for interaction between the two schools. The interactions that I heard of were rumbles between the senior boys of the separate schools. I did not attend a school of this type, so I cannot speak from personal experience.

The new system in Inuvik was made up of two residences, with one each being run by the churches under contract to the Government of Canada. Each residence could accommodate about 250 students. The students in each residence were divided into four dormitories: junior boys and junior girls up to twelve years old and senior boys and senior girls ages twelve and over.

All of the students from both residences, as well as all of the children who lived in Inuvik, attended the same school, which was the only school in Inuvik. First, it was called the Inuvik Federal School. The next year it became Sir Alexander Mackenzie School or SAMS. The Catholic residence was called Grollier Hall, and the Anglican residence was called Stringer Hall. Both of these names were for two of the church's early missionaries to our country.

Grollier Hall was run by Catholic priests, nuns, and brothers with various lay people in the kitchen, sewing rooms, and so forth. In the first year, there was a lay assistant supervisor for the senior boys named Roger Moore. I don't know why I mention his name, as he is, at best, just a passing memory. Maybe I remember him because he ran the commissary where we could buy chocolate bars and pop. There was a part-time lay assistant supervisor for the junior boys named John Comeau, whose full-time job was being the manager of the local bank. He was eventually caught and convicted for molesting quite a few boys. The junior and senior girls were supervised by nuns.

Oh, and each residence had a chapel, so we, in Grollier Hall, had mass and benediction every day as well as morning and nighttime prayers on our knees. Quite a change from our home lives.

At the time the Government of Canada made the decision to move the people from Aklavik to East Three, which would become Inuvik, not everyone from Aklavik agreed to move. As a result, there were not many students from Aklavik in the Inuvik school system. Judging from the yearbooks from that time, it appears that students from Aklavik did not start in Inuvik until they were in grade nine.

I should emphasize again that the previous systems were actually residential schools, as the students lived and went to school in the same building. The system in Inuvik should be more properly called residences only, as we all went to a public school, which was a separate institution from the residences. Another important distinction of the residences from the residential schools is that they were not race-based institutions. The residences were for all students living in the communities that they were from. Consequently, the residences were populated by Indian, Inuit, Métis, and non-Indigenous students. Unlike the earlier residential schools, the parents of the Métis and non-Indigenous students no longer had to pay for their children to be educated there. The overall objective was to create public institutions that were paid for by the Government of Canada, which, at the time, was responsible for the education of all students in the NWT.

Although the overall plan appeared to be an integrated school, the churches hung on for a few more years. The Catholic Church, in particular, negotiated an extension of their religious control. The first year for this new system was for the 1959/1960 school year. That year the school only offered grades one to nine. The school itself was comprised of two wings. One was a Catholic wing, and one was an Anglican wing. I hope I don't have the two confused as one, the Catholic wing, was called "B" wing, and the Anglican one was called "A" wing. Thus, the Catholic priests from the local parish were able to come to the Catholic wing to teach catechism every day.

The yearbook for the 1959/1960 year shows all of the grade nine students, who were called "Graduates," as one unit without distinction to religion. However, I am relatively sure that they had separate classrooms based on religion. The remaining grades were presented, in the year book, in groups that were clearly based on religion.

The gradual integration of religions in the classroom started in the 1960/61 school year when the school offered grade ten, grade eleven the year after that, and finally, grade twelve in 1962/1963. The students for grade ten in 1960/1961 had, for the most part, been in the Catholic and Anglican wings in grade nine the previous year, but were now together in one class regardless of religious affiliation. This is the way the high school eventually reached full religious integration for grades ten, eleven, and twelve. I suppose that the Catholic Church was satisfied that it could complete the indoctrination of the Catholic students before they entered high school.

It wasn't until a few years into this system that the two residences were allowed to compete against each other in sports. I believe this occurred as a result of the downtown fracases that would often happen on weekends. These fracases were a carryover from the schools in Aklavik. Sport competitions released some of the pent-up hormones that were raging away. I chuckle when I remember that the Catholic champion was Kenny Hodgson, and the Anglican champion was Ernest Firth, in the rumbles.

When the sports events took place, they were filled with tension by everyone playing and attending. There were not many of these events. As the high school progressed to integration, it formed its own basketball team, the Lions, that played in the local league, which had three or four other teams made up of men from the community as well as the local Navy base. The school team was made up of players from both residences. Finally, the Catholic and Anglican students had something in common to cheer for. The ridiculous walls finally began to come down.

∞

Again, I am getting ahead of the story. We left Fort Norman, off to what I thought would be another great adventure. We finally landed at Shell Lake, which is just outside of Inuvik. From there it gets a little hazy. The Catholic priest(s) would have been waiting for us with a panel truck, which we were loaded into and taken to Grollier Hall, which was brand new, and it smelled brand new. The next thing we knew, we were told to take our clothes off, so that we could take showers. Most of us didn't know what showers were. I think a nun, the one and only Sister Hebert, who I had met at the Aklavik Hospital, supervised us. We had to keep our underwear on, so as not to scandalize the sister, I guess. She told us what to do in the shower and in our underwear, and we eventually got through that ordeal.

It was a common shower that could accommodate ten to twenty of us at a time. When we were done and dried off, we turned in our wet underwear, which was our own, and were given our new play clothes. Of course, we had to stay wrapped in a towel, again so as not to embarrass poor Sister Hebert. The play clothes were a set of blue coveralls that were too big for us. We were also given boxer shorts for underwear, which most of us had not seen before. Once we were in the "uniforms"—yes, we were all given the same outfits—we were put in line for our haircuts, quick and short.

We were given another set of clothes, which were our school clothes. Then we were marched off to the open dormitory. Oh, how could I forget? We were all given a number, which became very important, sometimes even replacing our names when being called on. Interestingly, some of the students remember their numbers to this day. I don't. But I do remember that I was no longer free.

Some of us asked where our suitcases and our clothes were. I don't remember the answer, but we didn't get them until later in the year. We had taken our first steps into the dehumanization process. After that, everything became blurry again. I know we immediately learned how to line up and march to everything: meals, study periods, the weekly movies, masses, and benedictions. We were even prompted when to kneel, stand up, and sit down in the chapel by a "clicker" that Sister Hebert used. I was miserable. The senior boy's supervisor was Brother Morin, a bastard if there ever was one. He ruled with his fists. I looked forward to going to school every day, if for no other reason than it got me out of the hellhole and away from him. My teacher was Miss Sherry MacEachern. She was kind but firm.

∞

Notwithstanding the few hours a day that we had at school, my life was completely upside down, as I had never been exposed to such discipline and lack of love. I thought Mama was strict, but I now realized what a loving person she was. I wanted to go home.

Boys will be boys, and they need to find where they fit in the pecking order. I was young and small and, to some extent, had been spoiled by my life up until then. However, I didn't mind fighting to keep my dignity. That is, unless we were caught by Brother Morin, or as we quietly called him, "Moron." Once, one of the Green boys from Paulatuk, Frank—if I remember correctly—and I were fighting in the gym, and in walked the Moron. "Okay, you little bastards, into the equipment storage room." In we went, and it was, "Down with your pants, and bend over." He picked up a piece of plywood, which I think might have been a shelf. It was big enough that he had to use two hands to hold it. It was probably three quarters of an inch thick. I was trembling even before he hit. *Whack!* He used both hands and all the strength that he could muster. Three whacks each for Frank and me.

I had learned to stand up for myself before being locked up here without being beaten for it. I wasn't going to change, and the "minders" were just as determined to break me along with the other boys.

Hockey was a big thing for the boys at Grollier Hall. Those of us from Fort Norman were experienced with an outdoor rink, where we learned to skate, play shinny, and shovel it every day. So, we were not surprised with what we had to do to play hockey. What we did not expect was a coach who was as mean as Brother Moron. He was a good player and seemed to get a great deal of pleasure out of crushing us. One day as we were getting ready to go play a game on the rink, he said, "We need a goalie. Hardy, get the pads on." I did not want to play goalie, and I said so. "Hardy, I said get the pads on." I refused. Suddenly, he grabbed me by the scruff of my neck and threw me at the goalie pads, which were on the floor. Fortunately, I landed on them and not the hard floor. He roared at everyone that when he told us to do something, we damn well better listen.

While these sorts of things were going on, I was trying to get a letter to Mama and Daddy to tell them what was happening and to bring me home. I was caught twice, in study period, by Sister Lapointe, who took the letters away and read what I had written that far. The letters were very critical of the residence and the supervisors. She ripped the letters up right in front of me. I don't know what the punishment was for, but I was punished.

Eventually, I got a letter through to Mama and Daddy. I don't remember how, but it was likely that I wrote it while at the school and not the residence. I would have then given it to a friend at school, who lived in town, to mail it.

∞

As I was getting near the end of the third round of editorial reviews for this book, I found some materials that I had not paid much attention to previously. One item of those materials was a taped interview that had been made with Mama on April 4, 1984. This was approximately eight months before she died. The interview was conducted by a field worker with the Métis Heritage Association. The interview was wide ranging and covered Mama's whole life. Mama told the interviewer about going to the Catholic residential school in Fort Providence at the age of six. She said that initially it was not a bad experience for her, other than the loneliness.

She went there without any education but gradually learned to read and write. Eventually, she was able to write letters to her parents in Fort Norman. However, she said she had to be careful what she said in the letters, as they were all reviewed by the nuns before they were mailed. As she got older, she became less and less enamoured with the situation and wanted to go home. However, she could not say anything in a letter that would cause the nuns to destroy it.

The solution ended up being very similar to mine. One of Mama's friends had completed school and was returning to her home in Fort Good Hope on the mission boat, early in 1928. She told Mama to write a letter, and she would take it with her, personally delivering it to Mama's parents when the boat stopped in Fort Norman. Once Mama's parents got the letter, they withdrew her and Aunt Jane from the school. Mama had spent ten years in that school without seeing her parents. She said that she actually forgot them and thought that the "convent" was her home.

In chapter eight I briefly referred to the book written by Bridget Harris Volden in which she described her experiences in Fort Providence. With regard to letters home, Harris Volden had this to say:

The nuns did not allow us to pour out our hearts in our letters. We had to lie to our parents that we were happy and treated wonderfully. The nuns dictated on the blackboard what to write:

Dear Mother & Father, We are so happy here. Blah, blah, blah. . . Your loving daughter, Bridget.

Our parents had no idea how we lived, because we were so far away from our homes! There was no way to get to our parents or for our parents to get to us.

Mama did not like injustice and unfairness. In the interview she also spoke about all of the students being ordered not to speak in their mother tongue, which was Slavey. They complied until it became impossible. A young girl who could not speak anything but Slavey was brought to the school after her mother died. Again, the students were ordered not to speak to her except in English. Mama said it was terrible. The poor young girl had lost her mother and was in a strange place amongst strange people and could not communicate with anyone. Mama said that after three days and nights of listening to the poor young girl cry and cry and cry, Mama finally went to her and spoke to her in Slavey while comforting her.

Mama was severely punished for doing this.

PART III

155

∞

I wouldn't be broken at the residence, so the minders resorted to shaming me. I was demoted to junior boys. That meant I was sent to the upstairs dormitory with the five- to eleven-year-old boys under the supervision of Sister Hebert. I also had to line up with the juniors and march to all the activities with them. I thought I stood out like a sore thumb, which I likely did, and I was shamed. The pervert, John Comeau, was "supervising" the junior boys at night when I was being shamed. I do not remember him trying anything with me.

Then the lifeline arrived. Mama and Daddy sent a one-way ticket for me to go home for the Christmas holidays. The parents of most of the children could not afford to do this, so they all stayed in the residence for Christmas. The ticket was sent to the residence office, and the minders had no choice but to comply. I remember the ride to the Inuvik airport, in the panel truck, with one of the devils from Grollier Hall, Father Max Ruyant. If I remember correctly, Ruyant was not yet the superintendent of Grollier Hall. I believe the position was held by Father Franche that year. A number of years later, Franche was shot to death by a former student who had stayed at Grollier Hall.

At that time the terminal at Inuvik was a 512 building where Ruyant dropped me off and left me without a word. Such buildings were common in Inuvik and were used mostly for housing the natives in the west end of the community. The number "512" referred to the 512 square feet that made up the building. Try to imagine a family of six or seven or more people living in such a small house.

The airline was Pacific Western Airlines, and they operated a DC-6 aircraft that flew from Edmonton to Fort Smith, Norman Wells, Inuvik and back three times a week. I do not remember getting off the airplane at Norman Wells or how I got from there to Fort Norman, but I was back home, at last, with Mama, Daddy, and Diane, who was seven at the time. I think Walter and Rod were also there. I believe they picked me up with Walter's Bombardier. It was the best Christmas ever. I might have even served Midnight Mass, wearing my own clothes.

∞

My big Christmas present was that I did not have to go back to Inuvik after Christmas. The new school principal at the Fort Norman Federal Day School, Mr. Bob Elliott, had agreed that I could complete grade seven under his supervision.

As I said earlier, I have been blessed by Mama's saving of many items from my growing-up years, including report cards for my brothers and me. There is one for that school year issued by Mr. Elliott. My highest mark was in science and health (87), and my lowest mark was in handwriting (60), with an overall average of 75 percent. I was promoted to grade eight.

That was great, but it also meant that I had to either do correspondence on my own the next school year or leave home again. Mr. Elliott was moving to Inuvik! One of the good things about the Elliotts moving to Inuvik was that the boys from Fort Norman had a place to visit. The Elliotts, unlike the Freys, did not abandon us. In fact, four of us spent one Christmas with them after we ran from the devils of Grollier Hall.

∞

One of the things that we did that school year in Fort Norman was produce what I believe to be the last issue of the *Norman News*. This was a project that had run the previous year, and four issues were produced then. They are excellent snapshots of community life during those two years.

For example, the February 1959 edition had a full page of "Hunting News." A full page was an eight-by-fourteen-inch page produced on the school Gestetner machine. A Gestetner machine was state of the art in 1959 and 1960. The only place you will find one nowadays is in a museum. It was like a printer and could produce many copies by cranking a "master copy" through the machine. One of the items reported on in that edition of the "Hunting News" was as follows:

> *One day when Napoleon Kenny of Franklin was going along his trapline he came across some mink tracks. He followed them and came up on his house. He was about to set a trap at the doorway when he caught sight of the mink in his house. He reached in, caught him by the neck, and pulled him out. He then killed him by hitting him over the head with a stick. He got thirty dollars for the mink.*

The "News" section of that edition had a report on my trip to Aklavik. There was also a report on Randy and Marlene Stowell's stay in Ponoka, Alberta, where they went to a school that had about 1,000 children. The report also told us that Randy and Marlene watched television every day and included a list of their favourite shows. When they came back home to Fort Norman, they brought three hula hoops with them.

The final edition of the *News* included a "Magazine Section." It looks like we were now pursuing advertisements. We probably helped the advertisers write their ads. For example, the ad for The Bay said:

When shopping there are two good reasons why you should shop the Bay first: 1. It is the only store in town, 2. They may have what you want.

I suspect that the junior grades teacher, Mr. Wilf Plosz, who was helping us, was making an editorial comment! Mr. Plosz left Fort Norman and teaching the next year and moved to Hay River, where he started a newspaper, the name of which I don't remember. It may have been the *Mackenzie News*. In any event, we always looked forward to seeing the latest edition of that paper for the two or three years that it was published.

∞

Life in the community was pleasant even though we were quite isolated. There were no telephones, no television, and mail was intermittent. However, we had movies twice a week. In those days there was no community government. The only quasi-public body was the Indian Band, which was run by a chief and was for the Indians only. Frankly, the band at the time did not have much interest in the community, as it focused on hunting and trapping issues and the annual treaty payments.

As a result, the Whites, the Half-Breeds, the Others, the Almost Whites, and some Indians formed a Community Club. The club was open to all, and all were encouraged to participate. The club was non-political and was focused on providing entertainment for the community. It organized dances, carnivals, and similar events. The club also provided movies for the community.

A community hall was built by volunteers in the mid-1950s, and it became the venue for the movies and the dances. Movies were ordered well in advance and the supply would last six months or longer at a time. The movies for the winter would all come in on the last barge, and a schedule would be agreed to as to what movies would be shown when. Volunteers ran the projector and collected an entry fee to help pay for the rental of the movies. The system worked well and was a centre of community life, especially in the winter.

The building of the community hall and the operation of the Community Club gave the community a sense of existing in togetherness, based on volunteerism. Sadly, this changed with the emergence of race-based politics, with some sad results.

Earlier I mentioned how the original community hall was built by volunteers. This included Daddy's tractors and other equipment as well as his and Walter's labour. All of this was freely given for the benefit of all.

∞

A few years later, as the government began to creep into people's lives, the community decided that the hall needed to be enlarged. Everyone thought this would be a great idea, and besides that, the government was now running make-work programs. Harvesting logs, hauling them to town, and building the extension would certainly make work. The fly in the ointment was that the program was run by the Indian agent, and the work went to the Indians. The Whites, Half-Breeds, Others, and Almost Whites didn't mind as they, mostly, were employed or, like my family, had businesses. So, they continued volunteering to improve the community. The extension was completed and really improved the hall.

Then the Indian agent, who had replaced Kenn Stowell, whispered in the chief's ear, telling him that as Indian money had been used to build the hall, it should belong to the Indians. That's what happened over time, and it became known as the Band Hall, with no acknowledgment of all the volunteer work that the non-Indian population had contributed over the years. This was the beginning of the end of any sense of community in Fort Norman, at least until the introduction of a community council by the Government of the Northwest Territories.

∞

I was thirteen years old by this time and, as is normal for thirteen-year-old boys, my thoughts began turning to the other sex. The Dene people of Fort Norman were not prudish. They had a game that allowed male and female players to come into physical contact in a way that was fun without being overtly sexual. The game was called moose-skin ball. The ball was about two to three inches in diameter and was made of moss covered by tanned moose hide. The cover was sewn tightly because the game could become rough at times. I call it a game, but that might be a misnomer.

There was no discernable object to the game, such as scoring points by getting across a goal line. The players were divided into two teams. One team would be made up of all the girls and women who wanted to play, and the other would be all the boys and men who wanted to play. I don't recall how a game would start, but someone would put the ball in play by throwing it to a member of his or her own team.

The object of the game was to keep the ball away from members of the other team and vice versa. The object of the members of the other team was to get the ball and keep it. The game would start gently enough with members of one team trying to intercept the ball as it was passed around the members of the other team. Eventually, the action would ramp up, and

PART III

159

"gang tackling" would be introduced to the attempts by one team to get the ball from the other.

For example, if the men had the ball, and the holder of the ball did not toss it soon enough, he would be smothered by a half a dozen or more girls and women, and they would do their best to wrestle the ball away from him. Sometimes the hands of the girls and women would wander to areas of the man's body where the ball wasn't, even though there were other balls there.

Of course, a lot of shrieking and laughing happened throughout the game. Everyone had a great time. The young men showed their prowess by knocking the ball as far as they could. It looked like they were serving a small volleyball. Others would throw it overhand, as in throwing a baseball. Then the two teams would move in the direction that the ball was going.

Let's say that the girls and women managed to catch up to the ball first or had wrestled the ball away from a man, and one of them now had it. If she didn't quickly toss it to a teammate, she would be swarmed by the men and boys. Sometimes, in this situation, the woman would stuff the ball down the front of her blouse or shirt. Nothing was off limits. It was like an invite to feel the woman's chest, if you know what I mean. Men and women were also known to stuff the ball down the front of their pants! Sometimes the women would put it between their knees and squeeze as hard as they could. These tactics were usually used by the older women. As rough as it sounds, there was a certain gentleness to the game, as everyone was sure not to hurt anyone else.

There were no limits to the field, and the game would move throughout the community for hours at a time, usually in the evening. Players joined and left the game as they felt the need. The laughter associated with the game continued throughout.

I recall a couple of games when the priest descended from his church, high up on the second bench, overlooking the fun. He ranted at us about what horrible sinners we were. So, everyone left, but once the priest returned to his perch, the game would start up again. If the priest was Father Grias, he was probably just itching to get into the game.

With the benefit of hindsight, I can now see that there were objects to the game. One object was to teach the young ones not to be prudish or be embarrassed by their own sexuality. The other object would be to allow the older ones to feel their youth again. There were always lots of spectators, usually the elders of the community. Of course, everyone had fun. I don't know if the game is still played.

CHAPTER FIFTEEN

INTO THE ABYSS

I returned to school in Inuvik in September 1960. I was raped and sexually molested a number of times by Martin Houston between September 1960 and June 1962. Martin Houston was the new supervisor for the senior boys at Grollier Hall. He replaced Brother Moron in the fall of 1960 and was there waiting for us when we arrived to start the school year. I was thirteen years old and still very innocent, notwithstanding playing moose-skin ball quite often during the time that I was finishing grade seven in Fort Norman. He was in his early twenties and had a grade-eleven education. He was a big man. I would say at least six feet tall and around 220 pounds. He had broad shoulders and was slim at the hips. His domineering feature was an overly large head topped by bristly flaming red hair. His face was pock-marked, and he looked evil. I have an enduring picture of him in my mind—black slacks, a red shirt, and a pair of homemade moccasin slippers with beaded embroidery. I believe the slippers were made by Adeline Benoit, who was a local native and worked in the sewing room of the residence. I also believe she was an unwitting foil in Houston's game as he pretended, from time to time, that she was his girlfriend.

Houston and his assistant, Wayne Thomas, came from Pine Falls, Manitoba. His "application" to become our supervisor had been reviewed by the Father Provincial in Winnipeg and by Father Max Ruyant in Inuvik. I don't know if there was specified criteria and a job advertisement. I suspect not as it is more likely that the requirement was simply made known to the various Diocese's in western Canada. While doing research for this book I learned that Houston had been ". . . a Boys Supervisor at St. Philip's Indian Residential School on or about school terms 1956-58 inclusive." I assume that was disclosed in his application to come to Inuvik and had been looked into by the Father Provincial and by Max Ruyant.

With the benefit of hindsight, I can see that Houston hated women. He would become enraged whenever he thought that "his" boys were getting too close to the girls. On one rare occasion, we were invited to the girls' end of the residence for a social evening. We were dancing with some of them. The dances included slow waltzes. What thirteen- or fourteen-year-old boy would not want the opportunity to snuggle up to the girl of his dreams?

PART III

161

Houston suddenly exploded and ordered all of us back to our end of the residence. When we got there, he ordered us into the study hall, where he gave us a violent dressing down for getting too close to the girls. The dressing down included him throwing a table and some chairs at us. I was in the front row and was hit by the table. We were all shocked and scared. Other students recall that he used the strap on many of us at that time. I could see from the contortions on his face and the flashing of his eyes that he was a crazy person.

He was able to watch us almost all the time. His room was elevated above our dormitory and had a large window through which he could watch us walking to and from school. If he saw us mingling with the girls, we would then be in for another violent dressing down. There was another larger window, overlooking the dormitory, through which he could watch us at night.

During the 1960/1961 school year, we were allowed town leave for a few hours on Saturdays. Although he tried, he could not watch all of us while we were on town leave. He fixed that for the next school year by having Father Ruyant abolish town leave. I don't recall what flimsy reason Father Ruyant used, but with the benefit of hindsight, it is now clear that the action was just more evidence of the two of them acting in concert. We spent a whole year in the residence without being able to go to town and being terrified about getting close to the girls in our residence or at school.

Houston and Max Ruyant also tried to control which people were allowed to see us. One example was Richard Slobodin. He was an anthropologist from McMaster University in Hamilton and had been hired by the federal government to study the Métis of the Northwest Territories. One of his topics was "education," which included "the post-war federal school programme." His work brought him to Inuvik, where he lived for a while. He used to come to the residence to visit us and would play basketball with the boys in our gym. He was an avid supporter of the NDP, and this led to many lively discussions. Many of the boys, like Mike, were also supporters of the NDP. I wasn't and would argue for the Conservatives. When Houston and Ruyant found out about these harmless discussions, Slobodin was banned from coming to the residence. Again, with the benefit of hindsight, I think the banning was more related to the possibility that one of us might start spilling the beans about Houston's conduct to an adult who would know what to do about it.

Slobodin completed his work, and the report was published in 1966 under the title *Métis of the Mackenzie District*. While doing research for this book, I found out more about Slobodin. He was an American who was born and educated in New York City. He fought in WWII. After the war he began his academic career with appointments to two universities in California. Then he was "blacklisted" by McCarthy. He eventually cleared his name, but the cloud hung over him, so he moved to Canada and became a citizen here in 1970. He died in 2005. David Damas (deceased), from the Department of Anthropology at McMaster University, wrote his obituary and said: "He perceived socialism as a means to achieve social justice." Those were the days when the Catholic priests would thunder at us from the pulpit about the evils of communism. I clearly recall Father Adam almost foaming at the mouth while doing so. We had to pray to the Virgin Mary to bring about the end of communism.

I don't recall the incident, but other students have told me about the time when Houston went to the school and went on a rampage about "his" boys interacting with the town girls. Wayne Thomas must have suspected that something bad was happening. He managed to get himself a job in town and left the residence. If Wayne were inclined to report what he was aware of, he was likely discouraged by the lack of action resulting from others, such as Sister Hebert, raising the alarm. Wayne was replaced by a little weasel called Gerry Jobin, who was also, I believe, from Pine Falls, Manitoba.

Again, with the benefit of hindsight, I can see how we were terrorized so as not to do anything about the much more heinous crimes that Houston was committing against some of us. Houston especially hated those of us who came from Fort Norman and Norman Wells. Generally, we would fight back, and the older boys in this group did complain to Max Ruyant about what Houston was doing to us. Houston would, derisively, call us the "Fort Norman gangsters." There were times when it was not just some of us who were subjected to his sickness. The whole dormitory of about fifty to sixty boys between twelve and eighteen years would sometimes be included in his sick punishments.

From time to time, he would wake all of us up in the early hours of the morning. He would make sure that we were all stripped naked, and then he would herd all of us into the gymnasium and make us run laps. While we were running laps bare naked with our penises and balls flopping around, he would screech at us to run faster. He would also use a towel to snap at those he thought were not going fast enough. Some boys have recently reminded me that he also took pictures of us at these, I don't know what to call them, torture sessions?

When he finally got his jollies, or whatever it was that he wanted, we were allowed to go back to bed.

When the older boys complained to Father Max Ruyant about these sick punishments, he simply ignored the complaints. As a result, many of the older boys quit school and returned home.

PART III

163

I often wonder if these boys would have completed school and, maybe, had a better life but for Max Ruyant. Ruyant hired Houston and ignored his crimes. Most of those boys had tough lives, and at least one committed suicide.

Additionally, Ruyant was Houston's confessor. I am sure that the sick bastard confessed everything he did to us to Ruyant. Still, Ruyant did nothing and later denied any knowledge of what Houston did to us. I know that Houston's confessions were subject to his Catholic confessional privacy rights. However, Ruyant could have easily fired him without having to disclose what was said in the confessional. The complaints that were made by the older boys were not in the confessional and could have at least been investigated.

As I go on with my story, it will become clear that what happened to us was not the act of a single person. What happened to us was an act of the Roman Catholic Church. Houston was simply the tool. Why?

Houston would kick us out of bed in the morning to go to early mass, and we had to watch him piously kneeling at the altar to receive communion, knowing he had raped one of us the night before. We had to endure the same mental torture on Sundays when we were marched over to the Igloo Church to attend high mass with the townsfolk who made up the parish. Again, Houston would piously take his communion in front of hundreds of witnesses.

I know that Sister Hebert also complained to Ruyant about what was going on. Her room was immediately above Houston's, and she could hear what was going on in his room. Again, Ruyant ignored what he was told by a most reliable person. Why?

By this time, it was clear that a reign of terror over us was being enforced by Houston with the complicity of Ruyant. Our dormitory was a large, open room split into three areas separated by pony walls. When Houston came during the night, we would all bury ourselves as deep in our blankets as we could. That didn't stop him if he wanted one of us that night. Once a boy was picked and taken to Houston's room, the other boys could relax, at least for that night.

I was picked a number of times. It was about thirty years until I started losing the rotten smell of his body, which was ground into my senses. That rotten smell came from the many times that he lay on my back and breathed over my shoulder as he molested me. It was not only the smell of his body odour that lingered with me for all those years; it was also his foul breath. In addition to the foul odours, I vividly recalled his grunting sounds. For many decades I suffered from panic attacks triggered by being in the presence of larger people whom I felt

Robert Clement. Credit: Author.

Mike Gladu. Credit: Author.

threatened by. This still happens, albeit not as frequently. Why were we not offered counselling after Houston was caught?

There were many others picked, including two of my best friends from home, Mike Gladu and Robert Clement. One time Mike and I were taken together to do things to entertain him. My statement to the RCMP about that incident was as follows: ". . . but once he took MICHAEL GLADUE and I both into his room together and tied our pricks together with a string and made us pull."

Whatever happened to Mike and me, it would never be as bad as the abuse Robert received. Robert, unfortunately, died a number of years ago. I am sure his death was triggered by the constant stress that he lived with as a result of the horrors of Grollier Hall. Nowadays, it is called PTSD. He died of a massive heart attack when he was just thirty-eight years old. If only we had received proper help after the preliminary hearing.

∞

We did have some survival tactics. Some of us were fortunate enough to have battery-operated transistor radios, which were new at the time. They were small enough that we could hide them in our bed or in our locker. We were able to listen to the late-night request shows from CHAK, the local radio station, if we didn't play it too loudly.

The tears were streaming down my face as I added this to the manuscript. My late friend Ernest Firth hosted many of these late-night request shows. I will always remember his voice reading the dedications and the titles of the tunes and names of the artists: the Drifters and "Save the Last Dance for Me," Hank Locklin and "Send Me the Pillow you Dream On," Ray Price and "City Lights," and, of course, Jim Reeves and "He'll Have to Go." The sign-off tune for the show always stuck in my mind, but, for the life of me, I could not remember the name of the artist or the tune. Finally, I remembered: "Last Date" by Floyd Cramer. I found it on the Internet and started to listen to it on YouTube. As soon as the first chord was played, my emotional dam burst. Not only did I remember the happy emotional thoughts that I enjoyed while I surreptitiously listened to the late-night request shows, I also remembered my friends who were being sexually abused by Houston in his room while I listened to the poignant music.

∞

As I grew older, I spent a lot of time in therapy trying to deal with the effects of what happened to me in Grollier Hall. I learned that, in many cases, victims of such abuse become frozen emotionally at the age when the abuse took place. For me that would be from thirteen to fifteen years old. This helps explain why I still treasure the photograph that I have of Joanne. It has the fold lines where I reduced it so that it could fit into a picture sleeve in my wallet. It has an inscription, on the back, in her handwriting, that says, "To my 'honey' from Joanne." I have not seen or been in touch with Joanne for almost sixty years, but there she is, forever fourteen years old.

I see "Joanne" as another survival tactic. Someone who I really cared about cared for me, and it was my secret. The picture, which I kept hidden, was one link to a world that was not filled with insanity. Joanne was a "town" girl, and we only saw each other in the school. She was in grades seven to ten in the Catholic wing with Mike, Robert and me. We used to pass love notes in school, and she gave me the picture while we were at school. I do not remember her in grade ten, most likely because of the aftermath of the Houston criminal proceedings. It may also be that because, at fifteen and sixteen years old, girls usually move on to older, more mature boys.

∞

After two years, Houston became overconfident or, perhaps, simply more mentally deranged. I was reminded recently by Mike of the time Houston took all the boys to a local swimming hole in Inuvik that summer and took movies of us, naked. The testimony given by the five of us during Houston's preliminary hearing in September 1962 confirmed that he was spinning out of control before the end of the school year. He took Robert south with him for the summer holiday that year to his home in Manitoba and elsewhere in Canada. While they were staying in a hotel in Ottawa, Houston wrote on a men's bathroom wall words to the effect that if you wanted a good time, you should come to room such and such.

Joanne. Credit: Author.

Fortunately for us, a conscientious desk clerk saw the words in the bathroom and called the Ottawa Police. When the police arrived, they found Houston and Robert in the room and took them into custody. After Robert gave a statement to the police, they released him. Houston was held for possessing pornography. I speculate that the pornography, which was seized by the Ottawa Police, likely included the photos and home movies that he had taken of us. The Ottawa Police then contacted the RCMP in Inuvik to alert them to the potential crimes that had been committed by Houston in Grollier Hall. Sergeant Hugh Feagan of the RCMP began the investigation. Feagan travelled to Fort Norman and interviewed me on August

21, 1962. I was fifteen years old. He also interviewed Mike then, as well.

Mike and I had summer jobs working at Daddy's sawmill when Feagan came to interview us. Our job was to bag all the sawdust produced from the cutting of the logs for shipment to Imperial Oil in Norman Wells.

I recall, what I thought was the local RCMP corporal coming to our workplace and telling Daddy that I had to be interviewed. Daddy came with me and sat through the interview. I recall very little of the interview except when it was finished. I remember Daddy sitting on the top step of the long stairs that led up to the RCMP barracks from the lower bench of the community. I don't remember him saying anything, but I did know that he was extremely angry and upset.

From that time on, my life was a blur, including the preliminary hearing that took place in Inuvik. My brother, Rod, told me, later, that our other brother, Walter, had a plan to travel to Norman Wells on the day they would transport Houston south to go to jail. Walter was going to shoot Houston with his rifle.

Because everything was a blur, neither Mike, Robert, nor I remembered very much after the court proceedings, and we never talked about it. However, I do remember Max Ruyant marching the five of us, who were witnesses at the preliminary hearing, including Mike, Robert and me, to the courthouse from the residence and back. He was extremely cold to us. Neither he nor anyone from the residence or the Church offered us any support. There was talk about what happened to us as being our fault. I also remember the parish priest, Father Joseph Adam, telling us to pray for Houston.

Only five of us were chosen to be witnesses despite many more boys being victims of Houston. I don't know exactly how many boys Sergeant Feagan interviewed, but I would estimate that between twenty and thirty boys were victimized by Houston. I understand that the five of us were chosen because of the extent of the abuse that we suffered and the possibility that we would be more articulate than the other boys, on the witness stand.

The preliminary hearing was held in Inuvik on September 13, 1962. At the end of the hearing, the finding was announced:

> . . . *the Crown has established a case, which should come before a higher court of competent jurisdiction. Therefore, I commit you for trial at the next hearing of the Territorial Court.*

Houston, as was his right, then elected to be tried by a judge without a jury. The final words spoken at the preliminary hearing were by the Justice of the Peace, Barney MacNeil:

PART III

And I also wish you to be remanded into custody without bail.

I didn't think about it at the time, but Barney MacNeil was not only a leader of the community. He was also a stalwart of the Catholic Church. He would have witnessed Houston piously taking communion on Sundays over a period of two years. I wonder what he thought after hearing our testimony and if he ever raised the matter with the parish council.

A trial was held without any further involvement from us. Houston pleaded guilty in front of Judge Sissions in Yellowknife, where Houston was being held in jail. This was the same Judge Sissions who had escorted me home from the hospital in Aklavik three and half years earlier. I wonder if he remembered me. The Crown then applied to have Houston declared a dangerous sexual offender. The Crown was successful, and Houston was sentenced. There is confusion over whether he was given an indeterminate sentence or if it was for ten years. Notwithstanding the confusion, he was eventually released, after serving nine years. Strangely, to the best of my knowledge, none of the victims or our parents were advised of his application for release.

∞

Beyond that, the sleeping dog was let to lie while it tortured all of us who had been called as witnesses, as well as the other boys who had been molested by Houston and a number of other male supervisors in Grollier Hall over the years. All of these cases exploded in the 1990s. Alcoholism and drug abuse, as well as suicides, were becoming obvious among the group that became known as the "Survivors." Some of these Survivors had found sobriety and began to ask questions and organize the other boys. There were two primary leaders in the movement, Harold Cook and Lawrence Norbert.

These two brave men began to go public with allegations of abuse. Of course, the Church fought back and denied the charges. This was not surprising. What was surprising was the number of prominent individuals who publicly defended the Church and the perpetrators. Included among the defenders were many Dene elders who were Roman Catholics. In addition, there were many prominent individuals from Inuvik who were familiar with the history but who were in denial of the facts. Sadly, this included our family friend, Cece MacCauley.

With some vicious allegations, the deniers attacked the individuals who were taking the stories public. The deniers claimed that the Survivors were just making the stories up to get money. Survivors were accused of being "town drunks".

Some of the Dene elders attacked, saying that the priests spoke for God and should be believed when they said that nothing happened. This was the same rationale that the chiefs used in 1921 when Bishop Breynant helped hoodwink them during the making of Treaty 11. The chiefs called him "the man who spoke for God."

This would not have surprised me if I had known what the "bishop who cared," Paul Piche, had to say about this before he died on September 11, 1992. The deniers, no doubt, took his words to heart.

While this was going on in the Northwest Territories, there were also allegations from across Canada about the abuses committed in school residences and residential schools. Finally, because of growing pressure from the public, the Government of Canada decided to offer an apology for the abuses suffered across the country. I reached a turning point while listening to then-Minister Jane Stewart deliver the apology in early January 1998.

I had been slowly getting angrier about what the deniers were doing to the Survivors. The "apology" pushed me to the point of doing something about the deniers and the apology itself. At the time I was a prominent lawyer in Yellowknife and had considerable prestige in the community and throughout the Northwest Territories. Few people knew about what had happened to me and my friends at Grollier Hall. I decided to go public to support the Survivors who were trying to tell their stories. I did this by writing a letter to the editor. My point was that, "Yes, it happened. If you want to call me a liar, go ahead." My second reason for going public was to point my finger straight at the Roman Catholic Church. It seemed to me that with the apology, the government was setting the stage to let the Church off the hook.

My letter was addressed to the Roman Catholic Church and was published on pages three and five in the January 12, 1998, edition of the *News/North*.

The letter was read by many people in the Northwest Territories, and I received many calls, emails, faxes, and letters of support for my action. No one called me a liar. My friend and former law partner, the late Don Cooper, QC, simply said, "Now I understand."

PART III

NEWS/NORTH, MONDAY, January 12, 1998 **A3**

The residential schools experience
Readers speak out

An open letter to the Roman Catholic Church

Editor:

On Tuesday, Jan. 7, 1998, I, as most other Canadians, was inundated with media coverage of the so-called "apology" from the Government of Canada.

I sit here with tears in my eyes as I am forced to relive the horror of my experience of being in your care for four years, between 1959 and 1963. I have tears for all my friends who suffered the same terror that I did.

Especially those who have already died and have taken their shame and anger to the grave. I have tears at the thought that you (whoever and whatever you might be) might think that the government of Canada has somehow got you off the hook. NO WAY! You will admit the wrongs that you allowed to be committed on our young, precious bodies, minds and souls. You will unequivocally apologize and you will ask our forgiveness.

My parents and the government of Canada, believing that you were a kind, caring and loving institution, turned me over to you in September 1959, at the age of 12. I, along with my friends, were shipped to Inuvik like cattle in a single-engine Otter aircraft. There must have been at least 20 of us, along with our belongings, jammed into that airplane that was designed for 10 passengers, trying to breathe air that was rancid from the puke of all of us children who were flying for the first time.

When we arrived in Inuvik, we were immediately subjected to the start of your dehumanizing process when we were herded into showers, then our heads were shaved and we were forced into the standard uniform of those horrible blue coveralls even though we had our own decent clothing. You refused to let us be individuals.

But, I was an individual and refused to bend to you willingly. This resulted in four months of hell during which I was severely punished for such major crimes as writing to my parents to complain of my treatment. Do you remember how your priests, brothers and nuns used to read all of our incoming and outgoing mail? Do you remember how your priests, brothers and nuns used to beat us at the slightest provocation? Do you remember, brother Morin? Do you remember, sister Gallant?

Well, I got lucky that first year. One of my letters got through to my parents and they brought me home at Christmas and I finished the school year by correspondence. Unfortunately, I had to come back to your hell hole the next year. It must have been some year because I don't remember a damn thing about it. You see, there is a lot I blocked out. But I could not block out the next two years entirely because you brought Martin Houston to Grollier Hall to destroy us. You remember him, he's the one who was expelled from one of your seminaries for attempting to molest the other seminarians. You knew this and yet you brought him to Inuvik to take charge of us.

You knew that he was into things such as getting the entire senior boys' dorm out of bed around midnight and have us run around the gymnasium bare-ass naked for hours for his enjoyment. You knew and you did nothing. You knew that he was sexually assaulting us in his room beside the dorm. You knew and you did nothing. You knew he was physically assaulting those who

Please see **Troubled, A5**

Silence no more

This poem is dedicated to the former Inuit students of residential schools and also to their spouses, parents and children who have suffered with them in silence throughout the years.

Breathing, listening, looking and feeling,
the changing world around me.
Hungry thoughts dance in my head,
craving to share my hopes and dreams.

Once I used to talk with laughter,
freely around the shimmering qulliq.
Huddled inside the comforts of our igloo,
Eyes smiling sleepily inside my soft, fur blanket.
Feelings of contentment in the warm air,
as the Northern Lights dance around the moon-lit night.

Then out of the blue a loud metal bird,
swallowed us into its cold hard belly.
Leaving behind only the smoke that burned the eyes of our parents,
who cried in silence as they stand wordless by the shores.

This way! That way! No, not that way!
Wrong! Wrong! Wrong!
And hallowed be thy name,
as though squeezing out my identity.

Quivering and shivering tiny bodies lie there;
Not knowing which way to turn.
Shame and broken hearts screaming,
only in silence, never to be heard.
Innocence lost to the four corners of the cold, grey halls.

How long must we torture ourselves,
we are not at fault.
We did nothing wrong,
we have been silenced too long,
by the filthy hands of the so-called blessed and once trusted.
And they know who they are.

Today I refuse to be silent,
for the sake of my loved ones,
Because they too,
have suffered in silence.

— Leocadia Emingak

Third page of the *News/North* showing part of the letter. Credit: Northern News Services Ltd.

Fifth page of the *News/North* showing the second part of the letter.
Credit: Northern News Services Ltd.

At about the same time, the Survivors were moving ahead with their plans and incorporated a society called the "Grollier Hall Residential School Healing Circle." The society negotiated an agreement with Canada, the Northwest Territories, and the Roman Catholic Church to enter into a validation and redress process on behalf of twenty-nine named Survivors. Amongst the Survivors were family members who were representing those that had already died.

I was one of the twenty-nine named Survivors. The other four witnesses who testified at Houston's preliminary hearing were also named. Because one of us, Robert, had already died he was represented by his family members. The validation and redress process was limited to Survivors who had been victims of male supervisors that had been convicted of the crimes which were committed between 1959 and 1979. As far as I know, three other male supervisors, in addition to Houston, were caught and convicted. Despite the fact that Houston was caught and convicted in 1962, Ruyant continued hiring the same kind of perverts and pedophiles. How did he get away with it? Why did he do it? What did people like Barney McNeil do, if anything?

PART III

171

Those of us that had been witnesses at Houston's preliminary hearing needed documentation because of the "memory bank wipe" that most of us had suffered. Collectively, we recalled very little about the abuse we had suffered and the legal process that had taken place approximately thirty-six years earlier.

The validation and redress agreement committed all of the parties to "produce all documents in their possession" relating to the claims.

If I remember correctly, the lawyers for the Circle asked for the records of Houston's legal proceedings to help us with our memory difficulties and were either told that they couldn't be found or were met with obfuscation.

∞

While writing this book, I became aware of a blog called *Sylvia's Site*. The site has a heading: "Martin Houston – The Devil of Grollier Hall," which provides quite a few of the facts of Houston's sordid life and the "celebration" of his life by the Catholic Church. The site also includes the names of the other male supervisors from Grollier Hall who have been convicted.

CHAPTER SIXTEEN

SERENDIPITY

"Serendipity" is defined by the Cambridge English Dictionary as "the fact of finding interesting or valuable things by chance." That is exactly what happened to me after my letter of January 1998 was published. I do not recall the exact date of the serendipitous event, but I believe it would have been in the spring of either 1999 or 2000.

At the time, I was a partner in the law firm of Davis & Company LLP. Davis was one of the largest law firms, if not the largest, in western Canada and was embarking on an ambitious plan to grow into a national firm. At the time, the firm had its head office in Vancouver with offices in Whitehorse, Yellowknife, Edmonton, Calgary, Toronto, and Montreal. We also had an international office in Tokyo, Japan. I joined the firm in the early 1990s and became the resident partner in Yellowknife.

One of the partners who helped recruit me to Davis & Company was the late David H. Searle, CM, QC. David was very well known in northern Canada as he had been raised in Yellowknife and had spent the first twenty or so years of his career there as the head of what was then the largest law firm in the Northwest Territories. We knew each other from his time in Yellowknife, during which David had rescued me from a potentially embarrassing situation caused by another lawyer. While we had differences of opinion about the future of the Northwest Territories, we were friends. After I joined Davis & Company, we became closer as David mentored me in the new experience of being a partner in a very large firm with many partners and many offices. I grew to respect him very highly. Unfortunately, David passed away before I was able to complete this book.

The partners of Davis & Company would have two in-person meetings a year. One would be held in Vancouver and the other in a resort, where we could get a reasonably priced package in the off-season.

The meeting, in the year of serendipity, was held in Scottsdale, Arizona. The business of the meeting usually took about a day and half to complete, and the afternoon of the second day would be open for social activities. Most of the younger lawyers and their spouses would go hiking, golfing, or other activities of that type. At the time neither David nor I were much into exercise, nor were either of us married. David's first wife, Dorelle (Dodi for short) had recently died, and Bea and I were divorced. So, we met at his cabin at the resort and had coffee on the front porch and told stories.

∞

My brother, Rod, was meeting me in Scottsdale the next day, after the partners' meeting, and we were going to do a week-long driving holiday to California and back. We made the trip and had a great time. I am sure that Rod would have loved to have sat with us, as Rod loved to tell stories too, in a colourful fashion.

∞

So, David and I were sitting on the front porch of his cabin. David was not only a very good lawyer; he was also quite a raconteur and loved to tell stories about his many experiences practicing law. These stories included ones about his early career when he worked under contract as a Crown prosecutor in the Northwest Territories. He told me a few stories and then started another one with, "I can't remember the bastard's name, but I clearly remember prosecuting this supervisor from a hostel in Inuvik." I almost fell off my chair.

"His name was Martin Houston," I said, "and I was one of the witnesses." Then David almost fell off his chair.

Of course, David did not remember me from that time, as I was only fifteen years old. I was one of five boys of the same age group that David had examined during Houston's preliminary hearing in Inuvik. On the other hand, I did not remember David from the preliminary hearing because of the memory bank wipe. David told me details of the hearing and his impression of some of the witnesses. He said it was unfortunate that the five students, including me, were so young. Consequently, we were not able to completely tell our stories. I was not able to tell the whole story of what Houston did to me because he was sitting right there in the courtroom glaring at me. I was, at once, embarrassed to say the things that he did to me in front of all the strangers in the courtroom, and I was also extremely afraid of Houston. I will never forget him sitting there in the prisoners' box.

David H. Searle, CM, QC. Photo taken in 1965, three years after he conducted the examinations of the young witnesses and communicated directly with Paul Piche. Credit: Celia Stock.

At the end of the last chapter, I mentioned the difficulty of getting the documents from these legal proceedings. I spoke to David about this, and he was flabbergasted at the suggestion that the records could not be found. Based upon David's advice, we were able to have the lawyers for the Circle ask the right questions to get the documents. As individuals, we were not given everything from the records, but we did get enough to counter the memory bank wipe.

One of the documents that concerned me only was the statement that I gave to Sergeant Feagan on August 21, 1962. That statement is attached as Appendix A to this book. I would like to thank my friend, Mike Gladu, for agreeing to leave his name unredacted in the statement, as well as in the examination of me by David, which is attached as Appendix D.

The next two documents are what I consider to be "cover your ass" activities by the federal employees who should have been on top of this from day one. I attach these documents as appendices B and C. The first is the August 31, 1962, letter from the administrator of the Mackenzie to a Mr. Gillies but marked to the attention of a Mr. Needham. The letter references three other documents that I, unfortunately, do not have copies of. The three letters are: ". . . a memorandum dated August 27 from Mr. Sivertz to the Administrator of the Mackenzie, a letter dated August 24 from Mr. Sivertz to Bishop Paul Piche and a memorandum dated August 29 from the Administrator of the Mackenzie to the Director." I would dearly love to see the letter that was sent to Bishop Paul Piche on August 24, 1962, about Martin Houston by Mr. Sivertz. I assume that this Mr. Sivertz was the person who either was or was soon to be appointed as the commissioner of the Northwest Territories.

The letter also instructs the lesser officials to meet with Max Ruyant and Reverend Holman, of the Anglican residence, to "inform them of the details of the Houston case as they are known to you."

The document, marked as Appendix C, is "Minutes of Meeting of Hostel Superintendents to pass on Confidential Information concerning Martin Houston," which took place on September 10, 1962. The minutes were prepared by Bill Bock, the school principal. Ruyant's responses to questions are laughable at best. Based on these two documents, it is clear that everyone in positions of authority knew what had happened to us, but not one of them came forward to comfort or counsel us. Why didn't Bishop Paul Piche come to Inuvik to speak to us and tell us that none of what happened to us was our fault?

The fourth document is the transcript of the examination of me at the preliminary hearing, which is attached as Appendix D. The witnesses included the five of us, Max Ruyant, and Sister R. A. Hebert. I have copies of all of the examinations but am only publishing mine to protect the privacy of the other Survivors. However, I do not feel any need to refrain from quoting from both Max Ruyant's and Sister Hebert's testimony. One of Max Ruyant's answers, which I found interesting, was his response to Mr. Searle asking him:

PART III

Did you ever have any complaints, Father, from the boys, about Mr. Houston?

Max Ruyant's answer:

Yes, not often but we had a few boys who ran away from the hostel, and sometimes in the evening we had to search the town, and bring them back. I would ask why they ran away, and they would say their main complaint was that he was using the strap on the boys.

What I found interesting had nothing to do with the strap, which, frankly, I don't recall the use of by Houston, notwithstanding what I said in the examination. My failure to recall the use of the strap is likely part of what I have been calling the memory bank wipe. Other students have said that Houston did use the strap, especially on the night of the debacle that was supposed to be a social evening at the girls' end of the residence. Ruyant's assertion that he questioned the students when he found them jumped from the page when I read it.

I was one of the students who ran away. I ended up in what was called Tent Town or Happy Valley. I had no place to go, and it was cold because it was wintertime. I was very fortunate, and I will be forever thankful to Joe and Mabel Thrasher for taking me in and giving me food and a place to sleep. They didn't know me well but knew that I was from the residence because they would visit their relatives there from time to time. They saw me, likely in distress, and took me in without asking any questions. I stayed with them in their tent frame for two nights. On the third day, I was wandering around and had just left Tent Town and was on the main road connecting it to the rest of Inuvik. I heard a vehicle horn honking just behind me. I turned around and saw that it was Ruyant driving the residence's panel truck.

I felt some fear at first. He motioned to me to get into the panel truck. I thought I could run, and he couldn't catch me, but where would I go? I did not want to go back to Joe and Mabel, as they had already done enough, and I did not want to get them in trouble. Then I thought, *Well, okay, I've been gone three days, so I'll probably get expelled and sent home. That would be better than continuing to live in the hellhole.* So, I got into the panel truck.

The ride to the residence was surreal. He never said a word. We arrived at the residence, and he parked the panel truck and pointed to the door to the boys' side of the residence. I went in by myself. I don't remember anything more about the incident. As far as I know, my running away was never reported to any authorities and certainly not to my parents. Ruyant never questioned me about why I had run. It was almost as if it didn't happen. Why?

Years later, when I was in therapy, I learned that victims are not people to their abusers. To the abusers, victims are simply objects. It seems to me that I was nothing more than an object to Ruyant.

Had Ruyant cared about me at all as a human being, he would have offered some comfort and would have asked why I had run. The man was as cold as they came, and he certainly knew nothing about empathy. To think that the town of Inuvik still has a street named after him makes me sick. The other answers that Ruyant gave to Mr. Searle's questions make it clear that he was, at a minimum, willfully blind to Houston's crimes. This becomes even clearer from the questioning of Sister Hebert.

∞

I must say one thing about Sister Hebert. She was not loved or even liked by many of the boys she "raised" during her time with the residence and previously, in the residential school, in Aklavik. I have heard many people disparage her. Personally, I did not mind her even if she was an old-school nun and a disciplinarian. I will always appreciate how she fought for Houston's victims. She complained to Ruyant many times about what was going on in Houston's room but was completely ignored. Her story is set out in her answers to Mr. Searle's questions. Unfortunately, Sister Hebert's first language was French, so the examination of her was difficult. She did testify that she heard boys in Houston's room:

> *I heard the boys talking, and laughing downstairs too late after the time they are supposed to be in bed. I told him* [Houston] *many times. He said he wanted to keep them for a good reason, to know them better, and help them. I told him that it was no good, and once he was in his tub and one boy was there. I was thinking he was giving a bath to one kid . . . and I told Father, and always when Father questioned the children, the children don't talk. Then he don't take my part, and he say he have to take Mr. Houston's part. I said I will question the children in front of you I said 'XXXXX why take your bath in Mr. Houston's tub'. He said 'I am not taking a bath, I am washing Mr. Houston'. That is true; XXXXX told me that.*

Mr. Searle then asked her how many times a week she noticed boys in Houston's room late. She answered: "I mean every night."

Ruyant was also asked: "You are aware of the charges that have been laid against Mr. Houston, are you Father?" His answer:

PART III

177

"Yes, I am." The next question: "Did you have any suspicion that this could have been going on?" His answer: "Never."

Why was Sister Hebert ignored? Why were the boys who complained ignored? Why wasn't I questioned after I ran? Why did Ruyant turn a blind eye to the clear evidence that Houston was sexually abusing us? Why did he perjure himself at the inquiry? Why was the Church's reaction to Houston being sent to jail to tell us to pray for him? Why did the Church do its best to bury the whole story? Why did the Church do nothing to help the Survivors until they were forced to do so? I believe, beyond a shadow of a doubt, that there is much more to the story than the actions of one sick, depraved individual, Martin Houston. Why was Houston admitted to a seminary when he was finally released from prison for his crimes against the five of us and many others? Why was Houston ordained in 1990 and sent out to Native communities? Yes, he became a priest in the Oblate order of the Catholic Church!

With the benefit of almost sixty years of hindsight, I appreciate the difficulty that David Searle faced when questioning me and the other victims. We were all in the same age range. I was fifteen years old. As much as anything, I was horribly embarrassed, and I was not going to admit to anything more than I had to. When you add the devil, himself, sitting in the prisoner's box, to the atmosphere, it was amazing that we were able to get at least part of our truth out.

∞

When I was dealing with my claim for compensation for the abuse that I suffered at Grollier Hall, I asked for a face-to-face meeting with Bishop Croteau, who had succeeded Bishop Piche. The meeting took place at Trapper's Lake, which is where the bishop's residence is just outside of Yellowknife. Croteau expressed shock and a complete lack of knowledge of any abuse that might have happened at Grollier Hall. I did not and do not believe him. He was the parish priest in Inuvik for a decade or so. People talk. What about the letter sent to Bishop Piche on August 24, 1962? What about all the knowledge that Ruyant had? Surely, he reported to Bishop Piche. Surely, Bishop Piche kept a record. The Roman Catholic Church has a corporate memory like few other institutions in the world.

I asked Croteau to question other priests who were "ministering" to the communities at the time of the crimes to see what they remembered. The answer that I eventually got back was that no one knew anything. I found this strange, as these priests would gather from time to time in Inuvik, and they would stay at the residence. Some would even come and play volleyball with us in our gym. Didn't Ruyant share, at a minimum, the results of the criminal proceedings with them? These priests were ministering to our parents. Other priests who worked at Grollier Hall included Father Franche, Father Colas, and Father Beaulac.

As this book was nearing completion, I came across another piece of information that does not put Croteau in a very good light. The information was in an article written by Ed Struzik in the *Edmonton Journal* on May 11, 2002. The article was primarily about the settlements that were being reached pursuant to the validation and redress process. Struzik had interviewed me, Croteau, and others, and Croteau stated that he first learned about Houston becoming a priest from my open letter, which was published on January 12, 1998. Croteau "said he was shocked by the letter and called Hardy for a heart-to-heart talk." The only time that I remember talking to Croteau was on my own initiative when I asked for a meeting with him, as outlined previously. I do not recall any "heart-to-heart" talk with him.

Croteau also told Struzik that "Houston was only 19 years old at the time." I don't know what point Croteau was trying to make, but Houston was twenty-five years old when he was caught and he had only been at Grollier Hall for two years. Struzik may have been querying Croteau about Houston's time, as a boy's supervisor, at the residential school in Kamsack, Saskatchewan but it is not clear from the article.

∞

I can come to no other conclusion, based on my experience and what I have come to know, other than the Roman Catholic Church is a corrupt institution that preys on children as a matter of policy. I think there is a code of silence imposed on the priests, which is enforced by their vows of obedience. I believe that Bishop Paul Piche knew all along what was happening. Bishop Piche did nothing to help us. Yet, ironically, his biography is titled *The Bishop Who Cared – A Legacy of Leadership.* Cared about what? The biography was written mostly by Sister Agnes Sutherland, with the help of "the Bishop Piche Memoirs Committee." The book is particularly cruel because it missed the opportunity to deal with what happened in Grollier Hall under Paul Piche's watch. The book has "Bishop Piche's Last Message," which was written by him eighteen days before he died. The book also has an extensive chapter on "The R.C. Church and Education in the Mackenzie Diocese." Again, not a word about Grollier Hall.

However, the book does speak generally about "residential schools" in a defensive mode. I am really incensed by a quote from Paul Piche:

I always tried to listen to those who had complaints and when there was any serious problem I always looked into it and tried to make life better for the youngsters. I am also very concerned that some missionaries could be falsely blamed. Accusations can be exaggerated. It is so surprising to hear only those who have complaints come forward in the media and get all the attention. I believe that some of them are doing that to try to earn some easy money. I can't believe our former students who got so much from the missionaries would do such injustice.

The book reports that, while speaking about Grandin College, Piche ". . . never ceased to voice his great disappointment that not a single church vocation came forth in twenty-six years."

I found another aspect of the book to be disconcerting. One of the forewords is written by Stephen Kakfwi, "former student of Grandin College" and a former premier of the Northwest Territories. I was surprised and disappointed that Stephen would have participated in a whitewash of the life of a man who could have made a real difference in the lives of so many students but didn't.

∞

Part of the settlement that we reached with Canada, the Northwest Territories, and the Church during the validation and redress process was a requirement for each of them to provide a written apology to each Survivor and their family members, if asked for. I still have the originals of the apologies from Canada and the Church to me. I have not paid much attention to the involvement of Canada as I did not feel that I had much of a dispute with them. My dispute and my anger have been and continue to be aimed directly at the Catholic Church. The Catholic Church was the institution that was on the ground with us, and it was the one that my parents trusted to take proper care of me. Not only did the Church abysmally fail to take care of me, they also engaged in a vast cover-up of what happened to me and so many others.

The apology to me from the "Roman Catholic Diocese of Mackenzie" is dated June 21, 2002. It was supposed to be signed by Bishop Denis Croteau, OMI. It was not signed by him. It was signed "per" by some scribbled name. I think the scribbled name was that of Father Pochat, who represented the Church in the validation process. That final act of petulance by Bishop Croteau, like the final acts of the "bishop who cared," certainly lessened, significantly, the words of the apology. Where was the "bishop who cared" when we so desperately needed him in 1962? We were his lambs, severely injured and lost in the wilderness. He did not come to look for us. Had he acted in a Christian way then, he might have seen the vocations that he was so bitter about not having.

Interestingly, many years later, Croteau contacted me about a piece that I had written which was published in the October 4, 2021, edition of the *News/North*. I was writing about the calls for an apology from the pope and referred to the "non-apology" by Croteau nineteen years earlier. Croteau tried to explain the circumstances surrounding the lack of his signature. Surprisingly, he also asked me for a copy of the letter that I had complained about. I thought about his request for a while and looked through the documents that I have copies of. Amongst those documents is a copy of the agreement that the twenty-nine Survivors had entered into with the two governments and the church.

The agreement included a section on what would be in the redress package. Two items caught my attention: "acknowledgement of the wrong done" and "apologies to claimants, and where desired, to their families and communities." I had not previously done so, but Croteau's request made me contact the family members on my list to see if any of them had ever received an apology. No one had.

I also took a closer look to see if a real "acknowledgement of the wrong done" to me had ever happened. I don't think so.

I sent the letter to Croteau as well as the list of my family members who had never received what they should have. He responded almost immediately in a bizarre way. As with his first letter to me, he tried to lay the groundwork to make the Church look as good as possible. The Catholic Church plays a long, long end game. He also sent me a document that I had not previously seen. It was an "apology" that he had written and sent to the winding-up conference for the Survivors represented by the GHRSHC. Croteau claims that Pochat read the letter out to the conference. I have no confirmation that this happened. Whatever happened I absolutely, completely, and unequivocally reject this so-called apology. Pardon my language, but the so-called apology is nothing more than a "fuck you" letter to the Survivors.

Croteau's letters to me were not only petulant; they were also arrogant and filled with sophistry.

I started my young life as an ardent Catholic and even believed that I had a vocation. Since the abuses and the actions that followed them, I have tried, from time to time, to return to the Church, to no avail. I have lost my faith. Speaking of vocations, it was one way of escaping the evil regime at Grollier Hall. If a student was found to have a vocation, he or she would be moved to Grandin College in Fort Smith, to further his or her

PART III

181

pathway. Of course, it was standard fare at every high mass that everyone was urged to pray for more vocations for the Church. The Father Provincial for the diocese would travel to Inuvik once a year to check on the progress toward vocations. I volunteered that I had a vocation and wanted to be a priest. I was told that the Father Provincial had determined that I did not have a vocation and that I would, therefore, remain in the hellhole. I have no idea how he came to this conclusion.

I think there may be more to the story of Grandin College and vocations to come. That will be for another Survivor to tell.

∞

I am forever grateful to my friend, David Searle, for being there, serendipitously or not, when I needed him. David could have chosen to say nothing, but his strong sense of justice steered him in the right direction. Without the documents that he helped us find, I and others would still be struggling with many more lost memories than those that I continue to struggle to regain. Many of us might not even be here.

David also dealt with the Houston case in his private memoir. He was kind enough to include me in the circle of friends whom he gave copies to. With the permission of his widow, Celia Stock, I am quoting the following excerpt from *Gold, Diamonds, and the Law*:

> *In the course of the trial it was evident that there was no process in place to screen applicants for such positions. The only requirement seemingly was that one be Catholic. This was made apparent when the priest in charge of the residence testified that he had no knowledge about why Houston had left the seminary, nor had he heard any complaints from any of the boys, though he admitted to the practice of the sacrament of confession.*

> *By way of follow-up, I wrote to Ottawa, suggesting that the government require the Church to institute a screening process in the hiring of supervisors. Gordon Robertson, the deputy minister responsible, responded saying that the operation of such facilities, though under contract with the government, was the responsibility of the Catholic Church. Obviously, the Government of Canada was acting as Pontius Pilate had done, washing their hands of anything to do with residential schools, as they had contracted that business to the churches.*

> *Not to be put off, I then wrote to the Roman Catholic Bishop of the diocese of Mackenzie at Fort Smith, making the same recommendations, pointing out that the church should have shared*

the information, which it had with its priest in Inuvik. That in the future, such a practice should be initiated and followed. The response, on behalf of the Bishop, was that when next in Yellowknife, His Excellency would be most happy to meet with me to discuss the matter. Either the Bishop never made it to Yellowknife, which is unlikely, or the meeting with me just did not have the priority necessary to make it onto his busy agenda.

Many years later, as the claims, by First Nations people who had suffered under the residential schools, were made against the Church and Government of Canada were proceeding through a negotiation process; the exchange of correspondence with Gordon Robertson was discovered. With my consent, readily given, this correspondence became part of those proceedings and hopefully contributed in some small way to a just settlement.

The bishop whom David is referring to is the "bishop who cared," Paul Piche. Again, I say, no one from the Catholic Church ever offered any help, condolences, sympathy, counselling, or acknowledgment of the crimes committed against so many innocent children by Martin Houston, Max Ruyant, and other male supervisors who followed Houston until they were forced to do so by the Survivors themselves organizing to bring the Church, kicking and screaming, into the light of day.

David's manuscript flags an unresolved issue for me. David says ". . . when the priest in charge of the residence testified that he had no knowledge about why Houston had left the seminary. . ." I assume that the "priest in charge" was Max Ruyant but what was the reference to "the seminary" about? I have heard comments from more than one person that Houston had been a seminarian before he came to Inuvik. Could this have been between the time that he was a boy's supervisor in Kamsack and the time in Inuvik – 1958 – 1960? If Martin Houston was in a seminary, before being hired as our supervisor, why did he leave? His reasons for leaving would most likely have been known to the Father Provincial and Max Ruyant.

Canada is supposed to be in a time of "Truth and Reconciliation". Will Canada use it's strength and power to force the Catholic church to come completely clean?

PART III

183

CHAPTER SEVENTEEN

THE AFTERMATH OF GROLLIER HALL

The preliminary hearing took place on September 13, 1962 in Inuvik. This was twenty-three days after Sergeant Feagan took my statement in Fort Norman, twenty days after Bishop Paul Piche had been advised, in writing, about the facts, and three days after the "confidential" meeting of officials in Inuvik.

As I keep saying, I and the other boys suffered from what I have been calling memory bank wipe. I think the correct description is PTSD. I was surprised to read two questions in the transcript that David Searle had put to me and my answers. The first was, "Are you still going to school here?" My answer: "No." The second was, "And you are not staying at the hostel?" My answer again was "No." My memories, except for the more traumatic events, are very vague about those twenty-three days and the days after that. How did I get to Inuvik? Where did I stay? Why wasn't I going to school?

How is it that I do remember Ruyant marching us to and from the courthouse? I must have been staying at the residence if I was under Ruyant's control. How come I don't remember the examination by David Searle? After I read the transcript, I found out that I was the first witness to be questioned at the hearing.

Perhaps the answers to those questions will become clear someday. In any event, I know I went back to school and to the residence following the preliminary hearing. I was like a zombie, stumbling through that school year. For the first time in my life, I was getting failing grades. I was in grade ten.

If someone from the residence or the school would have put me into counselling, I might have pulled out of the tailspin. Those in authority certainly knew what had happened to me and the other boys. Yet, no help was offered to me or, as far as I know, the other boys. Ironically, one of the items discussed at the "confidential" meeting of officials on September 10, 1962, was the need for social workers. Mr. Needham asked, "What do you feel about the assistance of the Social Worker mentioned in the letter?" I assume that the letter that he is referring to would be one of the three that I do not have. Reverend Holman answered Mr. Needham this way: "The Social Worker is contacted as a matter of routine if problems are experienced." Mr. Needham then asked: "Is it agreeable to you then that the Social Worker comes in? Do you not feel that this will be interference in the internal affairs of the Hostels?" Reverend Holman's answer was: "Services of the Social Worker should be available when requested by the Hostels. That was agreed upon by all present."

No answers from Ruyant are recorded. To the best of my recollection, no social workers ever came to either residence while I was there as a student. A social worker assigned to me may have made a huge difference in my life.

I started drinking at school dances that year. There was always a student who could get an older buddy to buy us liquor. I had money, as my parents would send me an allowance regularly.

The previous year, when I was in grade nine, I had been the treasurer of the student council and the art director for the yearbook. I was not involved in either of these activities in my grade ten year. I think that grade ten might have been the year that I made the school curling team and made a trip to Fort Smith to play in the TPC championship for the Northwest Territories. We put up a good fight but didn't make it.

The 1962/1963 curling team that represented SAMS in Fort Smith. L to R: Cecil Hansen, Skip, Larry Gordon, Second, Fraser Biggs, Third; Mr. A. Robertson, Coach and Ricky Hardy, Lead.

One interesting side benefit of the trip was that I saw my first neon light! It was the sign on top of the Pinecrest Hotel. I knew I couldn't make the team the next year because an academic achievement component was added to the qualifications. My marks were getting even worse. However, I was elected as the president of the student council that year. I made a real mess of that, which resulted in no yearbook being produced that year.

1963/1964 Combined SAMS Student Council and Yearbook Committee. Back row, the young men, L to R: Mike Gladu, Fraser Biggs, James Wilson, Rod Vickers, Ricky Hardy, Fred Koe, Frank Hansen, Wayne Hewitt, Andy Tardiff, Happy Moses, Gary Butchart, Dave Wilderspin and Fred Bennett. Front row, the young women, L to R: Addy Tobac, Lucianne Barnaby, ?, Peggy Starling and Maureen Yorga.

At the completion of grade ten, we went home for the summer holidays, as usual. By then I was old enough to use the family boat and outboard to explore the Mackenzie River or just have some fun. There is an island directly across from Fort Norman called Four Mile Island. The island has nice sandy beaches and a snye between it and the western shore of the Mackenzie River. I was not a good swimmer, so I always made sure that I had some strong swimmers with me before I went in the water, just in case. On one of these occasions, Mike and Robert were with me. The snye emptied back into the Mackenzie River at the northern end of the island and was wider there than along the route. We decided to swim across that part of the snye. It seemed quite a distance for me, and I was nervous. I asked Mike and Robert to stay close to me in case I panicked. That was exactly what happened. They each took an arm and swam me to the far shore. They saved my life that day.

∞

Having the use of the boat and motor opened our horizons. It was usually just Mike and I doing the trips. We were able to get to and climb Bear Rock, which is the dominating geographical feature near Fort Norman. Bear Rock is about 1,600 feet high, and it takes about two to three hours to get to the top. The view from there is spectacular. We would also go duck hunting in the Four Mile Island snye and would proudly bring our kills home to our parents.

∞

During the year that I was in grade ten, the residence had a new supervisor for the senior boys. He was a bit of a strange duck named Mr. James Knowlton. He was married, and his wife and child lived with him in what had previously been Houston's room. They were Blood Indians from Alberta. The only thing that I could see that might have qualified him to supervise us was his ability as a hockey player.

He had a metal hook arm that I understood was a result of a farming accident. The hook was an ugly thing, and he wouldn't hesitate to threaten us with it. After a while it became obvious that he was a boozer. I don't remember if he lasted the full year, but he certainly wasn't back the next year. Gerry Jobin, the assistant supervisor who had come while Houston was still in charge, continued working in the boys' dormitory. There were also a couple of young American missionaries there at some point, helping with the supervising. As I said, I was zombie-like that year.

I don't remember any adult from the residence reviewing my report cards and speaking to me about what I would have to do to improve my academic performance. We were just warehoused. Somehow, I stumbled through the year and managed to get Bs in math, science, English, social studies, and industrial arts. I got Cs in literature and French. B represented a 50 to 64 percent mark, and C represented a 40 to 49 percent mark. Even though I was deemed to have failed literature and French, I was able to get credits for those subjects but could not take the next level in grade eleven.

My marks were even worse in grade eleven. I failed Math 20 completely and was required to take that course over the following year when I was in grade twelve. Strangely enough, I got an "Excellent" for "Conduct" while in grade eleven. Perhaps it wasn't so strange, as abused people tend to be nice, when we are sober, in order to avoid any attention.

∞

On the residence side of things, I made a huge change when I was in grade eleven. I came to Inuvik with all the other students at the start of the year and returned to Grollier Hall. I started grade eleven, but life continued to be horrible at the residence. We had another new supervisor, Brother Sarrault. It had to be some sort of a cruel joke that Ruyant was playing on us. Sarrault had no qualifications to supervise the senior boys or any other children, for that matter. He must have been in his sixties. His career as a brother had been as a carpenter and as a pilot on one of the mission boats. He was also a cruel bastard, which seemed to be a criterion to become a supervisor of the senior boys.

I seemed to be one of the main objects of his "supervising." I didn't last a month. I had some money of my own from working that summer, so I quit school and got a ticket home to Fort Norman. My parents talked things over with me. They told me that what was important was that I complete my education. After further discussion, I told them that one of my friends, Pat Lyall, who was in Stringer Hall, the Anglican residence, had spoken to the superintendents, Mr. and Mrs. Holman, and they were willing to allow me to stay at their residence, so I could go to school. My parents again said that what was important was my education, and they had no objection to me going to Stringer Hall, even if it was an Anglican residence. So, I flew back to Inuvik and returned to Grollier Hall. I stayed one night and saw that things were even worse. It seemed to me that they wanted to break me or get rid of me. I went to school the next day and asked Pat if he was sure that I would be welcomed by the Holmans. He said that would absolutely be the case.

I went back to Grollier Hall after classes had finished that day and packed my things. I walked out with my suitcase and went over the utilidor to Stringer Hall. Mr. Holman was waiting for me at the front door. He asked me, jokingly, what had taken me so long. At the time I did not know that Reverend Holman was fully aware of what had happened to me at the hands of Martin Houston. I was welcomed with open arms, and my life was saved. Strangely, I don't recall Mr. Holman or anyone else ever mentioning what had happened to me.

My friend Pat has, unfortunately, been dead for a number of years. I am forever grateful to him for being a true friend and taking the initiative for me.

Moving from Grollier Hall to Stringer Hall was like going from a very dark night to a day filled with sunshine. I and the other students in grades eleven and twelve were treated like adults. We had to dress up for dinner each evening. We learned proper table manners and etiquette. We did not have to line up for meals, as we were responsible for getting ourselves there on time. We took our meals in a separate dining room with the staff. I and others fondly recall Mrs. Holman's baked hams with cloves. The boys in grades eleven and twelve had a separate dormitory, and our supervisor was Reverend Holman. We would be invited to the Holmans' quarters for coffee or tea in the evenings, during which we had serious discussions about world and national affairs.

We had our own social room where we were encouraged to mingle with the girls and the staff. Mrs. Holman and Pat spent many hours playing Chinese checkers with each other there. We had a nurse named Mrs. Moorby who took lots of pictures of life in the residence and the town during those years. I particularly treasure one of those pictures, which is of me with

Reverend and Mrs. Holman, superintendents of Stringer Hall. Credit: Anglican Church of Canada, General Synod Archives (Mossie Moorby Fonds).

Reverend Holman and James (Orville) Wilson. Credit: Anglican Church of Canada, General Synod Archives (Mossie Moorby Fonds).

Margaret McDonald, Ricky Hardy, and Louise Reindeer. Credit: Anglican Church of Canada, General Synod Archives (Mossie Moorby Fonds).

Frank Hansen and Pat Lyall, arm wrestling at Stringer Hall. Credit: Author.

my friends Margaret McDonald and Louise Reindeer. I made many lifelong friends while I was in Stringer Hall.

However, there was still a large black cloud over my head. I was popular with my fellow students, including many young women. But that black cloud held me down. I didn't understand until many years later what was happening to me. Because of the sexual and other abuse that I had suffered at Grollier Hall and the failure of the "system" to provide counselling, I lacked confidence when I was around young women. Most of them were genuinely concerned and cared about me. Consequently, my drinking escalated to make up for my lack of confidence. As my drinking escalated, my marks continued to fall.

I scraped through the year, with the exception of Math 20, and returned to Stringer Hall in the fall of 1964 to begin grade twelve.

∞

Most of the boys from Fort Norman who attended the residences in Inuvik were still a bit too young to hold down regular summer jobs. Consequently, we would go home for the summers and help here and there.

During the summer of 1963, Walter was awarded a contract by Imperial Oil to provide one hundred power poles for use in Norman Wells. Robert Clement and I were "hired" to help Walter, Rod, Andrew Horassi (Abeyah), and Joe Lennie harvest the trees. Because tall, straight trees were not that plentiful near our home, we went south of Fort Norman by canoe with all of our supplies and tools to do the job. Walter estimated that it would take us about a week to do the harvesting, so he brought enough food for that time frame, bearing in mind that we would take wild meat as we needed it. Not!

We left Fort Norman planning on travelling fifty miles to the location for the timber. By the time we got close to our intended destination, it started to rain very hard. It did not stop raining for close to six days, and we could not work. We spent the first night in an abandoned cabin, and we and our sleeping bags got completely soaked. The sleeping bags never really dried out until the sun finally came out six days later. The bigger problem was that we had brought only a week's supply of food, and we were now on the sixth day without having harvested even one tree. Additionally, we had not been able to get out to hunt or set a fishnet because of the terrible weather. Not a problem; we were all native to the country, so we would get what we needed from the land and the river. Not!

Because of the amount of rain, the river had risen quite high, and fishing with a net was not feasible. As for fishing rods, that was also not feasible either because the Mackenzie River is dirty and full of driftwood, especially after big storms like the one we had just gone through. No problem; we'd just shoot a moose as soon as we saw one. If we don't see one, we'd get a beaver. That was not to be either. We saw nothing but black bears. None of us cared for bear meat, so we didn't kill one until a few days later when we realized we needed the calories if we were going to do the logging, which was all to be done by hard physical labour.

The older men did the falling, and Robert and I did the limbing. Then all six of us would get on the ropes to pull the logs to the riverbank and roll them down to the shore, where we would let them float while tied up to stakes driven into the ground. After Joe Lennie killed the first bear, we realized we had another problem.

Abeyah would not eat bear meat. It was not a matter of taste or anything like that. It was a spiritual belief held by the Shúhta Got'ıne. So, the hunt for other meat ramped up, to no avail. Poor Abeyah had to live on instant potatoes for the last five days of the job while the rest of us ate bear meat for breakfast, dinner, and supper. I felt sorry for Abeyah and also admired him for his strong convictions.

Walter Hardy and Andrew (Abeyah) Horassi. Home from the spring hunt. Credit: Hardy Family Collection.

We managed to harvest all the timber that we needed as well as some extra trees in case some were not accepted. We built one large raft out of the harvested trees and lashed them all together. Then we pulled the raft out to the main current of the river with the canoe and outboard motor. The raft was turned loose to let the current take it. The plan was to follow the raft in the boat and, as we got closer to Fort Norman, to hook up again and drag it out of the current to the shore and then drag the logs out of the water with one of our D4 caterpillar tractors. You know the saying, "the best-laid plans of mice and men"? Because we knew it would take some time to get to Fort Norman, we had set our camp stove on the raft and had a fire going in it and a pot of bear meat boiling away. We thought we were quite smart. Not!

Along came the *Y.T. Husky*, one of the newest and most powerful tugboats on the Mackenzie River, pushing a full complement of loaded barges. Of course, the *Husky* was also in the main channel and could not give way to anyone or anything. This was not deliberate but was a result of the conditions. A tugboat pushing a full complement of loaded barges under full power going with the current is not something that can be easily stopped or turned. Consequently, our carefully built raft was torn apart by the *Husky's* wake, and the logs were scattered asunder, except for the half dozen that were lashed together with the camp stove and the boiling bear meat on it.

By then we were getting just a bit discouraged, but we had no choice but to gather up the scattered logs and lash them back together as best as we could. We succeeded and got them all to Fort Norman. Then the logs were dragged out of the river to a low bank below the HBC compound and stacked with the D4 to be peeled by hand with drawknives. Once that was done, the power poles were loaded onto a barge going to Norman Wells for delivery. I don't remember if it was the *Husky* doing the delivery. I do know that I have never eaten bear meat again! After all, I am descended from the Shúhta Got'ıne, and I should honour their beliefs as best as I can.

∞

I spent the next summer working for Imperial Oil in Norman Wells as a deckhand on the *Taylor II*. The foreman of the production department that I was a part of was our family friend, Ed Hodgson. The "Captain" of the *Taylor II* was Father Antione Biname, one of the more outspoken and independent priests. He had nothing to do with Grollier Hall.

I recall wondering why Biname was not named the bishop, instead of Paul Piche, when Bishop Trocellier passed away. This was before we knew anything about Piche's involvement with the abuse that took place at Grollier Hall. Biname had the common touch, and I am sure he would have been on a plane to Inuvik to comfort us had he been the bishop. I remember a number of shifts with him on the *Taylor II* when he would invoke some salty language during bad storms as we were crossing the Mackenzie

PART III

191

River to pick up another load of crude oil. The salty language was sometimes directed to God for sending us such a bad storm!

I knew Biname from a few years earlier when he had been stationed in Fort Norman. I mentioned in an earlier chapter that he had helped organize the first boy scout troop there. He also taught me how to play chess and we had many games together.

I stayed in camp and partied along with all the other young "men" who were there for summer jobs. Near the end of the summer, I was switched from the *Taylor II* to a service rig that was contracted to Imperial Oil to service wells on Goose Island. The crew of the service rig mesmerized me with their stories of the good life travelling here, there, and everywhere with the rig. I was seventeen years old and impressionable. I was offered an opportunity to join the crew and leave with them and the rig when the contract was finished. I decided to quit school and go with them.

I don't know how relative the decision to quit school was to a severe beating that I got from my brother, Walter. He had come to Norman Wells by boat to pick up some engine parts, and we had been partying with friends of mine from Inuvik while they were waiting for repairs to the airplane being used for the PWA flight they were on. Walter and I were quite drunk and arguing about a number of things. One of those things was whether or not I should quit school. Walter kept shouting at me that I had to finish school, as I had to come back home to be the "auditor" for the family businesses. I basically told him to go to hell, and a fistfight started. He beat me very badly. I remember that he was in a rage. It seemed to me that all the pent-up resentments that he had against me for what looked like special treatment for me from Mama and Daddy had been released.

∞

That year the RCMP stationed a constable in Norman Wells for the summer. It was the first time they had done that. Previously the policing needs for Norman Wells had been handled from the detachment in Fort Norman. For the life of me, I can't remember the constable's name. I should because he intervened when he heard I was going to quit school and convinced me that it was a bad idea for me to become a rig hand. He spent a lot of time with the young workers doing what appears, now, to be social work. He helped a number of us get our driver's licences. I wish I could remember his name, so I could thank him for his intervention in my life. I returned to Stringer Hall instead of quitting school and started grade twelve.

My mother had quite a few of my report cards up to the end of grade eleven. Unfortunately, I can't find any from grade twelve. However, I know I didn't do very well. I was a few credits short, so even with a strong showing in the departmental exams, I would not graduate. I was preparing for the exams in early June 1965 and really wanted to do the best that I could. I also knew I would have to come back to Inuvik for another year to graduate. I had not yet explained that to my parents, and I was mulling over how to do that. Suddenly, it all became irrelevant.

A few days before the departmental exams were to start, I was walking back to Stringer Hall after school when I was met by Reverend Holman, who said he had some disturbing news for me. He told me that my brother, Walter, was missing in connection with a boat trip from Norman Wells to Fort Norman. It was possible that Walter had drowned, but no one knew for sure. Reverend Holman told me that I had to make a decision, and he said whatever I decided would be supported by him and Mrs. Holman. He said I could stay and write the departmental exams and then go home, or I could go home as soon as possible.

I made up my mind immediately to go home, so I could be with my parents. Reverend Holman said that was fine, and he would arrange a ticket for me to catch the PWA flight to Norman Wells, where someone from home would pick me up. He also told me that the departmental exams could be rewritten by anyone who wanted to try to try for a higher mark. He arranged for me to write my exams, that way, in mid-August.

I was very troubled by the deep grudge that I had against Walter over the beating he had given me the previous summer. I headed home to help wherever and however I could.

Alice and Walter Hardy. Taken two years before Walter drowned.
Credit: Hardy Family Collection.

PART IV

DIFFICULT YEARS

Rick Hardy with the truck used to run the PWA Agency in Fort Norman in 1966. Credit: Hardy Family Collection.

PART IV

195

CHAPTER EIGHTEEN

THE CROSSROADS

I arrived home while the search for Walter and his friend Gabe was just moving into full swing. Leo came up from Edmonton to help, and he joined Rod and our friend, Ed Hodgson, from Norman Wells in leading the civilians who were assisting the RCMP. Tensions were running high, and everyone was on edge. Mama and Daddy were distraught and angry.

Walter had been travelling with Gabe Mendo, and they were both missing. Everyone in the community still hoped they would be found alive, stranded on an island or some other safe place. As far as I can remember from what was told to me, Walter and Gabe made the trip to Norman Wells the morning that they went missing—June 14, 1965. One of the reasons they made the trip was to go to the liquor store in Norman Wells. The only liquor store in the region was there, and trips by boat from the outlying communities to "stock up" were not unusual. One theory that was in circulation was that Walter and Gabe had probably parked up a creek and were partying with the liquor they had bought.

The Mackenzie River, at that time of the year, runs very high. As a result, there is a lot of driftwood and what are called deadheads. These are logs that are just at or below the surface of the water and are very dangerous. Walter and Gabe were travelling in an older speedboat that Walter had recently acquired.

The circumstances around the drowning are not fully known. Walter had only recently returned from the spring hunt. As far as I know, Walter had a serious dispute with our parents, especially Mama. Walter wanted to marry the sister of one of his friends and trapping partner, Andrew Horassi, or Abeyah, as he was known in the local Dene dialect. Unfortunately, Mama had adopted the attitude of her father, Tim Gaudet, to her children marrying Indians. Although Granddad may have been more concerned about his children marrying someone who was uneducated and not a Christian, Mama took a harsher view. She would not allow it, or at a minimum, agree to it. Walter was going to go ahead with the marriage anyway and had recently received the materials, on the barge, that he had ordered to build a house for himself.

He was going to build the house "up the hill" on land that Daddy had purchased some time ago. The issue of the ownership of the land was contentious and continued to be so until recently, when I finally sold off the last of it. Our family quarrelled about the land right from the time when Daddy and Mama acquired the first parcel and built our family home there. They acquired what had originally been the whole of Lot 9 by pieces over a number of years as described in an earlier chapter. The quarrel was also linked to the issue of the ownership of the "business" that was growing. The ownership of the business was one of the main causes for the beating that Walter had given me the previous summer in Norman Wells. During the argument leading up to the beating, I remember him screaming at me that I had no right to call the business ". . . and Sons," as it should properly be ". . . and Son," and he was that son. The issue of land ownership and business ownership, among other matters, continued to tear us apart as a family for the rest of our lives.

When Mama took sick and was hospitalized, I took over her duties in the business, which included all the correspondence and invoicing. Prior to this, everything was in Daddy's name only. He had started using the name "Norman Freight" when he was partnered with Bob Hattie. When he and Bob parted ways, he and Walter worked in the business then. I was instrumental in getting Daddy to agree to call the business "Hardy and Sons Transport." At the time, Leo and Rod were living in Edmonton, and I was going to school in Inuvik. I had a dream of all of us coming back home and working in the business. I thought I would become a civil engineer in the future. Rod returned home a few years before Walter drowned. He was only peripherally involved in the business at that time. He worked full-time as the game patrolman for Bob Douglas.

∞

L to R: Rod Hardy, Jack Hardy, Ricky Hardy, Leo Hardy, Pierre Bavard, while the search was still going on. Credit: Hardy Family Collection.

The search continued, and as time stretched on, it became clear that Walter and Gabe would not be found alive. However, a family does not give up hope, and explanations that were more and more extreme came to the fore. Eventually, after a number of weeks, Gabe's body was found and brought home and buried. Not long after that, Walter's body was recovered. It was brought back to Fort Norman in an RCMP floatplane. As a family, it was as if the skies had opened, and God had reached down and punched each of us as hard as he could. The RCMP detachment included a warehouse behind the barracks. We were kept away until Walter's body was moved there. Then the RCMP corporal came to see us and told us that someone needed to identify the body. It was close to a month since the drowning took place.

I went with Rod to the RCMP's warehouse to help. I was not allowed to see the body, but I could smell it. It was foul. Rod had to do the identification. Rod carried that mental image for the rest of his life, and I carried the smell for quite a few years.

The speedboat had also been found. I never saw it, but I was told that the bow was smashed in, and it was clear that they had run into a drift log or a deadhead. It remains unknown what role alcohol played in the accident. Walter and Gabe were both young men and were still at the invincible stage of life. Walter was known to be a heavy drinker.

Whatever the truth was, they were both dead, and Walter now had to be buried. Mama took charge of the decisions that had to be made. She got Maurice Mendo, Gabe's older brother, to build the coffin out of some of the building material that Walter had purchased for his house. She found enough black cloth to cover the entire coffin. Because of the decomposition of the body, the coffin was closed. Mama decided he was to be buried beside his grandfather in the old Anglican graveyard.

Tim Gaudet and Walter Hardy, c. 1946. Credit: Hardy Family Collection.

She even went so far as to buy me a dark-coloured coat from the HBC store, so I would look proper for the funeral. The funeral service took place in the Catholic church, and then the coffin was hauled to the family area of the old Anglican graveyard.

My parents were devastated. They followed the coffin to the graveyard, crying all the way. They never got over Walter's death. I learned that the loss of a child is the worst pain that a parent can endure. Daddy had some conspiracy theories about the drowning, which he eventually let go of. He thought that some locals who did not like Walter had shot at him and then hit the boat, causing it to sink. It was a touchy subject for a few years as he refused to listen to reason about what really happened.

∞

I went back to Inuvik in August to write the supplemental exams, but even before I saw the exams, I knew I was not going to pass them. I still had to decide whether or not to return to Inuvik in September 1965 to restart grade twelve. After thinking the situation over, I decided not to return to school. I thought it was more important that I stay home to help Mama and Daddy through their pain. All of us had a difficult winter emotionally. I recall waking up in the middle of one night in the winter and getting dressed. I walked up to the graveyard and sat on the ground beside Walter's grave. I cried and I cursed. I cursed Walter for ruining our lives. I cursed him for the pain that Mama and Daddy were suffering from. I cursed him for what he had done to me. We had never resolved the beating.

When Walter died, he had a son who was three and half years old. I don't know if he knew about the son. I do know that no one else in the family knew. It was years later when the son sought us out.

There was no television in Fort Norman in 1965, so I subscribed to the Book of the Month Club and one other similar service. I became, and have remained, an avid reader. It is not unusual for me to be reading two or three books at a time.

Once the reality of that winter set in, I understood what it meant when people would say things like, "The living have to carry on with their lives." I needed to do my share to support the family until everyone worked through the grieving process. I was able to obtain the agency for Pacific Western Airlines, which ran both IFR and VFR operations in those days. The VFR operations, which had previously been operated by CP Air, connected Fort Norman with Norman Wells and the other surrounding communities. From Norman Wells, passengers and freight would be transferred to and carried on the larger airplanes, owned by PWA, to and from Inuvik, Yellowknife, Fort Smith, and Edmonton. The monthly pay was not high, but the benefits made having the agency worthwhile. I was allowed one hundred pounds of freight from Edmonton, on company service, every month. I was also allowed a return trip

PART IV

between Fort Norman and Edmonton every two months. The OCS freight helped reduce our cost of living.

The no-cost trips to Edmonton allowed me to make my first trip out of the Northwest Territories and my first visit to a real city. The airplanes that came from the North at that time landed and took off from what was called the Industrial Airport, which was practically in downtown Edmonton. I made my first trip in early March 1966. The plane landed at night, and Leo and Rod were supposed to pick me up. I stepped off the airplane and walked into the terminal with my northern gear on—mukluks, big mitts, and my parka, and I looked a bit out of place. That didn't bother me, as I was still digesting the beauty of the city lights that I had seen from the air. I was eighteen years old and still impressionable. Leo and Rod were there, but they were hiding. They had a good chuckle at what I looked like when I had realized no one had come to pick me up, or so I thought. I stayed in Edmonton for a week at Leo's house. I saw TV for the first time. I also went to my first A&W drive-in!

I didn't realize it, but Leo and Rod were planning the future of the business, which included Leo moving back to Fort Norman. When that was eventually agreed to in the spring of 1966, I saw my opportunity to leave. However, I needed to make some real money of my own, so I signed on with a company called Calgary Exploration (or Calex) and became a cat skinner, also called a heavy equipment operator. Calex had a contract to build the first road from Fort Norman to the new Bear River water plant. I worked on that job for about two months, during which time Leo and his family made the move to Fort Norman. They brought a small house trailer with them and set it up "up the hill." So, Leo and Liz and their two children, Corrie and Ben, settled in for what they thought was a long-term commitment.

I moved with Calex, along with the equipment and the camp, to Wrigley by barge. The company had a contract to build roads at the new townsite for the community. The old townsite, where Mama was born, was on the west side of the Mackenzie River. The move was to allow the residents quick access to the airport, which was on the east side of the river, and to keep them safe from flooding. That airport had been built in connection with the American Army coming in during WWII to build the Canol Pipeline.

Before I left Fort Norman to work in Wrigley, I applied to the Northern Alberta Institute of Technology (NAIT) in Edmonton to study business administration. I was accepted, and I was approved for funding to attend the school by the NWT government. My plan was to work in Wrigley until a few days before registration and then fly to Edmonton to start my studies. That would have worked fine except for the weather in early

September 1966 in Wrigley. A fog moved in, and I was unable to get out until a week after I had planned to leave. Nevertheless, I went to Edmonton and went to the admissions office at NAIT to register. To my consternation, I was told that my spot had been given to someone else, as I had not shown up by the cut-off date. So, there I was with everything in place except a program to start on. I asked if there were any other openings. It turned out there were still a couple of spots in the two-year architectural technology program. I would have preferred civil engineering technology, but what was available seemed to be close enough. So, I enrolled in architectural technology and started, a week behind everyone else in the program. Coincidentally, my cousin, Bob Overvold, was taking civil engineering technology at the same time at NAIT.

While I was in Wrigley, I had a whirlwind romance with a local Dene girl who was my age. I was not particularly experienced with sex, but she took the reins. We were—or at least thought we were—in love. The people who were being moved from the old townsite to the new one were living in tents until the houses that were being built for them were ready. Her family was in one of those tents, and I spent many nights there with her. She knew I was leaving for Edmonton, and we planned how she would join me there once I found a place to live. I wrote to her after I moved into the boarding house that I was going to live in, giving her the address and the phone number. I never heard back from her. Years later when we met again, we talked about this, and she said she had never received the letter. The reason that we saw each other all those years later was that she wanted to tell me that I had fathered a daughter with her. At first, I thought it was true, as rumours had swirled around between Wrigley and Fort Norman about the child, a girl, for years. I met the girl and spent time getting to know her. However, the claim ended up being false, as I found out after I had a paternity test done. I felt very sorry for the girl, as she had become quire attached to me, even calling me dad.

Rick Hardy in the mandatory "man on the street" photo in Edmonton in 1966 while attending NAIT. Credit: Author.

∞

Mama was in Edmonton when I got there to start at NAIT, staying with my cousin Mabel Hall. They had hatched a plan that would have seen me rooming and boarding with Mabel and her husband, George. I put my foot down and refused. I found a boarding house downtown where some other students from the North were living. I walked the three or four blocks from there to the bus every morning.

School did not go well. Not only did I never catch up from starting a week late, I was also in party mode. Many of my

PART IV

friends and acquaintances from the North were going to school or working in Edmonton then. We were young and invincible. And stupid. If someone wanted to find students from the North in Edmonton at that time, they just had to head down to the 97th Street area, where joints like Danceland, the Coffee Cup, and the New Edmonton Hotel were located.

I partied the next seven or eight months away, rarely going to school. Spring came, and a number of us decided it was time to head back North to find summer jobs. By that time, I had an old jalopy that I'd bought with the last of my earnings from the previous summer. Three or four of us piled what few belongings we had into the trunk, and off we went. We were heading for Hay River, where we thought we would get summer jobs with NTCL, working on the barges. Bad luck for us—the economy was in a downturn, and all available jobs had already been filled. We had more bad luck before we got to Hay River when the jalopy's engine gave up the ghost. We hitchhiked the remaining miles to Hay River.

We then made our way to Yellowknife, where my cousin, Charlie Overvold, and his wife, Adeline, put us up and put up with us for a few weeks while we looked for work. My cousin, Bob Overvold, had also returned to Yellowknife and was a supervisor at Akaitcho Hall, the student residence in Yellowknife for out-of-town students. Again, we had no luck finding jobs, so we made our way back to Hay River.

A friend of ours from home, Fred Clement, was living in Hay River. He gave us a ride to Pine Point, where we applied to work at the mine. We were told that they would be in touch. I don't remember hearing back from them. Years later when I became a member of the board of directors of Pine Point Mines Limited, I would chuckle about that incident.

By then we were broke and down on our luck. Another friend, the late Winston McNeely, was also in the area with his own car. Winston drove us to Fort Smith to see if there were any jobs available there. Again, no luck. By then the "we" had boiled down to just Larry Tourangeau and me.

Winston drove us back to Hay River, where we kept trying our luck. We slept here, there, and everywhere and begged for meals wherever we could get them. A couple of pretty Métis girls were waitressing at the Hay River Hotel. They would occasionally slip us a hamburger or something similar. Years later we would reminisce and laugh about it with them. Mike Gladu was working for CN Telecommunications, now Northwestel, and was on a job in Hay River. He and his crew were staying at the Hay River Hotel. Thanks to Mike, I was able to shower a couple of times and get a good night's sleep on the floor in his room.

However, there was a lot of roughing it. Hay River had suffered the ravages of a bad flood the year before, and there were a lot of shacks scattered around near the shore. One of these shacks was occupied by a friend of Winston's named Carmody. Winston dropped us off there once and told us we could sleep there. There was one old bare mattress on the floor of the one room. We were sinking fast. Then I did something that I regretted the rest of my life. I had been home for the previous Christmas. When I was ready to go back to Edmonton to continue at NAIT, my parents gave me a blank cheque, signed by Daddy. It was to buy some tools for him, but the need disappeared. Mama was worried about the cheque and called me at the boarding house about it. I lied to her and said I had destroyed it. I carried it in my wallet and still had it while we were in Hay River.

I knew it was wrong, but we were getting desperate, as we were not eating very much, so I went to Daddy's bank, the Royal Bank, and filled the check in for $100. The bank cashed it. I was ashamed and afraid, so I did not call home to tell them what I had done. Fortunately, they had enough money in the bank to cover it. When I finally got home later that summer, I had to face the music. I was humiliated and sorry.

Eventually, a couple who were originally from Inuvik, Elijah and Mabel Allen, took us in. This is another couple whom I am eternally grateful to. Elijah was a foreman on the Northern Alberta Railway. While he had no openings on his section of the railway, he was able to find us jobs on the High Level section.

There is an interesting side story to this. Earlier in the year, there had been a large robbery from the Hay River liquor store. Unbeknownst to Larry and me, the RCMP had two undercover officers working the case in Hay River. They were posing as out-of-work labourers looking for jobs. It didn't strike us that they were anything else. They seemed to have a lot of money on them. They were happy to buy a lot of beer for us and other down-and-outers in the bar of the Hay River Hotel. They were fishing for information on the robbery. They knew that Larry and I were both too young to be in the bar and were, at that point in time, ne'er do wells.

When Elijah and Mabel took us in, we stopped our lowlife ways out of respect for them, so we had no idea what had happened to those two fellas. When we got to High Level and started work, we went to a bar in High Level for a beer one evening. There they were, sitting there, drinking beer. We were happy to see them and tried to join them. To our great surprise, they hustled us out of the bar and gave us supreme hell. They told us that if they ever saw us in a bar again, they would make sure we were put in jail. It scared the shit out of me. I don't

PART IV

remember if they told us then who they really were or if we learned it some other way.

∞

Larry and I spent about a month shovelling gravel twelve hours a day, on the railway, for $1.65 per hour. When we couldn't take it anymore, we quit. We were the only two out of a crew of about thirty who could speak English. The rest of the crew were Portuguese immigrants. They were so talkative that the company put up a huge sign in the eating car that said, "No Talking During Meals." I assume that someone interpreted the words into Portuguese. We went into town to get our cheques. We were told that if we wanted our cheques right away, we would have to go to Edmonton. We didn't have two nickels to rub together, so we hitchhiked to Edmonton. This included many hours walking down the highway trying to get rides. Larry and I were both smokers at the time and were lowered to picking up butts off the side of the highway to feed our addiction. My life looked very much like I had taken the wrong turn at the crossroads.

CHAPTER NINETEEN

WANDERING

We reached Edmonton eventually and found our way to Larry's girlfriend's house. At first, she and her mother didn't recognize us, as it was dark, we were not very clean, we hadn't had haircuts, and we had tanned to a very dark brown. The tan came from working the twelve-hour shifts in the sun and riding the flat cars from site to site. At that point I'd had enough.

Before finding my way back home, I spent a few days staying with my cousin, Sarah Carr, and her daughters in Edmonton. Sarah was always kind to me and welcomed me to stay a while. While I was there, I saw the start of the Six-Day War between Egypt and Israel on television. That was between June 5 and 10, 1967. I was twenty years old.

I returned home to Fort Norman with my tail between my legs and took my punishment, in the form of a harsh lecture, for cashing the cheque. Things were not going well with the business. Leo and Rod were quarrelling, and Mama and Daddy were siding with Rod. Leo had a much clearer vision of the future and wanted to expand the business by borrowing money. Daddy and, to a lesser extent, Rod did not believe in borrowing money. Eventually, Leo lost the argument and had to move from "up the hill" with his family and the trailer. They were able to get some land, on a temporary basis, from the government, and they moved there. He found two local residents who were willing to provide him with financing and be silent partners in a new contracting business. Leo was now competing with the family business. Eventually, I went to work for Leo for a short period of time.

∞

Daddy and Mama had decided to tear down our family home and replace it with a smaller house the previous year that, in the longer term, would provide enough space for just the two of them and a guest. They hired Maurice Mendo as the carpenter and used all the materials that Walter had bought two years earlier for his own house. Additionally, they cut lumber with our sawmill for the studs, stringers, and beams. The regional electrician, Doug Bailey, gave me a crash course on basic wiring, and I wired the house. We also replanted the lawn and the flower gardens and rebuilt the picket fences. I mention the picket fences because I have been criticized by people that I grew up with for our family having them. Looking back at those times, it seems clear to me that we were living in settler mode and not as Indigenous people. Picket fences, flower gardens, lawns, and vegetable gardens were not things that the Indians cared about then.

The new house. Credit: Hardy Family Collection.

Alice Hardy and Irene Harrison. Credit: Hardy Family Collection.

It was now the summer of 1967 and I was their first "guest". During this time I fell in love with a young woman from one of the surrounding communities. For me, it was very real. I was head over heels. She was going to a residential school and wanted to return to finish grade twelve that fall. We talked about the future that we would make together. I was happy for the first time in a very long while. She returned to school, and a month later I got a Dear John letter. I was crushed. I locked myself in the small bunkhouse that Leo had purchased for the new business. I came out four days later a bitter person. I lost all my confidence in relations with the opposite sex. I thought there must be something really wrong with me if this could happen to me. Was it because of what had happened to me as a child in the Fort Norman Federal Day School and what Houston and Ruyant did to me? My drinking and anti-social behaviour increased. I wondered if I was a homosexual. That was not something that was accepted then, as it is now. I had a lot of difficulties accepting the homosexuality of anyone, as I equated it with Houston. Eventually, I learned that homosexuality had nothing to do with Houston's sickness, and I became more accepting of people's choices in the matter. I don't believe that gay people can change how their brains are wired. I now accept them as they are without judgment.

∞

After suffering through the affects of the Dear John letter, I picked myself up once again. I managed to duck the family dispute by taking a job with the government's area administrator, Frank Bailey, as his clerk. However, my parents did not forgive me for taking sides against them. I was lucky that my job with the government came with a house, so I was okay there. The house was the 512 that Maurice Cloughley had lived in during the two or three years he had taught at the school. Frank Bailey eventually decided that I had some potential in the accounting field, and he found me a training position at the regional office in Inuvik. I moved to Inuvik and became a trainee Clerk IV. I soon turned twenty-one and was old enough to drink in the bars and buy my own liquor in Inuvik. I had a full-time job and my own apartment. Of course, that meant I had a lot of "friends" then. The spiral continued.

Over the next five years, I held and lost twelve different jobs or contract positions. Every loss was a result of my drinking. I was arrested twice for public drunkenness. The first arrest was while I was at a curling bonspiel in Aklavik. My court appearance was back in Inuvik the following week in front of Reverend Holman, who was then the justice of the peace. He said to me, in a disappointed tone tinged with anger, that he wondered when I would show up in his court. At the time I was embarrassed, but I also thought the situation was somewhat funny. I still wasn't aware that Reverend Holman knew what had happened to me at Grollier Hall.

My second arrest was in Norman Wells, a couple of years later. I was drunk and violent in front of the old Rec Hall. I was placed in a cell, stripped naked, and handcuffed with my hands under my legs. I was later told that this was done for my own protection. When I wasn't drinking, I was smart and competent. When I was drinking, I was angry and violent. The only thing that kept me afloat in those years was the love of my parents and my realization of the pain and suffering that I was causing them. I didn't want to be what I had become. Part of my difficulty was that I was mostly associating with people who also drank a lot. Of course, I didn't think there was anything wrong with me then. I had many close calls with death.

I also made many life- long friends during this period of my life. These were primarily people that I had gone to work for. Amongst these people was the Stewart family in Hay River. Not only did they give me a job, they welcomed me into their home and made me feel as if I was a member of their family. I filled a number of functions in their various businesses as well as in Don Stewart's political adventures. I learned a lot from him.

I had similar experiences with the Phillip family in Fort Providence, the Anderson brothers in Inuvik and Norman Wells and Ralph Froment in Yellowknife. All of these people treated me well notwithstanding my failures.

I should have died one night in Fort Providence. I barely remember the details, but a local fellow was feeling very jealous about his girlfriend, who I had shown some interest in. One Saturday night he met me on the main road in the dark and dragged me over the riverbank down to the beach. I was quite drunk. He started beating me and banging my head on the boulders that make up the beach along the Mackenzie River. I guess he banged my head hard enough that I came to and realized how much danger I was in. I don't know how I got away from him, but I did. I crawled up the bank and made my way to Angus McLeod's house, where I was safe. As a young man, Angus had been stationed in Fort Norman, where he had worked with my grandfather when he was also a young man. Angus now had a family that were mostly adults, but he still "assisted" at the local HBC store in Fort Providence. I guess I didn't want to die just then. Other than that, I enjoyed my time in Fort Providence and still enjoy visiting there.

I returned to Inuvik one more time in the early 1970's. There was an oil-and-gas boom in the Beaufort Sea area, related to the proposed Arctic Gas Pipeline. There was lots of work in Inuvik, and I was hired by Mid-Arctic Transportation Company Ltd. My job was quasi-managerial. A Yukon airline, called Great Northern Airways (GNA) had developed a market for flying fresh produce and fresh meat and other goods to Inuvik, from wholesalers in Whitehorse, for the stores in Inuvik and the area around Inuvik, which, in turn, supplied the rigs in the Beaufort. If I remember correctly, there were five scheduled flights a week that needed to be ground handled. Mid-Arctic had just acquired that contract and needed someone competent enough to do the managing.

Basically, our job was to unload the airplanes and get the shipments to the customers as soon as possible, in good condition. This was not easy to do with fresh fruits and vegetables when it was minus 40°C or colder. Coincidentally, Diane was also hired by Mid-Arctic to work in the accounting department. She had recently graduated from high school in Inuvik. Part of my job was to take care of all the documentation and work with the recipients of the shipped goods to resolve issues. Of course, I also helped unload and load the airplanes. I made monthly trips to Whitehorse, which were usually just for one night, to meet with my counterpart there and GNA's management to ensure everything was flowing smoothly. I really enjoyed the work and all the people whom I worked with.

Diane was madly in love with her high school sweetheart, who was a local sports hero, Larry Gordon. Her love was reciprocated by Larry. As these things go, Diane became pregnant. She was terrified about telling our parents. So, she came to me and asked me to phone Mama and break the news. Holy smokes! I was just as scared as she was, but I was the big brother. So, I screwed up my courage and got on the telephone. I didn't waste any time chit-chatting and just got to the point and waited for the explosion to come. Not married and pregnant! Mama started talking to me urgently, in Slavey. I did not speak Slavey and, usually, didn't understand it. This time, for reasons I do not understand, I clearly understood what she was saying. The gist of the response was that I had better treat my sister kindly and not be angry with her and love her. What was important was Diane and the baby, and we would worry about the other issues later. What a relief. I think Mama was still hurting from the way her sister Bella had been treated by their dad.

Diane gave birth to a wonderful baby boy, Stewart Gordon. Because Diane still needed to work, our parents took Stewart for a year in Fort Norman. They were thrilled to have him and loved him to bits. In the meantime, the other issues—i.e., a wedding—were arranged. Larry and Diane were married by Reverend Holman in the Stringer Hall chapel the following spring. Diane was Catholic, and Larry was an Anglican. As far as I know, this never became an issue. Both sets of parents were there, and everyone had a great time. Larry and Diane had three sons and a daughter. They were all baptized as Catholics. Go figure.

Unfortunately, I was in the bush, providing security, along with my friend Frederick Andrew, Junior, for a drilling rig, at the Dahadinni River, south of Fort Norman at the time of the wedding, so I was unable to be there.

Larry and Diane (Hardy) Gordon with Jack and Alice Hardy on their wedding day in Inuvik.
Credit: Hardy Family Collection.

In 1971 and 1972, the Métis of the Northwest Territories started to become organized. They were helped substantially by Métis from southern Canada, who had gone through their own organizing a number of decades earlier. I did not like the direction that the movement was taking. First, the new organization was being led by Métis who were not indigenous to the Northwest Territories. Second, they were focused on social programs, such as housing and alcohol and drug treatment. While this was going on, the Indians had organized into the Indian Brotherhood, and their focus was on what became known as land claims. The Indian Brotherhood had successfully launched the *Re: Paulette* case, which put the whole meaning of Treaty 11 in question. I and other young Métis, such as my friend Jake Heron, began to organize within the Métis movement to change its focus to land claims. I thought of us as "young Turks" in terms of the fall of the Ottoman Empire. This resulted in me running for president of the new organization, the Métis and Non-Status Indian Association of the NWT at the annual assembly, early in 1973.

Somewhat like Mama, I have saved various documents over the years. One of those documents is my handwritten notes for the speech that I gave to that assembly. I began by thanking Agnes Semmler and Frank Laviolette, two elders who were instrumental in getting the organization off the ground, for nominating me. Then I iterated the three main points of my campaign. These three points, paraphrased, were: it was time for the Indigenous Métis to take control of their own destiny; we had to cooperate with the other native organizations in the NWT if we were to achieve a land-claim settlement for the Métis; and, instituting better practices in the management of the association's administration. I lost the election to Dave McNabb, who had moved to the NWT from Alberta a few years earlier. I also learned some lessons. One of those lessons was not to count the chickens in my own backyard unless they were hatched. I lost, in part, because my friends from Fort Good Hope did not vote for me.

So, I threw myself into organizing for the association. The association was made up of "locals" and were each assigned a number. For example, the Métis in Fort Smith became the first to organize, so their organization became known as "Fort Smith Métis Local 50." The next to organize were the Métis of Hay River, so they became "51" and so on. I became the president of the Norman Wells Métis Local # 59. My vice president was our old friend, Ed Hodgson, and the secretary-treasurer was Gerry Loomis, a Métis from Alberta who had settled in Norman Wells. I also helped organize the locals in Fort Norman and Fort Franklin. As the president of a local, I became a member of the board of directors of the parent organization. Now I had a platform to push for land claims for the Métis.

Early on, at the start of the land-claim movement, there was some talk of including the Métis as part of the Indian Brotherhood. This idea was rejected by the chiefs at a meeting in Fort Rae in the early 1970s. This led, in part, to the Métis establishing their own organization. However, the president of the Indian Brotherhood around that time was James Wah-Shee, and he favoured the coming together of both peoples. I told the assembly, "I support James Wah-Shee's statement that in a few short years, we will all be one people."

I did not know James then. He was only a couple of years older than me, and he was educated. More importantly, he had been born and raised in a community other than Yellowknife and understood the intricacies of community life. Some of my supporters had gone to school with James and had lived in Akaitcho Hall with him. They spoke favourably about him. Additionally, people in Inuvik, involved in establishing the

PART IV

Committee of Original People's Entitlement, supported him, and I trusted those people.

I was a lonely voice on the board, which was primarily made up of supporters of the then-president, Dave McNabb. I was viewed as a young hothead. I remembered the stories Mama had told me about our Métisness and my grandfather being at Batoche. I also remembered my first writings supporting the Métis. It was either in grade nine or ten, and it was in the social studies class. The textbook that we were using called Louis Riel a traitor to Canada. Naturally, I took exception to this. I wrote an essay on why Louis Riel was a hero and not a traitor. I finished the essay with words to the effect that "because my mother told me so." I got a high mark and encouragement for my thinking from my teacher, Bert Brin. I was also aware that my grandfather had refused to take treaty in 1921. Mama told me that he knew what the written terms of the treaty meant, so he opted for the scrip payments that were created for the Half-Breeds. I didn't know much more than that, but my gut instinct was that if the meaning of Treaty 11 was in question, as a result of *Re: Paulette*, then the effect of scrip payments should also be in question.

At that point, there did not seem to be much hope of advancing these ideas through our own organization. However, a new member of the board from Fort Rae, Richard Whitford, began to question spending and other administration matters, and Dave McNabb and the vice president were removed from office. They were replaced by a finance committee, which was headed by Richard Whitford. It seemed clear that the mess would be cleaned up, and Richard Whitford would emerge as our new leader. Richard was a Métis from the large Mercredi family in Fort Smith and was very personable. Because I thought that Richard would become our new leader, I accepted a job as a full-time civil servant. I became the manager of a youth development program for the Northwest Territories for the Government of Canada.

∞

However, another serendipitous event affecting my life intervened. The Liberal Party, which was in a minority government position, decided to go to the polls on July 8, 1974. They were tired of the NDP tail-wagging the Liberal dog. The serendipitous event was Jean Chretien asking Richard Whitford to stand for the Liberal Party in the Northwest Territories constituency. Richard accepted the invitation. Many of the Metis Association board members were supporters of the then-NDP MP, Wally Firth, a Métis from Fort McPherson. These board members were not happy with Richard Whitford and his supporters. Consequently, the board changed course, and part of the change was to ask me to become the executive director of the association. I was conflicted because I had just started my new job. I felt some loyalty to my new employer for hiring me, and I liked the pay and the stability.

I thought it over and decided that if I were to accept the executive director position, it would not be just for that job. It could be the stepping stone to the presidency of the association. At the time I had not fully crystalized my thinking, but eventually, it became clear that working for the rights of the Métis was my calling. By this time my cousin, Bob Overvold, had become a schoolteacher in Hay River and was also actively involved in the association as the board member for Hay River. I approached him and said I would be giving up the start of a new career to do what had to be done, but I wouldn't do it unless I had some certainty about what our team would look like. I told him I wanted his undertaking to become the executive director if I were to become the president. Bob agreed, but we had a major hurdle to deal with. His brother and my cousin, Charlie Overvold, also wanted to be the president. Charlie was one of three members of the finance committee that was reorganizing the association. Once Richard Whitford left Charlie became the acting chairperson. We managed to convince Charlie to stand for the vice president's position instead when the annual meeting was held. Charlie was always a reasonable person and would put principles ahead of personalities.

So, Richard Whitford was off campaigning to be elected to Parliament, and we had a plan in place to "reinvent" the Métis Association. Even though I was still only the executive director, I became the face and voice of the association. In fact, Charlie and I represented the association at a number of meetings with the Indian Brotherhood in the spring and summer of 1974. This included a joint assembly of the Indian Brotherhood and the Métis Association in Fort Good Hope in June of that year. The unity train was ready to leave the station. Charlie and I, along with Bob, attended the first formal land-claim meeting between Canada and the Métis in Edmonton in the spring of that year. That meeting explored, on a "without prejudice" basis, what our thinking was if Canada would agree to negotiate the land claim.

Richard lost the federal election to Wally Firth and had burned many of his bridges with the Métis of the Northwest Territories. Notwithstanding that the Métis were without an elected leader, the winds of change were sweeping through the Northwest Territories. Fuelling all of this was the Mackenzie Valley Pipeline Inquiry, which was headed by the late Mr.

PART IV

Justice T. R. Berger, a judge from the Supreme Court of British Columbia. Prior to ascending to the bench, Tom Berger was the leader of the NDP in British Columbia. The establishment of the inquiry and the appointment of Tom Berger to lead it was one of the concessions that the NDP tail had squeezed out of the Liberal dog in Ottawa prior to the calling of the 1974 election. The inquiry quickly became known simply as the Berger Inquiry.

The board of directors of the Metis Association finally called for an annual general meeting of the association to be held in August of that year in Fort Smith. I was nominated by Jake Heron to be the new president, and I defeated Joe Mercredi and Carl Carpentier in the election. Charlie Overvold was elected, by acclamation, as the vice president, and he resigned from his career job with the federal Department of Transport. Bea (St. Arneault) Goldney, who was originally from Hay River, was elected as the secretary-treasurer. She had held the position previously. Shortly after the annual general meeting, the board convened a meeting and hired Bob Overvold as the executive director. Bob put everything on the line by resigning his teaching position. We were all full of hope for the future and completely committed. We had no idea what a difficult time we would be going through for the next three years.

The winds of change were also blowing strongly through the other Indigenous communities of the Northwest Territories. When the four of us became the leaders of the Métis, James Wah-Shee was the popular president of the Indian Brotherhood and was inclined to work with us. The four of us were generally in favour of unity of the Dene and Métis people of the Northwest Territories. We realized this meant that a lot of details on how this would work had to be negotiated. We believed that with James leading the Indian Brotherhood, we could do it.

However, James's director of community development, Georges Erasmus, and a number of White advisers were not working on these details but were laying the groundwork for his removal. He was seen by them as not being radical enough. Not being radical enough meant that James was not inclined to Marxist-Leninism, like they were.

PART V
FINDING MY CALLING

Richard I. Hardy - College of Law graduation portrait, 1981.
Credit: Hardy Family Collection.

CHAPTER TWENTY
ACADEMIA

While I was the president of the Métis Association, I met Bea Bloomstrand, who was our executive assistant. Bea's father was a White trapper and businessman, and her mother was a Chipewyan Dene, who spent her young life in a residential school. This made our backgrounds common, and we could talk about things that we both understood. I was going through a number of relationships at that time, and Bea was about to leave the partner she was living with. She had a young daughter, Candy, from her first marriage. We began living together, and she gave birth to our daughter, Anna Marie, on February 25, 1977.

Rick and Bea Hardy. Credit: Hardy Family Collection.

Bea was the fifth person on our team at the Metis Association office. However, that created a bit of a problem as we now had two people named Bea working in the same office. A wag solved the problem when he named one big (tall) Bea and the other little (short) Bea. We worked well together, including preparing the association's positions in front of the Berger Inquiry. Berger finally delivered his final report in the summer of 1977.

Despite my opposition to Berger's findings, I must credit the inquiry with one thing—convincing me that I wanted to be a lawyer. As I watched the numerous lawyers perform their tasks, I realized that I could do many of those tasks just as well as they did. The Berger Inquiry was akin to a civil war amongst the Indigenous peoples of the Northwest Territories – albeit a virulent verbal one, that, only occasionally, boiled over into fisticuffs. I was one of the leaders of the losing side and needed to find a new path for myself and my family.

Earlier in 1977, when Bea and I were considering if we should seek higher education, we realized that we faced the same stumbling block. We were both, in effect, high school dropouts. However, Bea, like me, was an avid reader and had a thirst for knowledge. We knew we could apply to universities to be admitted as mature students. However, neither of us was confident that we had what it took. So, we both arranged to take the GED tests and did well on them. The next step would be to apply to a university to see if we would be accepted as mature students.

Bea and I decided that I would go first and see what a semester would be like. Because I had made the acquaintance of Doctor Lloyd Barber, the president of the University of Regina, and he had encouraged me to apply to his university, I did just that. Doctor Barber was also the chair of the Indian Claims Commission in Canada and had tried to mediate between the Dene and the Métis and Canada. That was when I met him, and we had talked about my academic ambitions.

I was accepted into the bachelor of arts program and moved to Regina in early September 1977. Bea stayed behind with Candy and Anna Marie and kept working. I had received funding from the Northern Careers Program, which had recently been set up by the federal government. The primary purpose of the program was to train Indigenous people to become mid-level management employees and thereby increase the number of Indigenous employees working for the federal government in the northern territories. However, they advertised that they were willing to train for any career that was available in the federal civil service. So, I called them and asked how they would train someone to be a lawyer, who could work in the Department of Justice. The answer ended up being a logical one. As this was not a career that could be started by on-the-job training, they would pay the cost of individuals, who showed some acumen at the law, to attend law school. The folks who ran the program were quite willing to think outside the box.

Based on my previous three years of work, I was judged to be someone who might succeed at law. If nothing else, I had broken the trail for others who might also want to go this route. It was very rare that anyone would be admitted to a law school without some successful prior attendance at a university. So, I started at the University of Regina. I enjoyed attending the courses and did well that first semester. I particularly enjoyed the courses in history. I also took two political science courses to study communism. If I was going to deal, in the future, with the gang that had taken over the Indian Brotherhood, I wanted to understand them better. Most, if not all of them, were peddling communist ideas to the Dene of the North. Included in the ideas was a strong anti-free-enterprise message. A lot of Dene took the message to heart and began opposing many of the small businesses that were owned by Métis individuals. I am told that the Indian Brotherhood kept a good supply of Mao's *Little Red Book* on hand to be distributed in the communities.

Another thing that I found interesting, and appreciated, while I attended university was being just another face in the crowd. I was no longer a big fish in a small pond. In fact, I was now the opposite—a very small fish in a very big pond.

∞

Bea and I became engaged before I left for university, and we decided to get married during the Christmas break and then move to Regina with the girls. We were married on December 10, 1977, in Saint Patrick's Roman Catholic Church in Yellowknife by Father Felix Labatt. Because Bea had been previously married, she had to obtain a special dispensation from the bishop "who cared." Getting the dispensation took some time, but we had it by the time I got back to Yellowknife. What had happened to me in Grollier Hall was shoved way down in the back of my mind. Bea and I really wanted to be a good Roman Catholic family, and we tried our best. The children were baptized, with some cajoling from Mama, and they attended Catholic schools. We attended Sunday masses. I did not realize how the abuse that I had suffered was eating away at me. While I never talked to anyone, including Bea, about it, the demon was beginning to stir, and I was drinking too much. Hindsight, hindsight, if only I and the other boys had been properly counselled at the time of the court proceedings fifteen years earlier, I might have been able to deal with what was happening to me.

Rick and Bea Hardy's wedding photo. Credit: Hardy Family Collection.

∞

One happy event took place. Because we were finally married, I was able to adopt Candy as my daughter, and we changed her last name to Hardy. Candy and I have had some differences over the years, but there has never been any doubt in either of our minds—she is my daughter, and I am her dad. Nurture overcame nature. We love each other very much.

Bea and the girls flew to Regina near the end of December and I drove our truck with our personal belongings and met them there a few days later. I continued with my studies and Bea enrolled in the BA program in the spring. I was driven and wanted to get on to law school. Our original plan was to spend two years at the University of Regina, after which I would try for a law school to accept me. That meant that I might be able to start law school in the fall of 1979.

At the time, the University of Saskatchewan in Saskatoon had started what was called the Program of Legal Studies for Native People. The program's primary purpose was to increase the number of Indigenous students attending law schools in Canada. The establishment of the program was spearheaded by Professor Roger Carter, QC, a man who helped me tremendously when I finally got into law school. Roger had been the dean at the College of Law for a number of years. He used to love to tell the story of the federal election when he ran for the NDP against John Diefenbaker. Of course, Diefenbaker routed him and the other candidates. The punchline of the story was that Diefenbaker phoned Roger after the election and told him that he shouldn't feel so bad—after all, he had beaten the Liberal. Roger would always laugh loudly at this point in the story.

Candy and Rick Hardy at a Métis Nation AGM.
Credit: Hardy Family Collection.

∞

The main focus of the Native Law Centre at that time was the summer program. The summer program was a six-week semester that compressed, in a reasonable way, the first semester of a first-year law program. The courses were taught to students accepted into the program by law school professors from across Canada. These professors basically gave their time, and I really appreciate what they did. I applied to the program, and, to my great surprise, I was accepted. To be accepted into the program, applicants had to get a reasonably good mark on the Law School Admission Test (LSAT). I wrote the test and did well, thanks to a number of mathematics-oriented questions. I did have an acumen for mathematics despite my inability to pass math 20 in high school. This meant that I had to move to Saskatoon for the summer and stay in the single students' housing on campus. As a result, I experienced what it would have been like to have attended university when I was younger and single. Bea enrolled for the summer semester in Regina and continued her studies there. Candy and Anna stayed with her, and we had a sitter to look after them.

The summer program in Saskatoon was tough. Approximately twenty of us attended the program, and of that number, only five of us were recommended for full-time attendance at a law school. I received a conditional acceptance to the College of Law at the University of Saskatchewan.

It was a tough year. Bea and I were struggling with our marriage because of what I was turning into—a heavy drinker and a womanizer. I really hurt Bea. Attending law school was difficult, but it became a convenient escape from the personal problems I should have been dealing with. I worked very hard. To continue from first year to second year, students needed to have at least a 50 percent mark in each course and an overall average of not less than 60 percent. I failed Real Property and my average was just shy of 60 percent. I had to rewrite all my exams if I wanted to raise my marks and get into the second year. I was in a panic. Everybody, or so I thought, in the North was watching me. I could not go home as a failure. I especially could not embarrass Mama like that.

So, I signed up to rewrite the exams and spent most of the summer studying. I rewrote the exams for all the courses, squeaked out a pass in Real Property, and got my average up to just over 60 percent. The movie *Paper Chase* was relatively new at the time, and it was a favourite of first-year law students because its portrayal was so accurate. The professors kept our feet to the fire to see if we had the acumen, strength and stamina to make it as a lawyer. Once I started second year, it got a bit easier. Somebody suggested that it might be the fact that I only spent a bit more than a year in undergraduate work that made the first year so difficult for me, the reasoning being that more time in the BA program would have taught me better research and study skills. Nonetheless I pressed on, and third year, while not a breeze, went much smoother than the first two years. However, in the process I had destroyed our marriage. For that I am eternally sorry.

∞

Of course, life was carrying on in the North. The Métis, now under the leadership of Charlie Overvold, had completed and presented their version of what a land claim might look like to the Government of Canada, in September, 1977. It was high on principles but weak on detail. The struggle between the Métis and the Dene continued under new Métis leaders. Ideas were being discussed about how to bring the two people together for the purpose of negotiating the land-claim agreement. I was hired by the next Métis president, Richard McNeely, for a six-week period in the summer of 1979 to work on a constitution for the new organization. Prior to bringing me "back," the Métis purchased a 50 percent interest in a downtown building for a new headquarters.

A federal election was called for May 22, 1979. To the surprise of a great number of people, Georges Erasmus, the president of what was now called the Dene Nation, sought the nomination of the NDP and won it. The Dene Nation was previously known as the Indian Brotherhood. The name change took place in 1978. Erasmus faced Dave Nickerson, a mining engineer and former territorial councillor from Yellowknife, and David Searle in the election. Georges garnered only 29 percent of the vote. Dave Nickerson, representing the Progressive Conservatives, was elected. David Searle was embittered for a number of years over losing the election. He was, however, pleased to be able to say, somewhat like Roger Carter, that he beat Erasmus, with a second-place showing, only 231 votes behind Nickerson. David decided to leave the North after that. When I returned to Yellowknife in 1981, he was just moving to Vancouver to join Davis and Company and head up its mining practice group. Little did we know how our paths would cross again in the future.

I continued my support for the Métis cause while in law school. My major paper was "Métis Rights in the Mackenzie River District of the Northwest Territories." I earned my highest mark in law school for that paper, and it was published in the *Canadian Native Law Reporter* in 1980. My minor paper was about the *Indian Act* and Section 12 and the Custom of the Band. Bea was a great help to me in writing the papers. I could not type very well, so while she was doing my typing, she also cleaned up the grammar and the punctuation. She was also not afraid to challenge some of my ideas.

Bea completed her studies at the end of December 1980. She had earned her bachelor's degree, majoring in psychology. She returned to Yellowknife with Candy while Anna Marie stayed with me in Saskatoon. My sister, Diane, and her husband, Larry Gordon, and their children were living in Saskatoon at the time, and Diane looked after Anna during the day while I was in classes. Larry was completing his bachelor of education degree. Convocation, for Bea and me, was in May 1981. Bea flew down from Yellowknife for it, and we picked up our degrees together. Mama also flew down from Fort Norman, and I was so proud that she was there to see us graduate. Of course, she was also bursting with pride. Additionally, Mama finally got to go to Batoche and see the site of the Métis' last stand. Batoche was just a two-hour drive from Saskatoon, and we made a day

Alice Hardy at Batoche, holding her granddaughter Anna Marie's hand. Next to Anna are Aaron and Stewart Gordon, also Mama's grandchildren. The boy at the end was a friend of Aaron and Stewart's when they lived in Saskatoon. Credit: Hardy Family Collection.

PART V

trip of it. She was amazed that the church still held so many bullet holes from shots fired by the Canadian soldiers. Anna Marie would have been four years old at that time and was very attached to Mama. She remembers being with Mama but doesn't remember that she and I drove back to Yellowknife through Banff and Jasper a few weeks later.

One of the good things that happened to me while I was in law school was quitting smoking. I had been a two-pack-a-day smoker. The stress of studies was getting to me, and every time I lit up a cigarette, I would throw up. I finally said, "Okay, God, I get the message," and I quit—cold turkey. It took about six years to finally get rid of the nicotine cravings, and now I can't stand the smell of tobacco smoke, or that other kind of smoke!

Once I graduated, I was no longer supported by the Northern Careers Program. I was fine with that, as I really appreciated all that they had done for us to see me through to my degree. If I wanted to practice law, I needed to find a lawyer who would accept me as a student, and I needed to work in that position for twelve months. Of course, there were also quite a few articling courses that I needed to pass and seminars that I needed to attend during that year.

Before returning to the North, I seriously thought of staying in Saskatchewan. I would have done my articles there and joined a firm in Saskatoon. It would have been a clean start for me, and hopefully, also for Bea and the girls. We really enjoyed living in Saskatoon. I still didn't realize that it didn't matter where I was. I needed to face my devils. On the other hand, I knew that a lot of people from back home had cheered me on and expected me to return. So, I did.

∞

I had offers from the two largest firms in Yellowknife. I accepted the one from Cooper, Johnson and Wilson based on the amount of money that they were willing to pay me, as well as my personal affinity for Don Cooper. I knew Don before I went to law school. He had recently divorced his first wife and was dating Bea's sister, Marlene. Don realized I was no ordinary student, as I was able to attract a lot of business to the firm based on my family's history in the NWT. I completed my articles and was called to the bar of the Northwest Territories on June 14, 1982. I was thirty-five years old, married, and had three children. Our third child, James Joseph Peter, had been born on April 27, 1982. In honour of Aunt Jane's prediction, made when I was a child, that someday I would wear a grey suit to work, I bought one and did just that.

The Honourable Justice Mark deWeert, QC, who had been the Hardy family's lawyer many years earlier, conducted my call. He spoke highly of me and his expectations for me as a lawyer.

Many years later, Bea told me that she had intended to leave me when we returned to Yellowknife, but when she became pregnant with James, she changed her mind. She also told me, a few years later, that we had separated for a short period when we got back to Yellowknife. I honestly have no recollection of that happening.

L to R: Rick Hardy, Mr. Justice M. M. deWeert, QC, Donald M. Cooper, QC. Credit: Hardy Family Collection.

L to R: Candy, Bea (with James), Rick (with Anna) Hardy, Mr. Justice M.M. deWeert, QC, after the call to the NWT bar. Credit: Hardy Family Collection.

CHAPTER TWENTY-ONE
PRACTICING LAW

I was carrying a full practice by the end of my articles, so I hit the road running. Once someone gets called to the bar, the banks are more than willing to loan them money. Early in 1983 we bought our first house. It was a nice-looking two-storey house in School Draw. It had a beautiful flower garden and vegetable garden in the backyard beside a creek that emptied into Great Slave Lake. There was also a white picket fence around the front yard. Shades of growing up in Fort Norman. We were able to lease a brand-new vehicle. We also bought a cabin at Walsh Lake, just outside of Yellowknife. Of course, we needed a snowmobile to get to it in the winter and a boat and motor to get to it in the summer. It seemed as if we had arrived. Bea was working as the executive assistant to Dennis Patterson, who was the Minister of Education at the time. It didn't take long for me to be offered a partnership in the firm. I was a rainmaker and a hard worker. We had all the trappings of material success.

My parents celebrated their fiftieth wedding anniversary in July 1984. The Hardy boys were all doing well in their businesses, and we put on a big dinner, with wine, for the whole community of Fort Norman following Mama and Daddy's renewal of their vows at a mass at the Saint Teresa of Avila Church. At the time, I did not know that Mama was dying from cancer. She only lived another six months. By Christmas she was a permanent patient at the Yellowknife Hospital. We did our best to make it a happy Christmas for everyone. By then Leo and his family were living in Yellowknife, and Diane and Larry were back in Inuvik. Rod continued to live in Fort Norman. All of them flew to Yellowknife, and Bea put on a great Christmas dinner at our house. I think this was the only time that we were all together, so we got some photos. A problem taking family group photos is someone has to press the button. Fortunately for us, our cousin, Charlie Gaudet, was with us and he did the honours.

Mama passed on near the end of December 1984. I clearly remember being told that she was dead. I knew she was going to die, but it still hurt in the extreme. Physically, it was as if I had been clubbed with a baseball bat. I fell to the floor. She would have turned seventy-three years old in just a few weeks. I was furious that she had been taken just when she was beginning to enjoy her grandchildren and see her children succeed in life, and she no longer had to work so hard. In hindsight, I can see

L to R: Cecilia (Blondin) Hodgson, Alice (Gaudet) Hardy, Jack Hardy and Hib Hodgson, in Fort Norman, July 1934. Credit: Hardy Family Collection.

now that it was likely a good thing that she died then, as we were about to come apart at the seams as a family. I am not talking about just Bea and me but about the entire family.

Jack and Alice (Gaudet) Hardy at the Hardy's fiftieth wedding anniversary party in Fort Norman in July 1984. Credit: Hardy Family Collection (Elizabeth Hardy).

Alice (Gaudet) Hardy and Jack Hardy - wedding picture, July 1934. Credit: Hardy Family Collection.

We chartered a twin Otter from Yellowknife to bring her body home for burial in the old Anglican graveyard beside her parents and Walter, as well as various other family members. It was a relatively mild day for January, and we had a blazing sunset all the way there during the three-hour flight. It was as if God was guiding her home. The funeral was held the next day, and the church was filled to overflowing. I collapsed again during the final viewing of the body at the end of the High Mass. Bea was with me and the children, and she held me up until we got back to our pew. I was an emotional basket case. Mama was gone.

Jack and Alice (Gaudet) Hardy on the church steps after renewing their vows to celebrate their fiftieth wedding anniversary. Credit: Hardy Family Collection (Elizabeth Hardy).

Hardy family gathering at Christmas 1984, a week before Mama died in Yellowknife. Credit: Hardy Family Collection.

We returned to Yellowknife. Business was booming, but our marriage was imploding. Later, in 1985, Bea and I formally separated and sold our house and the cabin. I agreed that Bea should have full custody of the children, and I paid a generous amount of support every month. I took full responsibility for what happened. After about a year, we reconciled and bought another house, this time on Latham Island. While my drinking continued to get worse, unfortunately, so did Bea's. About three years after we reconciled, our marriage collapsed permanently. We were drinking and fighting and were being awful parents. We separated again. We were able to work out a separation agreement with the help of our lawyers, and it was completed on March 25, 1991.

During this time, the Dene and Métis had also reconciled and were working together to bring a joint land-claim agreement forward while maintaining their separate existence. They worked through what was called the Dene/Métis Negotiations Secretariat. The claim would be called the "Dene/Métis Comprehensive Land Claim Agreement." Former members and supporters of the Dene Nation were now gravitating to the government they were supposed to be against and becoming career civil servants in the government of the NWT. I was in the thick of it, acting as legal counsel to what was now called the "Métis Nation – Northwest Territory," under the leadership of Gary Bohnet. The workload, my marriage difficulties, and my drinking were all pushing me to the edge.

I accepted that I was an alcoholic and recognized that I needed professional help. I applied to go to Henwood, which was a well-regarded alcohol rehabilitation centre south of Edmonton. I was accepted, but it took three tries for me to get there. On the first attempt, I was unable to maintain the required five days of sobriety prior to starting the program. I was able to do the sobriety thing on the second try but got cold feet at the airport just before I was to fly to Edmonton. My spiral continued. I had started a new relationship with a long-time friend and, within a short period of time, wrecked both the relationship and the friendship in a blackout. That really shook me and forced me to look even more seriously at myself. I finally managed another five days of sobriety and got to Henwood on April 8, 1990. My road to recovery would continue the next morning at 9:00 a.m.

∞

A humorous event occurred as I was about to leave for the airport in Yellowknife on April 8. The Dene/Métis were trying to salvage the collapsing land-claim agreement, and they were

PART V

229

in the second week of joint leadership meetings. The meeting that day was being held in the community gym in Ndilo, which is the Indian village at the south end of Yellowknife. I stopped in at the meeting to say goodbye and tell some close friends where I was going and why. Of course, most of them were part of the Métis leadership group. Then I left for the Yellowknife airport. Following that, one of my nemeses, from over the years, who was a very suspicious person, began telling people that I had secretly left for Ottawa and was going there to negotiate a separate deal for the Métis. I understand that this individual remained convinced, for a long period of time, that this is what had happened.

The last thing on my mind, once I got to Henwood was the Dene/Métis Comprehensive Land Claim Agreement. I didn't know that when I checked in, my life was going to be saved in the next three weeks. I had reached that proverbial point of either dying or sobering up. Interestingly, the patients lived in open dormitories that were similar to those used in the residences in Inuvik. We lined up for meals, made our own beds, had chores, and kept to strict schedules. We even had numbers—mine was 23. If nothing else, I felt that my life was getting back to some semblance of organization.

The hard part was looking at myself honestly. I started in the Alcoholics Anonymous program and admitted my shortcomings and all the harm I had caused to everyone around me. The AA meetings were held in the evenings. During the day we took part in different types of sessions, usually in small groups. It was a three-week program, and it was difficult. We drilled down into my life honestly and in detail. Near the end of the second week, I had a breakthrough. The words "Martin Houston" and "sexual abuse" started coming out of my mouth. I was shocked, as I had buried what had happened to me in alcohol, workaholism, and other inappropriate behaviour. It had been thirty years since I was first molested by Martin Houston and twenty-eight years since my court appearance as a witness. I had spoken to no one about it other than Mike in our drunken stupors, which I could not remember. Now, the dam was open, and the words poured out. I was forty-three years old.

∞

I completed the rehabilitation program and returned to Yellowknife. I knew I had to make some serious changes to the way I lived if I wanted to stay sober. The biggest problem that I had to deal with on my return, in addition to custody of Anna and James, was my law partnership. When I joined the firm, I helped build it up, and we had bought an office building right across from the courthouse. We added a third floor onto the building and renovated the first two. We included a separate posh room that was called the lounge. It was always well stocked with liquor. Some of us were heavy drinkers, and this led to an eventual breakup of the partnership, which coincided with my marital problems. I had driven home many an evening impaired as a result of stopping in the "lounge" after work for a "quick" one that turned into too many "quick" ones.

Because of the breakup of the partnership and my continued sobriety, I gradually began to feel that I no longer fitted in. However, I did not want to leave the firm immediately out of loyalty to my remaining partners. The firm had survived the breakup of the partnership, but it would be a terrible blow if I were to leave so soon. The firm was now known as Cooper, Hardy & Regal. Another problem that I had with leaving the firm was our partnership agreement. If I did not refrain from private practice in Yellowknife for a period of two years, my buy-out would be significantly reduced. I did not want to leave Yellowknife because of the custody dispute over Anna and James, which was now part of the divorce proceedings that the separation agreement had turned into.

Cooper, Hardy and Regel and associates, students, and staff, shortly before Rick Hardy left the firm. Credit: Donald M. Cooper, QC.

A break for me came in mid-1991 when the government of the NWT and all of the Native groups of the western part of the then-Northwest Territories agreed to form a Commission for Constitutional Development to lay out the basis for governing what would be left of the Northwest Territories after Nunavut was created. I was nominated as the representative of the Métis Nation – Northwest Territory. The commission was formally created in June 1991 and was chaired by the late Jim Bourque. Jim was a Métis originally from northern Alberta who had spent most of his life in the NWT. Jim worked his way up in the government of the NWT to become the deputy minister of the department of renewable resources. He had also served a term as the president of the Métis Nation in the early 1980s and was well regarded by most people in the NWT.

Don Cooper and Rick Hardy. Credit: Donald M. Cooper, QC.

We were given a timeline during which we were to deliver an interim report to be followed by a final report, both within a period of two years, at the end of June 1993. It was almost a full-time retainer for me and would run out the clock on my non-compete covenant with my old partners. I would not have to leave Yellowknife, and I would be doing work that I enjoyed. More importantly, I would be near my children - James was nine years old, Anna was fourteen, and Candy was twenty.

That was a great plan. We delivered our interim report in April 1992, and then the premier, my fiend Nellie Courneya, pulled the plug on us. The GNWT was funding the entire process, and she thought we had reached too far to the sky to try to satisfy everyone. When I was doing the research for this book, I searched the Internet for information on the commission's work. There was none to be found. The only mention of it was in connection with Jim Bourque having been the chairperson. Even though Nellie might not have liked the interim report, the commission did do lots of good legal research. I wonder where it all is.

The commission had six members: Jim Bourque, George Braden, Francois Paulette, Bertha Allen, Les Carpenter, and me. Sadly, only Francois and I are still alive. All six of us had high profiles in the NWT and were well respected. Francois was the chief of the Fort Smith Dene in the late 1960s and early 1970s. He was the Paulette in *Re: Paulette*, the court case that led to the decades-long negotiations for a comprehensive land-claim agreement.

So, with about fifteen months left in my non-compete covenant, I was unemployed and unemployable in Yellowknife. I had to leave, and the question was where to? I had three offers from law firms in Vancouver, including Davis & Company. The firms all wanted me to buttress their Aboriginal law practice groups. The problem was, I still didn't know if I would have custody of one or more of my children.

The negotiations for the divorce agreement were not going well, so I had filed a petition asking for custody of Anna and James before I left for Henwood. The day that I started the program at Henwood, Bea filed a counter-petition, also asking for custody of Anna and James. Included in her petition was a damning affidavit by her about my behaviour, including physical abuse against her by me. There was truth to the allegations. However, they were exaggerated.

The timing was coincidental with the breakup of the law partnership. One of the disgruntled departing partners made a bad choice. That partner got a copy of Bea's affidavit from the courthouse, copied it a number of times, slipped the copies into unmarked brown envelopes, and delivered them, anonymously, to all the banks in Yellowknife and other major clients of our firm. Fortunately for us, most of the bankers sent the copies and envelopes that they were in to us. The other banks and the other clients also did so eventually. Don Cooper then obtained an order from the court to seal the file, so this could not happen again. We filed a complaint with the Law Society about the conduct of the lawyer in question. After a hearing, he received a thirty-day suspension.

When I returned to Yellowknife, after completing the program at Henwood, we agreed to set the court proceedings aside and jointly retained a psychologist to do home studies and assess all of us: Bea, Anna, James, and me. The psychologist recommended joint custody of both of the children, provided that Anna was sent to a private boarding school. We agreed, and that got us through the next year and a half. So, Anna was off to Queen Margaret's School (QMS) in Duncan, BC, and James lived with Bea and spent most weekends with me. We had sold the Latham Island house in the fall of 1989. Bea and I had each found places to rent for ourselves.

Anna did very well during her first year at QMS (1991/1992). I travelled back and forth to Duncan to visit her quite often. I was very impressed with the school, and Anna was happy. Our lives seemed to be stabilized, except that Bea's drinking continued to escalate. By that point I had maintained sobriety since leaving Henwood. Anna returned to QMS the next year for grade nine but only lasted until Christmas. I was still in Yellowknife working as an "employee" primarily for the

PART V

233

Sah-Tu Dene Metis Council, helping them prepare to submit a land-claim agreement to Canada for negotiation. I was also "employed" by the Metis Nation – Northwest Territory as an advisor with regard to the Charlottetown Accord negotiations which led to the national referendum in October 1992.

∞

By early October 1992, I concluded that Bea's lifestyle had become completely inappropriate for James. I moved ahead with the divorce and asked for custody of James. The divorce proceedings had been put on hold as a result of the custody agreement. Anna had changed and made it clear that she did not want to live with me. The legal battle was on, again, and I moved to Edmonton in early 1993 by myself. In May 1993 we retained the same psychologist to assess us, once again. The psychologist's report, dated July 15, 1993, reads, in part:

> *In talking to Rick, it became quite evident that there is a tremendous amount of anger that is still directed towards Bea . . . Probably the most difficult part of this file, is that the parties have not been able to disengage from each other. Certainly, the anger evidenced in Rick's voice in speaking about Bea supports this observation.*

What I was most angry about was forcing James to, in effect, choose between the two of us. Of course, I was not the most objective person in the room, as I completely blamed Bea for not seeing the need for James to live with me. The psychologist had been retained, this time, just to advise on what would be best for James in terms of custody. She recommended that I have sole custody of James. Looking back, I can now see what a horrible experience it was for James, having to, in effect, decide which parent he wanted to live with. James was a gentle person, and he loved both of us dearly. I think it is very likely that the experience contributed significantly to James's difficulties later in life. I can't help but feel guilty about my part in the whole tragedy.

At the time I did not understand how much the negative experiences of my childhood and the failure of my first real love had shaped me. I was extremely jealous and insecure. With the benefit of hindsight, I can see that there was no need for these feelings with Bea. However, they were there, and they blinded me.

A few years later, Bea and I were able to sit down, without anyone else being there, and talk rationally about what had happened to us. I owned up to my bad behaviours and asked for her forgiveness, which she gave to me.

Both of us had spent many years in residential schools, and neither of us had the tools to be proper parents. Based on my time at home with my parents, my own view was that the mother should stay at home and raise the children, and the husband should work hard to support the family.

∞

I bought a house in Edmonton, and James joined me there for the start of the school year in September 1993. My non-compete period was up, but I wanted to make a fresh start with James and still had hopes that Anna might come to live with us. Unfortunately for me, Anna preferred to stay with Bea.

Our divorce was finalized later that year. I read an article in the *Toronto Star* a year earlier that was titled: "Years after divorce, friends at last." I kept the article as a source of inspiration and hope that Bea and I would eventually become friends again. We did after time dulled the hurt that we both suffered. Bea contracted MS but, unfortunately, continued her drinking. She did have periods of sobriety, but she could not hold on to it. When my open letter was published in January 1998, she sent me a note, saying, "Let the healing begin." She was still alive when I remarried, and she wished me well. We talked occasionally, and she would ask about my new wife, Maryann, in a kind way. Bea died in February 2013, and I was there with the children at her bedside. I spoke at her funeral at the Sacred Heart Church in Edmonton. I still have the article from the *Toronto Star*.

∞

When I was mulling over the offers from the three firms in Vancouver, I realized that Vancouver was too large of a city to bring James to. So, I decided that I needed to find a place to practice law that was closer to Yellowknife and not as overwhelming as Vancouver. I contacted a lawyer whom I had worked with in recent years. His name is Fred Martin, and I had the highest respect for his ability as a lawyer and as a human being. Fred was a partner in the Ackroyd firm in Edmonton. After being interviewed by the firm's managing partner, Sean Day, I was offered an associate's position. Ackroyd's had a significant Aboriginal law practice in western and northern Canada. Consequently, my practice fit well with theirs. My largest client, by far, at the time was the Sahtu Tribal Council, the new name of the Sah-Tu Dene Métis Council.

I was a member of Northwest Territories bar, so I was able to work for clients who were located there. However, if I wanted

PART V

235

to practice with Alberta clients, I needed to become a member of the Alberta bar. My confidence was not high, but I hit the books and studied. I didn't realize how much I had absorbed about the law since 1981, but most of it was still there. I passed all the requirements for admission in Alberta on the first try and was called to the Alberta bar in Edmonton in May 1993. Once James moved to be with me in the fall of that year, I thought I would be making my life permanently in Edmonton. James was doing well in school and hockey, and he had made some friends in our new neighbourhood. However, I was travelling too much to the Northwest Territories in connection with my practice. I was always able to get good babysitters, but I was worried about the effect that all of this would eventually have on James. We spent a comfortable year in Edmonton during the 1993/1994 school year.

PART VI

STARTING OVER

Maryann and Rick shortly after they met. Credit: Hardy Family Collection.

PART VI

239

CHAPTER TWENTY-TWO

RETURN TO THE NORTH

When James finished the school year in June 1994, he went to spend the summer with Bea in Yellowknife, leaving me to think about our future. James was beginning to drop hints about wanting to move back to Yellowknife, and I sympathized with him. Ackroyd's made it clear that if I wanted to join their partnership, I would be welcomed.

Then came an unexpected development. David Searle contacted me and told me that Davis & Company had decided to open a Northwest Territories office in Yellowknife. Davis had already opened a Yukon office in Whitehorse and wanted to become the lawyers for the North. David said that Davis wanted me to become the managing lawyer of the Yellowknife office. I flew to Vancouver to meet some of the other potential partners and to see what sort of compensation I would be looking at. I was very happy with the breadth of skill and knowledge that the Davis partners could offer. I was also quite happy with the offer of compensation.

So, with a lot of sadness, I told my friends at Ackroyd's that I was going back home. I returned to Yellowknife for the start of the school year and rented a large four-bedroom house on the edge of the downtown area. No, I wasn't planning on running a boarding house, but that was all that was available. Yellowknife was in diamond boom mode, so housing was hard to come by. This boom was the primary reason for Davis wanting to open the office in Yellowknife. David Searle was one of the primary legal advisers to BHP, which would be the first mining company to get a diamond mine approved and opened in the NWT. I played a role, in the background, providing legal advice on aboriginal law issues.

Coincidentally, Candy was looking for a place to live, after having completed her bachelor's degree in Native studies at the University of Saskatchewan, and she moved in with James and me. Anna would occasionally stay for a few days at a time. Bea was slipping further and further into homelessness, so she would show up occasionally to use one of the downstairs bedrooms. She struggled to maintain sobriety, to no avail. Even if we were dysfunctional, we would sometimes all be together as a family.

I opened up the office for Davis & Company on the eighth floor of the Northwestel Tower and went to work. Now that I was back in Yellowknife, a number of old clients moved their business to my new firm. I was also very fortunate that one of the paralegals who had worked for me at Cooper's joined me and took charge of the administration of the practice. Her name is Debbie Moss. It was our good fortune that Debbie agreed to join us. During all the years that I practiced law I was fortunate to have nothing but excellent support workers. I did my best to treat them decently, and this helped our working relationships.

∞

In a short period of time, I attracted a new client—Northwestel. Up to that point, the company had most of its legal work done in house, in Whitehorse, where its head office was located. However, the lawyer who did that work was leaving, and the company wanted someone with a lot of northern experience. As a result of this need, the company, in the person of the president and CEO, Bill Dunbar, decided to offer me a contract, through Davis & Company, to be their corporate secretary and maintain their legal records. Bill's Yellowknife office was three floors up from mine, and one day, he appeared at our reception desk and asked to see me. Fortunately, I was in and had the time. I started a ten-year engagement as the corporate secretary for the company. I think I did a good job. I learned a lot of new things while doing my work, and I tremendously enjoyed my time with the company. A lot of what I learned about the telecommunications industry came from Murray Makin, who was the chairman of the board and CEO during my first few years. Of course, I already had the skills needed to carry out the duties of a corporate secretary.

Coincidentally, David Searle was on the board of Northwestel before I was hired, and this continued during my tenure. He was quite surprised that I had obtained the contract without his knowledge. After I retired and moved to Atlin, BC, at the end of 2005, the company moved the job back in house. However, to my great surprise, I was then asked to join the board of directors. I accepted the invitation and spent ten years on the board. So, what I had learned from Murray Makin came to benefit the company after all. During my time on the board, we had an excellent president named Paul Flaherty, who eventually assumed the CEO role as well. Sadly, Paul passed away while still living in Whitehorse after I finished my time on the board.

I had spent close to twelve years with Davis & Company, and it was a great experience. I was well treated and learned a lot from the other members of the firm. Davis featured me in a 2005 publication of the history of the firm, titled *Davis & Company Partners in History*. With the successor firm's kind permission, I now reproduce what was published:

PART VI

Davis & Company writeup about Rick Hardy.
Credit: Davis LLP.

Although my years as a "practicing" lawyer were cut short by cancer and depression, I thoroughly enjoyed those years with all three firms that I was a member of: Cooper Johnson, Ackroyds, and Davis. I made many lifelong friends and continually learned more about the law with each new file that I took on.

∞

Daddy was living in the Avens Senior Centre in Yellowknife by this time. I was forty-seven years old, and he was ninety-one. By living in Yellowknife, I got to spend more time with him, and he saw his grandchildren a lot. Diane's son, Stewart, had also moved to Yellowknife and was a tremendous help to Daddy. In the summertime I would take Daddy out for boat rides up the Yellowknife River, which he really enjoyed. We would also go out for dinner from time to time. After a while I didn't have to ask him where he wanted to go. It was always the Red Apple, and he would order fresh pickerel, pan-fried. After he died, I would sometimes go to the Red Apple and have the pickerel just to remember him. He died on March 1, 1997, at the age of ninety-five. He was quite healthy up until a few months before he died, when dementia began to set in. He really wanted to live to a hundred. As with Mama, we flew his body home to Fort Norman, and he was laid to rest beside her. I had his headstone engraved with the following words: "A Man Who Came From Away, He Chose To Spend His Life With Us, And Helped To Build Our Community."

During the last few years of his life, Daddy got to meet and spend time with his grandson, Maurice Blake, who is Walter's son. While he was growing up, Maurice did not know who his father was. When he did grow up, he wanted to get married but also wanted to be sure that he wasn't marrying a close blood relative. He went to see his birth mother, Annie Cook, from Fort Good Hope and explained that he wanted to know who his father was and why he needed to know. She told him that his father was Walter Hardy from Fort Norman. I said earlier in the book that we don't know if Walter knew about Maurice when he drowned in 1965. As far as I know, no one in the family knew. Maurice was born on December 7, 1961. If I remember correctly, Annie worked at Grollier Hall, either at or after that time. Walter would have been twenty years old when he fathered Maurice, so I would assume that she was still living in Fort Good Hope at the time. Maybe she was working at the PWA hotel in Norman Wells. In any event, Annie gave Maurice to her sister, Jane, who was married to John Blake, and they lived in Fort McPherson, where Maurice grew up. After Maurice learned who his father was, he began reaching out, tentatively, to his birth family. I think the first contact would have been with Rod. Before he began looking for us, I knew Maurice through my legal work with the Métis and found him easy to get along with. When I found out that he was my nephew, I welcomed him to the family. However, Rod, while he was alive, was the main contact for the relationship.

Alice (Gaudet) Hardy's grave on the right, Jack Hardy's on the left and Ray Overvolds in the background. Taken after Bob Overvold and Rick Hardy cleaned up the family graves in the old Anglican graveyard in 2020. Credit: Author.

Maurice and his oldest daughter, Charlene, came to Fort Norman for Daddy's funeral. Just before I started the eulogy, I introduced them to the community as Walter's son and granddaughter and welcomed them as members of our family. We had a picture of Daddy, in whites, playing a guitar as a young man in Fort Norman, placed on top of the casket. Once the funeral was over, we gave the picture to Charlene, who was very happy to receive it.

I was very happy to have helped Maurice get the closure that he needed before Daddy died. Maurice and his children, from his second marriage, have all become members of the Fort Norman Métis Community, creating closer ties with those of us who are left.

I was able to find a number of things that belonged to Walter while I was cleaning up the family property in 2020, including his traps, which I gave to Maurice. I hope those items bring him some comfort.

∞

In the spring of 1997, I was about to turn fifty years old. It was nine years since I had gone through the treatment program at Henwood. Unfortunately, I did not maintain my sobriety. However, I was mellowing out and was no longer the angry young man that I had been. I had grown the Yellowknife office of Davis & Company by hiring local lawyers as well as two students. We had a lot of good clients, and the future looked solid from a business perspective. I continued to represent a number of Aboriginal groups, and our Vancouver office continued to act for a number of mining companies. Sometimes, this clash of interests created some tensions, but we were able to manage it.

In 1998, the pressure for governments to acknowledge and settle the claims for abuse, sexual and otherwise, of students who attended residential schools continued to grow. This affected me both personally and professionally. There was a terrible event in the offing that would shake me to my core.

One of the local lawyers that I had hired was named Charles McGee. I had known Charles and his mother for many years, starting in Inuvik when I was going to school. The family was originally from England and were staunch Catholics. Charles was a litigator, while my practice was that of a solicitor—business law. The Grollier Hall group of abused students had hired me to advise and represent them in the upcoming negotiations, but I was not comfortable doing that. On the one hand, the Survivors were comfortable with me, as most of them knew me personally, and they saw me as someone who had suffered just as they had. On the other hand, I was also a Survivor, and my claim would be advanced through the process that I was advising on. As lawyers, we are taught from the start that a lawyer who represents himself has a fool for a client. The Survivors all knew Charles as well and were comfortable with him, at least to begin with. So, I transferred the files to Charles and stepped back.

It appeared that Charles was really throwing himself into the challenge and was making progress. I thought we had the right lawyer, as he was a pillar in the community, certainly in the Catholic community. He, his wife, and his mother were regular attendees at the Catholic church, and he was the director of the choir. He was doing well in the firm, and we offered him a partnership, which he accepted.

He and his mother were thrilled, and we had a celebratory barbeque at his house when David Searle was next in town. The offer of the partnership was not fully acted on when the roof caved in. We were advised that Charles was being investigated by the RCMP for sexual crimes committed against young girls. The alleged offences were claimed to have taken place over a number of decades, starting in Inuvik. We were shocked, and Charles denied all the charges. My instincts told me that what we had been told was likely true. I was very upset on both a personal and a professional level. We could not leave him on the Grollier Hall files under the circumstances. On a preliminary basis, the firm assigned a junior lawyer to maintain the files until we were able to find a lawyer with the right experience. The junior lawyer was very competent, but the Survivors were quite upset, and rightfully so. The managing partner of the firm at that time was Paul Albi, who worked from our Vancouver office. He took charge of sorting the issues out. That was a good decision, as Paul was not only bright but was also a person with a lot of empathy. He managed the situation well for all concerned, including the Survivors.

Charles's denials crumbled after he was charged with a number of offences. We withdrew our offer of a partnership, and we parted company with him. There was more than we were initially made aware of, and Charles was eventually disbarred and spent some time in jail. I believe he went to work for the Catholic diocese after he completed his jail time. I was not only extremely angry; I was extremely embarrassed. It was I who had brought Charles into the firm. I had mentored him, and I had put him on the Grollier Hall files. Some of the Survivors were also furious with me and the firm for putting Charles on their files. Some of this anger continues to this day. I certainly don't blame any Survivor for what they may feel and I extend my humblest of apologies to them, for my part in placing additional hurts on them.

Eventually, we were able to identify a very competent lawyer in the firm who had experience in settling such cases. That lawyer took over the files and reached settlements for almost all of the Survivors, including me.

The settlements were reached by using a negotiation agreement between the twenty-nine Survivors (represented by

PART VI

245

the Grollier Hall Residential School Healing Circle), the Roman Catholic Diocese of Mackenzie, the GNWT, and Canada. The negotiation agreement was entered into in early 1999 and the settlements were reached in mid 2002. The agreement set up a validation and redress process, which I discussed earlier in chapter fifteen. The process was made up of three phases. The first phase was the gathering of documents and other facts. The second phase was the appointment of an independent fact finder to review all of the facts that were gathered in phase one. The independent fact finder would also meet with any of the Survivors who wanted to tell their story, in private but in the presence of lawyers for the Church and the two governments. Once all of that was done, the fact finder would prepare a report that would be used by the parties to settle the compensation that would be paid to each individual Survivor taking part in the process.

The twenty-nine Survivors were all witnesses to the various criminal proceedings held for the four pedophiles who had been supervisors at Grollier Hall, including Martin Houston. Thus, the five of us who had been witnesses at the Houston preliminary hearing were included. Those who had already passed on, such as our friend Robert, were represented by their estates, in the person of close family members. The key to being included among the twenty-nine was that the individual had to have taken part, as a witness, in one of the criminal proceedings against the four pedophiles. Because all four pedophiles had either pleaded or been proven guilty, there would be no further dispute that the Survivors had been abused.

The independent fact finder agreed to by all the parties was Katherine Peterson of Yellowknife. Katherine was a well-known northern lawyer who was appointed as Queen's Counsel a few years later. My hearing was held on April 13, 2000. The hearing and the subsequent report were satisfactory to me. The most difficult aspect of the hearing was preparing for it. I, as with the other Survivors, was allowed to have a support person with me to provide emotional support. I was seeing a therapist at the time, and the Grollier Hall group urged me to let my therapist sit with me. I declined and, instead, asked Irene Roth to be my support person. Irene's maiden name was Clement, and she was Robert Clement's sister. Irene was very involved in the entire process up to that point, helping out wherever she was needed. I felt that she understood me better than my therapist, and she also needed to hear what I had to say, as much of what happened to me was similar to what happened to her brother. I am forever grateful to Irene for supporting me through this difficult time.

Katherine Peterson's report is confidential to the parties to the negotiation agreement. That is so,

> *. . . except that a claimant may choose to have the record of his own story included in any memorialization undertaken alone or in concert with other claimants.*

This book is my memorialization. Part IV of the report, which is titled "Effects and Consequences," is attached as Appendix E. The report concludes with the following:

> *During the course of the validation hearing, Rick was requested to provide some insight into his perspective of the effects and consequences of his Grollier Hall experiences. He was extremely articulate and candid in his evidence and he did not hesitate at times to indicate that it is difficult to determine in hindsight, exactly how his life would have been different had these events not occurred.*

This was certainly a long way from the frightened and reluctant fifteen-year-old being examined in a courtroom in Inuvik in September, 1962.

I received the report on October 3, 2001. Then it was on to phase three—the negotiations for compensation. I left the negotiations in the hands of our lawyers, and an offer was made by the co-disputants on May 30, 2002. I let it sit for a week as I thought about it. I accepted the offer on June 5, 2002. I am forbidden, by the final release and settlement, from disclosing what the amount of the settlement was. It took a few more months to pay the entire amount out, and then it was over—or so I thought.

There were more apologies and payments of compensation to come. In 2008, Murray Chatelain, the new Catholic bishop, apologized globally. This was after Prime Minister Stephen Harper rose in the House of Commons on June 11, 2008, to apologize to former students of residential schools on behalf of Canada. Then there were the Common Experience Payments in 2007 and the Day School payments in 2020. Notwithstanding all the apologies and the compensation, I am still emotionally damaged. I still have some temper problems. I still drink too much. I lack confidence. My relationships with my children and grandchildren are strained. I live in fear that manifests itself in my nightmares. A theme runs through my nightmares that I am a fake and will be caught soon. There are many times when I realize that I am still fourteen years old, from an emotional perspective. Will it end before I die? I don't know. What I do know is that my wife, Maryann, metaphorically holds my hand and does her best to protect me. Thank you, Maryann.

PART VI

CHAPTER TWENTY-THREE

MARYANN

Notwithstanding what I said in the introduction to this book, life is not singular and does not move in a straight line. While I was dealing with the issues in the previous chapter, I also had a lot of other things going on in my life.

I met the woman who would become my new wife. Her name is Maryann, and she has been the most important person in my life since we got married. We met online. Maryann was a schoolteacher in a small border town in the state of Washington, close to Osooyos, BC. She taught middle school. In the summer of 1997, she and another teacher drove from her home in Washington to Inuvik and then flew to Tuktoyaktuk to swim in the Arctic Ocean. Yes, she is adventurous. When she returned home, she posted a message on the Internet, which was a new phenomenon at the time, about her trip and her wish to travel to Yellowknife the following year, so she could paddle on Great Slave Lake. I responded, telling her that I lived in Yellowknife and could help her along when she got there. We corresponded by email for a few months and then talked on the telephone a number of times. Eventually, we agreed to meet in person.

∞

Before we met, in person, I went to a place that offered therapy called the Haven and took the "Come Alive" program. The Haven is located on Gabriola Island, which is near Nanaimo on Vancouver Island. The Come Alive program is five days long and is a combination of individual and group therapies. The program worked well for me, and I believe that, in my penultimate exercise, I came into contact with the Creator.

The exercise was to release my anxieties and began by relaxing my body with the use of soothing music and the calm voice of a guide. Once I was relaxed, I began to travel to and do things in what I thought were imaginary places. I was swimming in the ocean in the form of a fish and gradually ascending out of the water, after having descended into a fathomless abyss, in the form of an eagle. The eagle then flew higher and higher into the sky and gradually came to a place where I became a man again and was guided into a room that was filled with riches beyond belief—gold, silver, diamonds, all kinds of jewels, and money—money beyond belief!

A voice told me that I could have all these riches if I wanted them without having to give anything in return, or I could go and see what was in the next room. The temptation was terrific, but my spirit told me that even though I did not know what was in the next room, all the riches in the first room would never bring me happiness. So, I chose to go into the next room. As soon as I stepped into it, a magnificent golden light began to shine and in the most kind and loving way blocked out everything else. There, sitting on the most beautiful of all thrones, was the Creator. As he—yes, he—reached out to touch me, I became one with him. I awoke with great cries and tears of absolute joy. To this day I am still overcome with joy at these memories.

After that experience, I was walking on clouds and was a changed person. That was the condition that I was in when I went to meet Maryann in Penticton, BC. I often tease Maryann and tell her that she got some false goods, as what she saw then was me at my absolute best—practically floating through life. I was still in that glorious state when I got back to Yellowknife. I remember meeting Harold Cook, one of the early leaders of the Grollier Hall group and a long-time acquaintance of mine, on a sidewalk in downtown Yellowknife. I gave him a gigantic hug and laughed at his bewildered look. "Where's the real Rick and what have you done with him?" seemed to be the question on his face.

Sadly, the effect did not last, as I did not work the program as I should have. I returned to the Haven a few more times over the years but never got back to that wonderful spike of joy.

∞

Prior to becoming a serious couple, Maryann and I agreed to make a boat trip down the Mackenzie River to test our tolerance for each other. The boat was not that big, and James had decided to come with us just in case we "old folks" ran into something we could not handle. The trip certainly had its trials and tribulations, including running out of power halfway across Mills Lake on the return leg. However, the most serious mishap occurred on the Blackwater River when James and I were "playing around" in the rapids with the boat. We were heading back to our camp at the mouth of the river when I lost control of the steering and smashed into a large boulder at a high speed. My forehead and the top of the windshield collided, and blood began flowing all over my face. I regained control of the boat but could not stop as the water was too swift and rough. We managed to make our way back to the camp, and gave Maryann a severe scare when she saw my face covered in blood.

Once we landed, the adrenalin dissipated, and I realized I had wrenched my back quite badly, in addition to the big gash on my nose and forehead. So, Maryann and James had to get me out of the boat and up to the tent, where they attended to me. Maryann cleaned and patched me up as best as she could. However, we weren't going anywhere for a few days, as my back was very sore. Finally, I decided that even though I was in a lot of pain, we ought to finish the next part of the trip, to Fort Norman. Maryann's recall is that I was very difficult to deal with. My tendency to be in "control" became a bit overwhelming for her and James. I could barely stand up or walk without their assistance, and I felt very threatened. Of course, that was a ridiculous thought, but it was there. It's part of residential school syndrome—don't trust anyone.

We were going to stay with Rod for a few days, so I called him on our satellite phone to give him an ETA. When we got to Fort Norman, the wind was blowing hard, and the waves were pounding on the shore. It was weather that I would normally enjoy. Rod was there with his four-wheel-drive truck and a trailer, thinking I would be driving the boat up onto the trailer. However, my back was so bad that all I could do was sit there like a sphinx, unable to move. Rod had a short fuse, and when he saw what the situation was—someone he barely knew and a White woman to boot was smiling at him and trying to get the boat up on the trailer—he barely hung on. However, Maryann knew what she was doing and got the boat up and out of the water without any difficulty. She was not a complete stranger, as Rod had met her earlier that spring, in Edmonton.

Rod was not to be appeased. Things were made worse when he realized I could not get out of the boat and had to ride in it as he pulled the trailer up to his house. Of course, I had to ham it up a bit and gave folks the royal wave as I rode my "carriage" to Rod's abode. The next few days were not pleasant. Rod got angry at James for not being able to help him service the trailer in a way that Rod demanded. In return, I gave Rod what for. The stand-off was on. He had the upper hand—our boat was on his trailer, and we could not move it without his help. Also, I was still barely able to get around. I had no control and fumed away in the cabin where Maryann and I were staying.

All I could do was struggle up to get to the bathroom once in a while. Meanwhile, Maryann had taken over his kitchen in Rod's house and was cooking up a storm in the hopes of appeasing him. She would send James over to the cabin with food for me a couple of times a day.

Of course, nothing could appease Rod when he got a bee in his bonnet. He blew up at Maryann and told her that she had to "stop with the frivolous hand-washing!" He was trying to tell her that water had to be used sparingly because it was hauled in by truck, and the tank could easily go dry. From my perspective, I thought he could have explained that in a kinder fashion. So, I finally did what I had to do. I limped over to the house and told him we wanted to leave and could he be so kind as to haul us, the boat, and our supplies and equipment down to the river the next day.

Rick Hardy about ten days after the accident on the Blackwater River—down to having to use just a Band-Aid. Credit: Maryann Hardy.

I suppose Rod could have told me where to go, but he swallowed his anger, and we were on our way the next morning. Maryann later told me that he was contrite and almost cried when we left. Of course, we made up later, and Rod was an honoured guest at our wedding. We continued on to Norman Wells and Fort Good Hope before starting back to Yellowknife. An incident, which some considered amusing, took place when we arrived in Norman Wells. By then I was well enough to be back in control, and I was driving the boat even though I was not fully focused on what I was doing. My back was still hurting. The boat was a new jet boat, and I had very little experience driving one previous to that trip. I did have a lot of experience with outboard motors though. When one is landing a boat driven by an outboard motor on the beach of the Mackenzie River, it is not unusual to give the motor a shot of gas to ensure that the bow gets about halfway up on the beach, if possible. Being distracted by my sore back, I did that when trying to land the jet boat. We flew out of the water, landing about twenty feet above the waterline. James, who was sitting beside me, turned and with a deadpan face, said, "Who do you think you are, James Bond?"

Unlike an outboard motor which has a leg and a propellor which causes drag on the exit from the water, a jet boat has an absolutely flat bottom. As a result, there was nothing to counteract the extra shot of gas.

As if that wasn't embarrassing enough, my friend, Larry Tourangeau, tipped off the local newspaper about what had happened. The next edition of the paper had a picture of the jet boat, high and dry, with the headline: "Local Lawyer Arrives in Town." All in good fun. But we still had the problem of how to get the boat back into the water. Fortunately for us, Larry's brother, the late Norman Hodgson, came down with a bobcat loader and two of his boys, and we were back in the water, lickety split. Additionally, Norman also loaned us his hunting cabin, which was on an island a bit north of Norman Wells.

We stayed at the cabin for a few days, and we would have stayed longer, but a forest fire drove us out. The island had a fairly lengthy, narrow strip of water, a snye, between it and the mainland. We took this route out without realizing how forcefully the fire was burning. It was an inferno on both sides of the water, and I felt a bit scared. On the other hand, James thought that it was quite spectacular.

We camped on the other side of the Mackenzie for a night and then continued to Fort Good Hope. We were met by our friend, Winston McNeely, who made sure that we had everything that we needed, including bringing enough gas to the boat, so we could get back to Norman Wells. Once we got back to Norman Wells, I made sure that we took on enough gas to make it to Wrigley, so we did not have to stop in Fort Norman on our way south. When we got to Wrigley, our cousin, Gabe Hardisty. took care of getting more gas to us.

We continued on and were met by Anna and her boyfriend in Fort Providence with our truck and boat trailer. As we got close to Fort Providence we ran into heavy wind and rain while crossing Mills Lake. Things got more complicated when our engine loss power and we had to call the RCMP on our satellite phone to come and rescue us. This resulted in quite a crowd waiting for us when the RCMP towed us into the community dock. Sigghh.

Maryann and I married two years later in Yellowknife. We invited one hundred of our friends and relatives and hired the *Norweta*, a Yellowknife-based ship, for the wedding ceremony and party. The ship was owned by Margaret Whitlock and her family. Margaret is a descendant of the Camsell and Carter families. Her great-uncle is Charles Camsell, whose work I used in chapter two of the book. Margaret was a certified captain, and when I first asked her to do the wedding, she thought I was asking her to perform the wedding as captain of the ship. We had a good chuckle about that.

Our friend, Captain Al Hoeft of the local Salvation Army, officiated with the help of his wife, Karen. I was very happy to see many friends from outside of Yellowknife make the trip to join the celebration. Mike Gladu was my best man, and Maryann's sister, Stephanie, who travelled from Florida, was the bridesmaid. Maryann, of course, was new to Yellowknife and was not yet familiar with my circle of friends and acquaintances. At first, she wondered what I was doing—I had hired a ship and was having a captain (Al Hoeft) perform the wedding. She was having visions of a peg-legged individual with a parrot on his shoulder, somewhere out in the middle of Great Slave Lake.

Family photo before Rick and Maryann's wedding on September 1, 2001. Credit: Bea Frost.

The only sadness on the day was the absence of Diane, who had succumbed to cancer earlier that year. However, her husband, Larry, and two of their children and her daughter-in-law, Valerie, were there and were a tremendous help in preparations. The date of our marriage was September 1, 2001, ten days before 9/11.

L to R: Rod, Diane, and Rick Hardy after Aunt Jane Gaudet's funeral in August 1992. Credit: Hardy Family Collection.

L to R: Rick, James, Anna, and Candy Hardy after Diane (Hardy) Gordon's funeral in Inuvik in January 2001. Credit: Hardy Family Collection.

We settled down and bought an older house on Latham Island and renovated it. Maryann made friends in the neighbourhood and started to fit into the community. We had a lakeside property with a brand-new dock where we kept a newer and larger jet boat moored and a beautifully renovated house. Despite the setback, which I described earlier, the Davis & Company office was doing well, and I was at my peak earning years. As is normal, there were a few small blights on the horizon, but all in all, the future looked secure and happy. Then God said, "Huh!"

∞

I was diagnosed with colorectal cancer in early December 2002 and was on the operating table in the Stanton Yellowknife Hospital within a few weeks. My surgeon was Dr. Michael Haskins, who did a fantastic job. Maryann also did a fantastic job as my "guide." When I was diagnosed, I went into a mental tailspin and wasn't really following much of what the doctors and technicians were saying and doing to me. Maryann made sure that nothing untoward was taking place, and I followed the advice of the doctors. Included among the doctors was my dear friend, Peter Kallos. I met Peter and his wife, Linda, when I first started going out with Bea in the early 1970s, and he became our family doctor. After I married Maryann, she and Linda became very good friends, almost soul mates.

Following the surgery, I was put into a recovery room and was given morphine to relieve the pain. Neither I nor any else knew that I would have a negative reaction to the morphine. Well, I tell you, I had my first drug trip at age fifty-five. The clocks were going backwards, monsters were crawling out of the walls, and Maryann was pulling my hair and beating on me, or so I imagined. While all of this was going on, I had a visit from an old friend, Father Felix Labatt, and I, apparently, said some very nasty things to him. The medical staff and Maryann eventually figured out what was going on and switched me to T3s. I certainly regret the things that I said to Felix, at the time, as he was always good to my family. He had married Bea and I and he had conducted the renewal of vows by my parents on their 50th wedding anniversary.

One of the things about the surgery was that I could not take anything solid until I was able to pass gas. It took five days until I heard and felt a little *beep*. I immediately said, "Bring on the food." If I remember correctly, I was rewarded with a small cup of yogurt. I was discharged a few days later, on Christmas Eve. When Maryann and I got home, we had a conjugal visit, and then she cooked me a steak, and I demolished all of it. At that point I felt confident about my recovery.

I was very fortunate that the cancer was still at stage two when Dr. Haskins performed the surgery. He performed a resection without having to add a colostomy. However, the cancer had spread, and it was not possible to say that it had all been removed. This meant that I had to undergo both chemotherapy and radiation treatments. After a few weeks of rest, I was sent to Edmonton to be seen by a specialist at the Cross Cancer Institute. His name was Dr. Anderson. When he began to interview me, he said he previously had another patient named Hardy from the North quite a few years earlier. He said that this Hardy was quite a tough old bird.

"Yes, his name was Jack Hardy," I said, "and he was my father." Dr. Anderson then related the story of Daddy's cancer treatment to me.

After examining me, Dr. Anderson determined that I should have six months of chemo, which would be interrupted by six weeks of radiation treatment. The chemo would be administered at the Stanton Hospital in Yellowknife, and the radiation would be done at the Cross Cancer Institute in Edmonton.

The whole process, starting with the colonoscopies, the surgery, various tests, the chemo, the radiation, and the travel took a toll on me, and I lost about thirty pounds over the twelve months that it all took. I did not lose my hair. I learned that each chemo "cocktail" is unique to the patient that it is meant for. As a result, some lose their hair, and others do not. I returned to work in late November 2003 and waited to see if all the bombardments of my body would yield the hoped-for result. Well, here I am, eighteen years later, writing about it. If I may, I would like to say that one of the things that helped me through the ordeal was my acceptance that I could die from what was happening to my body. This acceptance helped me relax and stay calm.

Of course, Maryann played a significant part in my recovery, and I may not have made it without her as my champion. I love you very much, dear. I also need to extend a huge thank-you to my partners at Davis & Company, who continued to pay me through the whole time and extended moral support throughout. I also have to commend the GNWT for the excellent support program that they have for cancer patients. They generously paid all of the costs that Maryann and I incurred in our travels to and from Edmonton. Thank you also to the nurses and support staff at the chemo treatment program in Yellowknife. Finally, and certainly not least, our good friend Dr. Peter Kallos. Peter continues to make sure that I get my colonoscopies every five years, just in case. Uggh.

∞

After I returned to work, I stayed with Davis until the end of 2005. After surviving cancer, I realized I needed to change my lifestyle, as stress may have played a significant role in me developing the family curse. To be honest, part of me just wanted to show the world that I could still do it. I also wanted to do the right thing vis-à-vs my partners at Davis & Company, who had treated me so well. I completed some significant files before I left.

∞

Maryann had some friends living in Atlin, BC, which is a couple of hours south of Whitehorse, Yukon. I was still the corporate secretary for Northwestel, and we were having a meeting in Whitehorse in late May or early June 2004. I asked Maryann if she wanted to come along, and we could then go and visit her friends, the late Brad Thayer and his wife, Diana, for a few days after the meeting. She agreed, and we rented a car and drove down to Atlin after I had completed my work in Whitehorse. Maryann had been to Atlin previously, but it was my first visit. I fell in love with the area. It was springtime. The ice was just coming off Atlin Lake, and the air was filled with all the beautiful smells of spring. On the way we stopped to enjoy the view created by Mount Minto. Also, on the way in, we spotted an acreage that bordered the lake and was for sale. We bought the property later that year and began planning to build on it.

That meant we were committed to retiring and moving from Yellowknife. I started getting cold feet—not about retiring but about building. Fortunately, a large property on the edge of Atlin was available, and, more fortunately, we were able to find a buyer for the original acreage. I gave my notice to Davis & Company, and we were going to put our property in Yellowknife on the market. Before we could, potential buyers started dropping by, saying, "We heard . . ." In addition, one of them said, "I will pay your asking price." So, we sold what we had in Yellowknife, bought the new property in Atlin, and moved our worldly possessions there. I hauled our boat over in September 2005 and returned to Yellowknife to complete my commitment to Davis & Company to stay until the end of the year. The law business basically closes down over the Christmas period in Yellowknife because all the government registries and courts close for the holidays. I was able to leave Yellowknife with my SUV on December 23 and got to Atlin late on Christmas Eve, 2005. It was so cold that I didn't realize I had driven into Atlin with a flat tire. To compound matters, I had to take our niece, Jamie, somewhere in town the next day. I still didn't know that I had a flat tire, as the roads were rough, and the tire was still frozen.

I finally noticed it a few days later, so I went to the local garage/gas station, owned by Pine Tree Services, to get it repaired. When I got there, I was greeted by a bewhiskered attendant who seemed to be quite agitated. He sputtered: "Oh no, oh no, we are not fixing that tire." I had no idea what was going on until he sputtered again: "You, you were seen driving around town with that flat tire, and it can't be fixed." So, I met Colin and was introduced to living in a small town where

PART VI

257

everyone watched out for everyone else. I eventually convinced Colin to put the spare on for me and order a new tire.

∞

The community of Atlin is located approximately in the middle of the eastern shore of Atlin Lake. The lake is about ninety miles long, south to north. The southern end is a short walk from the Llewellyn Glacier, which, some have said, is the size of Switzerland. It certainly is large, as we learned.

Maryann's niece, Jamie, lived with us for the five years that we lived in Atlin. She spent the last three living in a residence in Whitehorse and completed high school there. She did very well in school and won the Governor General's Academic Medal. She graduated in 2009, and her aunt and uncle, Hank and Stephanie Philips, came from Florida for the occasion. Jamie went on to obtain a degree in early childhood education from the University of Southern Florida. She has just recently been accepted into an MBA program.

While Hank and Stephanie were with us, we treated them to an airplane ride over the glacier and the lake. We chartered a Beaver, on floats, from a local operator. The glacier was certainly something to see from the air. Because the lake is fed by the glacier, it is spectacularly azure in colour, and the water is very cold. The lake flows into the Atlin River on the western shore which flows into the southern lakes and then into the Yukon River, which eventually empties into the Bering Strait.

We spent many a fine day in our jet boat cruising the lake and catching an occasional lake trout or grayling. We would also, occasionally, go down the Atlin River, through a few sets of rapids, and then cruise the big lakes that were there. The whole area is filled with mining history, and we enjoyed seeing many artifacts from the mining era. In addition to that, the scenery is spectacular. I was fortunate enough to have some of my grandchildren spend a few summers with us in Atlin. Great memories. Once when we were out on the lake with the grandchildren, we saw a mother moose with her calf resting on her back swimming across a narrow section between an island and the mainland. I have always been grateful for having been able to show these scenes to the grandchildren.

Maryann's mother, Grandma Frost, would spend every summer with us. She is an avid gardener and helped Maryann make our place look beautiful. So, we had Jamie, Grandma Frost, and some of my children and grandchildren, from time to time, stay with us, and we felt we had a family. We made many friends in Atlin and spent time in their homes, as they did in ours.

There is a lot of big game around Atlin: moose, caribou, mountain sheep and goats, grizzly and black bears, wolves, coyotes, and the occasional cougar. There are outfitters who make their homes in Atlin and earn their livelihood by outfitting. There is always a "community moose" that wanders around town, and no one bothers it. There were two, year-old calves that camped on our acreage and would come on to our deck to eat frozen flowers from our raised gardens in the winter. It was a bit strange the first time it happened. We heard the clopping noise of their hooves on our deck. We didn't go for the rifle, but we did go for the cameras and got some good photos.

We had pet dogs and cats, but we had some bad luck with them. The coyotes loved them and would stalk them right into our yard. One winter, Grandma Frost saved one of the dogs from an attack. She had the help of her little dog, Pickles, who was a holy terror. The year we were leaving, the coyotes got my favourite dog, Jack, who was a Sheltie. We were having dinner with family and friends when Jack went roaring out of the house. He was going to chase some coyotes off, but it was a trap, and we never saw Jack again. The grandsons who were with us were devastated. I hunted those coyotes for two days after that but couldn't find them. I fired a few shots into the bush just to release my anger.

Sadly, we decided to leave Atlin after Jamie graduated from high school. Maryann had suffered a severe heart attack the previous fall and found it very difficult to cope during the winter after she got back home from the university hospital in Edmonton. So, there we were, selling and moving again. Atlin does not have a particularly active real estate market, but we got lucky, again. Our family doctor in Atlin was Dr. Dick Fast. He was an excellent doctor and a good friend. I went to tell him that we had decided to leave and to thank him for all he had done for us. He told me that he and his wife, Maggie, had decided to retire in Atlin and how much he liked our house and property. Both he and I, being reasonable people, were able to put together a mutually satisfactory agreement for us to sell the house and property to them.

We thoroughly enjoyed our five years in Atlin. When we left Yellowknife to move there, I expected to fully retire and spend the rest of my days there. I thought I was going into full retirement, but that was not to be. It wasn't very long after we settled there that I moved to the status of semi-retired. I had hedged my bets and hadn't resigned from the Law Society of the Northwest Territories, just in case. I did resign as an active member in both Nunavut and Alberta, and I did not join the BC Law Society. I am a soft touch and usually try to help when someone asks for it. However, I was now living in BC and would have to be a member there if I were going to help anyone. Not being a member allowed me to honestly say, "I'm sorry, but I'm not licenced to practice in BC."

Unfortunately, while we lived in Atlin, my brother, Rod. died of a heart attack while on a trip to Edmonton. His death occurred on April 17, 2008. My nephew, Diane's son Michael Gordon stepped up and took care of all of the arrangements, including having Rod's body returned to Fort Norman. Rod was a lifelong bachelor, but almost all of his nephews and nieces attended the funeral on April 25, 2008. One of the interesting aspects of the funeral service was that the Shúhta Got'ıne leaders came to the church with their drums and sang the funeral songs. Not so many years before that, the leaders of the same church were preaching against things like that. Rod was laid to his final rest beside our parents and grandparents in the old Anglican graveyard.

Rod had asked me to write his will, but I had refused, because of what I perceived as a conflict that could lead to disputes in our family after his death. So, I was as surprised as everyone else when we opened the will. Rod died a rich man. He left substantial cash gifts to each nephew and niece as well as his long-time employee and friend, Helen Naedzo. He left all of the land that he owned to me. That still left a substantial amount of cash even after paying a huge amount in income taxes and funeral and probate expenses. He left the balance in a trust that was for the benefit of students from the Sahtu who would attend post-secondary institutions in the future. I was appointed as the trustee.

I have managed the trust in a way that the capital is still intact but have still been able to provide bursaries every year since then. Rod's memory will remain as a living gift.

I still miss Rod very much. I know how excited and interested he would have been by the writing of this book. No doubt, he would have had many suggestions on what to include. Unfortunately, I would not have agreed to all of his suggestions! As I said earlier, he was also quite a raconteur.

Rod Hardy who left so much for all. Credit: Hardy Family Collection.

CHAPTER TWENTY-FOUR

NÁÁTS'IHCH'OH

The call came about eight months after I got to Atlin. It was from Clarence Campbell, then the president of the Tulıt'a District Land Corporation. After the pleasantries were exchanged, he asked, "Have you had enough yet?"

"What?" I replied.

We both laughed. Tulıt'a District Land Corporation is an overarching body representing the three Aboriginal communities in the Tulıt'a District in the Sahtu Settlement Area. The three communities were called: Tulıt'a Land Corporation, Fort Norman Métis Land Corporation, and Norman Wells Land Corporation. Since then, the Fort Norman Métis have changed the name of their entity to Fort Norman Métis Community. Collectively, the three communities own and manage large parcels of land and have to be consulted by the Crown before a number of activities can take place on Crown lands, in their area.

The first call was about me doing a short-term contract with the group to help them with a number of non-renewable resource-based issues. The help that was needed was someone who was a skilled negotiator. At that point in time, I had gotten a good rest and was looking for a challenge. I realized I was not ready for full retirement yet. Frankly, I'd had just about enough of chopping wood, shovelling snow, building gardens, and other such chores, and then watching television. I was happy that I did not have to join a firm or start a full practice to accept this retainer. I made it clear that my services were limited, and I had no intention of opening a trust account, which would be required if I were to start a full practice. It would involve a lot of work that I was no longer interested in doing.

The Tulıt'a District would be my only client, and I would act as a consultant as much as I would act as a lawyer. The groups were from my home area, and I knew the leaders well. I worked out an agreement with them and advised on a number of files.

A few months later, Clarence called to tell me that the Government of Canada wanted to establish a national park in a part of the Mackenzie Mountains that is located in the Sahtu Settlement Area. Because of previous situations where the Parks Canada Agency ended up having its hands slapped, metaphorically, for dealing with Aboriginal peoples and breaching the law, they were insistent that the groups have legal

PART VI

261

counsel in all future negotiations. Frankly, there were very few lawyers, if any, who had the knowledge and experience that I had when dealing with issues arising from the Sahtu Dene and Métis Comprehensive Land Claim Agreement.

So, the group wanted to hire me to negotiate the Impact and Benefit Plan that was required by chapter sixteen of the land-claim agreement before the park could be established. I wrote to the executive director of the district, Louise Reindeer, on December 14, 2006: "As you know my current retainer agreement ends with you on December 31, 2006, so we have to discuss . . . as this issue [the park] could run well into 2007." We hammered out a contract, and I was instructed to make a trip to Whitehorse to meet with some Parks Canada officials to be briefed on what they were thinking. None of us had any idea that it would be mid-2012 before the agreements would be completed and signed off.

∞

So, thinking that I would be engaged for less than a year, I drove to Whitehorse for the meeting, which was held on December 19, 2006, on the second floor of the Elijah Smith Building. I met Gordon Hamre there for the first time. I had no idea how often we would be seeing each other over the next six years. Gordon was the negotiator for Parks Canada and worked from the Yellowknife office and had flown to Whitehorse just to meet with me! Gordon and I became friends over the time that we negotiated and collaborated.

The meeting in Whitehorse was to look at the big picture from a preliminary perspective. The proposed location of the park was in the southwest corner of the Sahtu Settlement Area, bordering on the Yukon to the west and the Dehcho Region to the south. Included in the Dehcho Region and abutting the boundary with the Sahtu was the Nahanni National Park Reserve of Canada. We were in the territory of the Shúhta Got'ıne, who I was descended from.

The first ask from Parks Canada was simply for an agreement to allow it to extend the Nahanni National Park Reserve, north into the Sahtu. I don't know if the folks from Parks Canada were aware of the recent history of the area, in terms of land-claims negotiations. They likely were, but a good negotiator sometimes just plays dumb. The area that they wanted made sense from a geographic perspective, as it included all of the headwaters of the South Nahanni River. However, borders and boundaries around the world haven't always been set from a common-sense perspective. In this case the boundary in question was the southern boundary of the Sahtu Settlement Area. That boundary had been roughly "drawn" on a map in the 1980s when all the Dene and Métis of the Northwest Territories were still working together. Since then, the Sahtu Dene and Métis had split off and reached their own agreement with Canada and the GNWT with rights limited to a smaller area. Not a great deal of thought had gone into placing the line in the 1980s, as it was expected that all Dene and Métis would have the same hunting, fishing, trapping, and gathering rights throughout the Northwest Territories. If some serious thought would have gone into the line, the area of land that Parks Canada was now interested in would have been included in the Dehcho Region. At the same time, the line that was north of the Blackwater River, which flows into the Mackenzie River from the northeast, would have been in the middle of the Blackwater River. This would have meant that all lands lying north of the Blackwater River would have been included in the Sahtu Settlement Area.

So, our counter to Parks Canada was that the boundary between the Sahtu and the Dehcho should be redrawn so that the Sahtu Settlement Area would be extended south to the middle of the Blackwater River, and the headwaters of the South Nahanni would be included in the Dehcho. By doing this, Parks Canada could do the extension that it wanted and would have to deal with the Dehcho First Nations only.

Even though our proposal was logical, Parks Canada did not want to become involved in opening the Sahtu land-claim agreement to accomplish it. I understood that the initiative to extend the Nahanni Park was a result of a commitment by Prime Minister Harper to the Dehcho First Nations, meant to expedite a settlement with them. I thought that with the prime minister involved, we could get the Blackwater back for the Sahtu. Not. Incidentally, fifteen years later, the Dehcho First Nations are still nowhere near reaching a settlement of their claims.

∞

As a result of the lack of interest on the part of Canada, in our counter proposal, the proposed new park would have to be done in accordance with the terms of the Sahtu Dene and Métis Comprehensive Land Claim Agreement—specifically, chapter sixteen. This chapter was a carry-over from the original negotiations for an NWT-wide agreement. The chapter dealt primarily with the establishment of new national parks in the Sahtu. We were surprised that it was actually going to come into use.

We formed a negotiating team for the Tulı́t'a District made up of representatives from the three communities, the two Renewable Resources Councils, the Tulı́t'a Dene Band, the

Sahtu Secretariat Incorporated, and me. Not all of these groups were entitled to be at the table, but we all agreed that it was best to include them, so all information would come to them firsthand. Fortuitously, Ethel Blondin-Andrew was appointed to represent the SSI. Ethel played a very significant role in getting the agreements done and the park established. She brought gravitas to the table, having formerly been a federal cabinet minister.

The first major issue that we had to deal with was what lands would be included in the park. When Parks Canada had prepared the early briefing materials, they used "Begádóh National Park" as a working name. Coincidentally, there was a move afoot to bring protected area status to Begádóh proper. We explained to Gordon and his team that the area that they were proposing did not extend to the area known as Begádóh. The dividing line between the two areas was the height of land that enclosed the South Nahanni watershed to the south and Begádóh to the north. We said we wanted Begádóh to be included as part of whatever national park that would be established. I set all of this out in a letter to Gordon on July 12, 2007.

We were not successful in getting Begádóh included as part of the national park but did achieve two other commitments. First, Canada agreed that Begádóh would be the subject of negotiations for the establishment of a national wildlife area. The second commitment resolved the issue of whether the new park would simply be an extension of Nahanni or if it would be a stand-alone park with its own infrastructure and staff located in Tulít'a. Canada agreed that it would be stand-alone. As a result of these decisions, a new name had to be found for the park. Chief Frank Andrew, who was a member of the negotiating team, worked with his brother, Leon Andrew, and Leon's wife, Ethel Blondin-Andrew, to hold a series of meetings with the elders, and they eventually recommended that the name be "Naats'ihch'oh." The name, I understand, means pointed like a quill. The description is in reference to the shape of what is legally called Mount Wilson, which is the dominant feature of the park.

The negotiations were long and arduous. The main barrier to reaching a final agreement was the government of the Northwest Territories under the leadership of Bob McCleod, who is now a former premier. Bob is a Métis originally from Fort Providence. He worked his way up in the GNWT's civil service until he became the top civil servant in that government. Then he entered territorial politics and reached the top position there as well. So far, he is the only member of the legislature who has been twice elected to the position of premier. His government had a trump card as the *National Parks Act* required the consent of the province or territory in which the lands were located to agree to the use of the lands for a new national park. Additionally, there were some mining interests in the area and some big-game outfitters. Our negotiating team thought that the park would include all of the lands that were included in the Land Withdrawal Order, which was put in place to allow the negotiations to proceed.

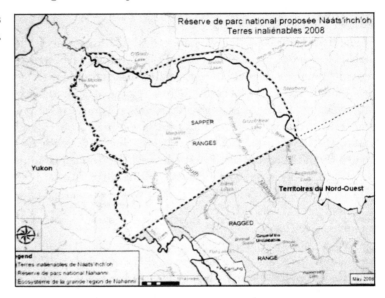

What the Tulita District thought it was negotiating for. Credit: Parks Canada Agency.

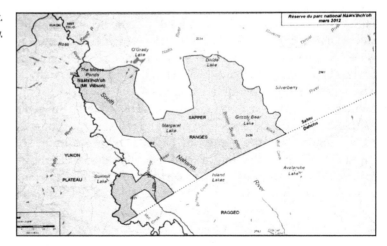

What the Tulita District got. Credit: Parks Canada Agency.

Eventually, it became clear that the federal government's position, at the insistence of McLeod's government, was that the land in the withdrawal order was the maximum and was not all going to be included in the park. Members of our team were quite angry, and the negotiations almost went off the rails. Gordon and his team were also very displeased about that development. Although the GNWT would not deal with our negotiating team, they did talk to the federal government representatives, and we were kept up to speed that way. It seems to me that Bob McLeod really personalized the issue and lost all objectivity. The negotiations inched forward with a lot of compromise. Fortunately for us the minister responsible for the Parks Canada Agency, Peter Kent, was on side with us.

The federal minister who was championing the GNWT cause was Minister of Indian and Northern Affairs John Duncan. Interestingly, John Duncan was the opposition critic for the department when the Sahtu Dene and Métis Comprehensive Land Claim Agreement was before Parliament in 1994. Even though that agreement had been negotiated with the previous Conservative government, John Duncan did not like it at all. He also had a very belligerent official advising him, who looked for technical ways to derail the park agreement. Fortunately, I had kept copies of all my old files and was able to deflect all of the technical objections.

As we inched along, we worked out all of the details, and the only outstanding issue was which lands would be included. This issue was still outstanding when Prime Minister Harper arrived in Norman Wells on August 21, 2012, to publicly announce the establishment of the park the next day. Both Kent and Duncan were with him, as was Loreen Harper, the prime minister's wife. Bob McCleod was also lurking around somewhere, sulking because he couldn't get a seat on the airplane that the prime minister and his wife would take into the park.

There were approximately 7,600 square kilometres of land in the Withdrawal Order, but only 4,300 square kilometres were included in the final agreement. The prime minister agreed to review the entire process and held out a chance that the area could be increased. There we were, between the proverbial rock and a hard place. Our team said, "Hoorah," or "Okay, let's go." Everyone knew that they would be alive to fight another day. We flew into the park the next day in beautiful weather. We spent about three hours there with the Harpers. Once all of the photos and press statements were finished, the press was sent packing back to Norman Wells in their plane. After that, Ethel Blondin-Andrew and I had some private time with the Harpers, and we walked and talked and enjoyed the scenery.

I knew that I couldn't waste this opportunity to try to convince the prime minister to enlarge the land area. He heard us out politely but would not commit. Finally, I asked him and Loreen if they watched many movies. Loreen said she did, so I asked her if she had seen *Out of Africa* with Meryl Streep. She replied that yes, it was one of her favourite movies. Then I asked if she remembered the scene where the character played by Streep had prostrated herself in front of the governor to beg for a school for the Kikuyu children. She hesitated, then indicated that she did recall the scene. I then said to the Prime Minister: "Well, Prime Minister, we will be publicly announcing the establishment of the park in Norman Wells later today. If you don't agree to enlarge the park by then I will prostrate myself in front of you and beg you for more land, in front of everyone including the media." Or at least words to that effect.

Rick Hardy flying to Naats'ihch'oh with the Harpers. Credit: Prime Minister's Office.

He looked at me with a steely twinkle in his eye and said: "If you do that, I will just give you a good swift kick," or at least words to that effect.

We continued walking to where our floatplane was parked, and the last few members of his entourage were waiting. When we got there, he said to an assistant, "Did you bring that bottle with you?" She said she had and then pulled an unopened bottle of Crown Royal out of her backpack. We all had a toast to the establishment of Naats'ih'choh National Park Reserve of Canada and then got into the airplane for the flight back to Norman Wells and the public announcement. No, I didn't prostrate myself, but when it was my turn to speak at the announcement as the elder representative of the Fort Norman Métis Community, I did my best to make the case for more land. I had turned sixty-five earlier that year. I also did not take offence at the prime minister's response to my threat. Sometimes you need to be able to make or take a joke.

Rick Hardy toasting Naats'ihch'oh with the Harpers and their party. Credit: Prime Ministers Office.

The park was formally established soon afterward. No more lands have been added to it since then. However, the lands that Bob McLeod wanted for mining activity are still not available either. The lands that Bob McLeod wanted excluded from the park are now subject to the provisions of the Sahtu Land Use Plan and are, colloquially, "no development" lands. This designation cannot be changed without the consent of the Sahtu Dene and Métis which means, practically speaking, the Tulita District. What goes around comes around.

Nááts'ıhch'oh National Park Reserve of Canada Plaque Dedication on July 17, 2013. Credit: J.D. McKinnon. Parks Canada.

CHAPTER TWENTY-FIVE
VANCOUVER ISLAND

By the time the team had completed the negotiations for the establishment of Nááts'įhch'oh, Maryann and I had moved from Atlin to Nanoose Bay on Vancouver Island. This is likely our last stop, but who knows? In between Nááts'įhch'oh and today, I spent six years as a member of the Sahtu Land Use Planning Board. The board has its head office in Fort Good Hope and holds its meetings throughout the Sahtu as well as in Yellowknife. I also spent three years as the chairperson of the Nááts'įhch'oh Management Committee. These meetings were held in Tulít'a, Norman Wells, Fort Simpson, and Yellowknife.

The work that I did as a member of the planning board and the management committee was, for me, giving back. I was giving back to the Sahtu Dene and the Métis for all the great opportunities that I had while working for them. The knowledge that I have gained belongs to them as much as it belongs to me.

I also spent two years as the president of the Fort Norman Métis Community. This term was, as much as anything, a call to duty. I have also advised the executive and board of directors of the Fort Norman Métis Community on issues related to the cash compensation received under the land-claim agreement, as well as on residential school issues.

In return for giving back and answering the call to duty, I got to spend more time in the Sahtu and remain active. Maryann would prefer to have me at home more often, but she is a trooper. Speaking of movies, do you remember how the character played by Brad Pitt in *Legends of the Fall* ended his life?

Rick Hardy, as a young boy, wearing his first suit.
Credit: Hardy Family Collection.

PART VI

CONCLUSION

Well, here we are. Back to the introduction and the questions that were posed there. Before I respond to the questions, I want to acknowledge that this memoir is written mostly about my family, so it may not be of that much interest to others. I hope that is not so, as everyone can learn from our experiences. I wanted to explore how the lives of one family in the Mackenzie River District unfolded over a period of over 200 years and how that unfolding contributed to who we are today.

"Where do I come from?"

My first Indigenous blood ancestors were Shúhta Got'ıne. I don't know what their names were, other than one of them had the last name Taupier or Toutpied. The one using that name could have been either the father or the mother of Elise Taupier. Then the Scotsman, Alexander Munro Fisher, fathered Marie Fisher with Taupier in 1843. Between the births of Elise Taupier and Marie Fisher, we took on the identity of Half-Breeds, now known as Métis. At that point we could say that we came from the country; that is, the Mackenzie River District.

As other unions, similar to ours, took place in the Mackenzie River District, we joined with those offspring to form a new people. Some Red River Métis joined in those unions, but that did not change the fact that a new people, known as the Mackenzie River Métis, were being created. Our brand of Métisism does not deny or discount our Indigenous roots, which, in my case, are the Shúhta Got'ıne. I can no more deny that I am Shúhta Got'ıne than I can deny that I am a Scotsman. Of course, the Gaudets brought French into my lineage, and the Hardy's brought the English. But the starting point for me is being a Half-Breed, a.k.a. Métis. Louis Riel told us that:

> It is true that our Indian origin is humble, but it is indeed just that we honour our mothers as well as our fathers. Why should we be so preoccupied with what degree of mingling we have of European and Indian blood? No matter how little we have of one or the other, do not both gratitude and filial love require us to make a point of saying, 'We are Métis'.

So, I think I can fairly say that I come from the Mackenzie River District and am descended from the Indigenous people who live there as well as three European nations. I can say that I am Métis, and we can say, as did Riel, "We are Métis."

My first wife, Bea, brought other lineages to our children, and they brought further lineages into the fold after they started their own families. From the Indigenous side, Chipewyan and Tlicho have been added, and from the European side, good doses of Scandinavian and Irish have been brought in. Who knows what the next generations will bring? Bea's father, Pete Bloomstrand, used to counsel us not to worry about it, as we were all just Heinz 57 anyway. I suppose that is one perspective. However, I prefer to see the continued formation and growth of ourselves as Métis. We can all say, if we so choose, that "We are Métis." I hope we have lived, and continue to live, up to that direction from Louis Riel.

"Where am/are I/we going?"

If it is "I," then it is not likely that I am going anywhere. This will remain true until I die. At that time, I will return to my country to lie eternally with my family in the old Anglican graveyard in Fort Norman. It is quite possible that I will join the Anglican Church before then, so there will be a proper Anglican burial.

If the second question is about "We," then the answer is difficult to see. The Mackenzie River Métis are small in number and struggle every day to assert their identity. This assertion becomes more difficult as the dominant societies in the Northwest Territories continue to grind the Mackenzie River Métis down. Our situation is further worsened by the ongoing refusal of the Métis National Council to recognize us as Métis from a distinct geographic part of present-day Canada which is outside of the purported boundaries of the Metis National Council. Our plight is further exacerbated by the fact that many, if not most, of the Mackenzie River Métis live in places in Canada other than the Northwest Territories. The latter is an issue that the resident Mackenzie River Métis and governments have yet to acknowledge and come to grips with.

"Why am I here?"

Doing the research for and then writing this book has forced me to wrestle with this question. As I have said in the book, I have realized that my calling in this life has been to help the Mackenzie River Métis find their place. This began with the stories that Mama told me about who we are. Then in grade nine, I took my first concrete step by challenging the social studies textbook that we were using. Fortunately, my teacher was francophone, and he encouraged me. Next came my surfacing from years of wandering to become involved in organizing the Métis of the Northwest Territories.

This was followed by law school and my major paper on the rights of the Mackenzie River Métis. Since then, I have continued the mission, which includes the writing of this book. I hope the mission will include a second book. In this book I have dealt, in a very cursory way, with the history, rights, and organizational history of all of the Métis of the NWT. Those topics can easily make another book. If the Creator is willing, I hope I can be the one to write it, or at least help. Perhaps my mission in this life may then be finished.

Bob Overvold and Rick Hardy working on the family graves in the old Anglican graveyard in Fort Norman in August 2020. Credit: Author.

"Who am I?"

I am still Richard Irving Timothy Hardy. Simply put, I am the person who the answer to question three speaks of. In addition to being a champion for the Métis, I am also a human being who has compassion for the rest of the human race. I am a truth-teller. I am a person of principle. I am a person with many mental, social, and emotional frailties that I continue to try to overcome. I hope that when I leave this world, I will be remembered with kindness and love. These answers may not be given a passing mark by a professor of philosophy, but they are what I believe. I studied logic, not philosophy.

I hope that our children and grandchildren will take notice of the photo of Bob and me and do their duty to look after all of our family graves in the old Anglican graveyard and elsewhere.

Residential Schools

I did not set out to write a book about residential schools. However, my life and the lives of Mama and her siblings and the lives of Grandad and his siblings and the lives of Granny and her siblings inevitably led me to having to deal with that elephant in my living room.

The easy way out would be to join the rage and choruses condemning the governments and the churches for the system of residential schools that they established in Canada. There is no doubt that these rages and choruses are based on truths, and the heat being placed on the governments and the churches is more than well deserved. However, in the case of my family, we need to face the truth of our particular situation.

We were not all forcefully ripped from our families. We did not have our culture and our languages suppressed. Our parents made the hard decision to send us to school, so we could be formally educated and make our way in the "White Man's World." Those were conscious decisions that clearly set us apart from the Shúhta Got'ine and other First Nations people.

Although Mama and her siblings were told, in no uncertain terms, that they could not speak Slavey while in the residential school in Fort Providence, they and others returned home as fluent speakers. Why was that? I don't know, but perhaps, in the future some scholar in the appropriate discipline might want to study and explain this phenomenon.

Mama and her siblings did not lose or give up their Shúhta Got'ine culture while in residential school. That culture was "given up" when they were born because their parents were

PART VI

very conscious that their children were being transformed. Part of this transformation was the sending of their children to Residential Schools.

However, I cannot believe that they, the parents, agreed to send their children away to be sexually, physically, mentally, and emotionally abused. They sent them away so they could be educated in the ways of the modern world. My grandfather and his siblings were sent to Saint Boniface College in Winnipeg, the school at Ile a la Crosse, and the residential school in Fort Providence. My grandmother and her siblings and their children were sent to the Anglican residential schools in Fort Resolution and Hay River. Mama and her siblings were sent to the Catholic and Anglican residential schools in Fort Providence and Hay River. I and my sister, Diane, and two of our Hardisty cousins, were sent to Grollier Hall and Stringer Hall in Inuvik.

My great-grandparents paid the churches to allow their children to go to school. My grandparents paid the churches to allow their children to go to school. My parents did not pay for Diane and me to go to school in Inuvik because, by the time we went to school, the Metis and the non-Indigenous students were, by law, to be provided with free education. In the case of Diane and I, we were sent to residential schools because a parsimonious government wanted to save money, so it herded us into Inuvik.

However, my parents trusted the Roman Catholic Church to look after me while I was in its care while attending the government school in Inuvik. Do you think that my parents or any other parents would knowingly hand their children over to the devil?

One thing I have to face up to is my mother's time in Fort Providence. Many of the details of this experience were told in her own words in the tape recording that I spoke of in chapter five. How could her parents do what they did to her? They "sent" her away when she was six years old and did not see her for ten years. She and Uncle Fred, and later, Aunt Jane, were sent away to make room for older siblings at home. They only brought her home when she finally got a letter to them telling them to bring her home. Neither the government nor the Church did this. My grandparents did it. Mama said she forgot who her parents were and actually came to believe that the "convent" was her home. My grandfather, while not as wealthy as his father before him, could have easily managed to travel to and from Fort Providence to visit his children each summer and show them some love. Our family cannot blame this on the governments or the churches. And what for? When Mama finally got home, she was employed as a domestic for the HBC. No doubt that whatever pittance she may have been paid for this "career" went straight to her parents.

If we are truly going to have truth and reconciliation, all of us need to look squarely into the mirror of history and admit our own shortcomings as well as those of our parents and grandparents. We may not like what we see but we will get some peace from facing the truth.

EPILOGUE

A Visit with Hugh Feagan

I travelled from my home on Vancouver Island to Edmonton, Alberta, on Saturday, August 14, 2021. I began by driving to the airport at Comox and then flew to the Edmonton International Airport. I overnighted at the hotel attached to the airport. Mike Gladu met me the next morning at 5:30, and we proceeded to make our way through the check-in process and then the security screening. We had breakfast and then flew to Calgary, Alberta, with connections to London, Ontario.

When we arrived at the London airport, we were met by Hugh Feagan. (I first mentioned Hugh in chapter fifteen.) He was a sergeant in the RCMP in 1962 and was responsible for conducting the investigation into the crimes that Martin Houston had committed against Mike, me, and the other boys. Hugh was the sergeant in charge in Inuvik. He could have easily assigned the matter to a number of junior officers. However, he recognized the seriousness and sensitivity of what had happened to us. As a result, he conducted the investigation himself. Hugh travelled to Fort Norman and interviewed Mike and me on August 21, 1962. This was almost fifty-nine years to the day that we were meeting him again. Neither Mike nor I had seen him in the intervening period.

Hugh Feagan around the time that he conducted the investigation into the abuses by Martin Houston. Credit: Hugh Feagan.

The *News/North* had published an article on July 19, 2021, about the unmarked graves that were being discovered near a number of former residential schools in various locations in Canada. The reporter, Blair McBride, had interviewed me to ask me what I thought about it all. During the interview I mentioned that I was completing this book, and there would be a lot in it about our experiences at Grollier Hall. Unfortunately, the *News/North* reported that the book would be about Grollier Hall and did not mention anything else that would be in it.

Hugh saw the *News/North* article and reached out to me through his son, Rob, to talk about his involvement in the investigation. After talking to him on the phone, I suggested to Hugh that a good way to connect would be for Mike and I to travel to see him at his home in Ontario. He agreed, and we worked out the arrangements.

This decision was very important, as the three days that we spent with Hugh allowed us to form a relationship and to think about what was being said. This was better than a Zoom call, where questions, answers, and comments might not be fully thought through.

While with the RCMP, Hugh had spent many years in the North as well as other locations in Canada. He retired from the RCMP on August 31, 1985, as the chief superintendent for the Northwest Territories. Most of his time in the North was in the Mackenzie Delta Region. He met and married his wife, Marj, in Aklavik on December 15, 1955. The marriage was performed by the Reverend L. P. Holman, who played an important role in my life a few years later.

Hugh and Marj Feagan's wedding in Aklavik. Credit: Hugh Feagan.

Following his retirement, Hugh and Marj lived in West Kelowna, BC, for approximately thirty years. Sadly, Marj passed away in 2019. Hugh then decided to return to his roots in Goderich, Ontario. That was where he took us to after he picked us up at the London airport.

Hugh was ninety-two years old at the time and was in excellent condition. He still had his driver's licence. He took us on a drive, and we got a good look at the country around Goderich. Neither Mike nor I had ever seen that part of Canada. We stopped at a local restaurant for dinner. After we had a good visit, reminiscing about people and events that we all knew or knew about, Hugh dropped Mike and me at a motel where he had made reservations for us, and we agreed to meet the next day.

Hugh came to pick us up a bit after 9:30 the next morning. We explored more of the area around Goderich. We enjoyed the drive and did more reminiscing as we moved around the countryside. Then we went to Hugh's apartment for a light lunch and looked at memorabilia from Hugh's career in the

PART VI

277

North. He expressed a great deal of pride about the certificate of honorary membership issued to him and Marj in the Fort McPherson Loucheux Indian Band, which today is known as the Tetlit Gwich'in First Nation.

Then we talked about his involvement in the Martin Houston investigation.

Hugh explained to us that he only took statements from the five of us who were later examined at the preliminary hearing. I had previously thought that he had interviewed many more students. He told us that he and David Searle believed that the five statements were enough to commit Houston to stand trial on the charges. They were right. Hugh also told us how he obtained our names as well as those of the other witnesses. Hugh told us that the names had been provided to the Ottawa Police by Robert when they interviewed him. They simply asked him if he knew of other boys who had been molested.

Up to that point, I had mistakenly believed that six of us had been interviewed and were witnesses at the preliminary hearing. I even knew the name of the sixth person. Talk about a manufactured memory. When I got back to my home, I reviewed the transcripts, and, lo and behold, there were only five of us. I offer my sincere apologies to anyone whom I said that there were six of us.

In addition to the five of us, Hugh had also taken a statement from Sister Hebert. He told us that when he interviewed her, Father Ruyant insisted on being present. Hugh told us that he started the interview by explaining to Sister Hebert what he was investigating. He said Sister Hebert then pointed and shook her finger at Father Ruyant and told him, "Father, I told you so," or words to that effect. Father Ruyant remained silent. Hugh told us that he found that Sister Hebert was being very brave in telling all that she knew in front of Father Ruyant.

Hugh did not recall whether or not he had also interviewed Father Ruyant. Whether he was interviewed or not, Father Ruyant was sworn as a witness at the preliminary hearing.

Hugh had a much clearer recollection of taking the statements from Mike and me in Fort Norman than either of us had. My recollection was that it was the corporal in charge in Fort Norman who had come to get us from the sawmill for the interviews. Hugh was clear that he was the one who came to get us.

Hugh also told us that he was expecting difficult interviews with us. He expected that we would not cooperate. However, he found the opposite. He told us that it was as if we had been waiting for someone to tell our stories to.

It became clear to me that it was very fortunate for Mike and me and the three other boys that it was Hugh Feagan who did the investigation. I found Hugh to be a man of integrity and compassion. This confirmed everything that David Searle had told me about Hugh. Many other police officers would have been dispassionate about what they were being told, but Hugh was strongly offended by what had happened to us.

Following the completion of the preliminary hearing, Houston was committed to stand trial on the charges. The trial was held in Yellowknife, so we had no opportunity to be there.

Hugh told us that the prosecutors had arranged for examinations of Houston by two mental health professionals. Then they proceeded with the trial and, based on the evidence that the five of us and Sister Hebert had provided and the reports of the health professionals, Houston pleaded guilty and was declared to be a dangerous sex offender. As a result, Houston was committed, subject to a review every three years. He was released after nine years.

Mike Gladu, Hugh Feagan, and Rick Hardy in Goderich, Ontario, in August 2021. Credit: Mike Gladu.

Mike and I wondered why we had not been notified about these reviews taking place. During this discussion, Mike told us that he had been solicited by Father Adam to give a statement that Houston was a "good" man. Mike also told us that Father

Adam wanted this statement to support work by the Church to obtain Houston's release.

Mike's recollection was that this request was made in 1968, which would have been the year of the second review. Mike told Father Adam exactly where he could go. I was angered, once again, at the Catholic Church, when I realized it had played an active role in obtaining Houston's eventual release. At the same time, it had been very busy doing absolutely nothing for the victims.

With regard to the boys whom Hugh had not interviewed, they eventually had their day in court. In 2004, Houston was charged with more offenses, for the two-year period from 1960 to 1962. Houston pleaded guilty to those additional charges and received a sentence of three years' probation.

I believe that Hugh was the last adult who was involved in the criminal proceedings that put Houston in a penitentiary for nine years who was still alive. I was honoured that he had reached out to us and spent the time that he did with us.

My Unanswered Questions and My Conclusions

The information that we received from and the discussions that we had with Hugh once again inflamed my questions of "Why"?

Why did the Catholic Church act as it did throughout Houston's life?

Why did the Father Provincial in Manitoba and the Church in the Northwest Territories, which included, among others, Bishop Piche and Father Ruyant, not properly vet Houston? Or did they?

Why did Father Ruyant not listen to the many boys who complained to him about Houston?

Why did Father Ruyant not listen to Sister Hebert after she told him, on more than one occasion, what was going on in Houston's room?

Why did Father Ruyant perjure himself at the preliminary inquiry?

Why was the only response from the Church—after the conviction and sentencing of Houston—to the victims to tell us to pray for Houston?

Why did Bishop Paul Piche not travel to Inuvik to comfort us after he was told, in writing, what Houston had done? Why did Bishop Piche never speak to us about what had happened to us?

Why did the Church not arrange for proper mental care for us after it learned all the facts?

Why did the Church, after it knew exactly what had happened to us, go on to hire three more pedophiles to supervise the boys in Grollier Hall?

Why did the Church ignore David Searle's offer to help them establish a proper vetting process when hiring supervisors?

Why did the Church take an active role in obtaining the release of Martin Houston?

Why did the Church allow Houston to become a priest after he was released?

Why did the Church bury Houston with full honours in what it considers hallowed ground?

Why did the Church deny any knowledge about what had happened after the truth became evident in the 1990s?

I can only conclude that the Church knew what was happening and condoned it. Houston was a tool in the hands of the Church, and it directed what happened. Why?

∞

A theory, that is plausible in my view, has emerged where it may have been Houston who held the power in his relationship with the Church. Hugh told me that while Houston was in custody, he showed no remorse for the abuse that he had inflicted and no concern about what future effect it might have on us. Hugh observed that Houston's sole interest was how a conviction could hurt his ambition to be a priest. Houston knew where the secrets were hidden, and if he were put on trial, they might be revealed. Did he reach an agreement with Fathers Adam and Ruyant and Bishop Piche to plead guilty and keep his mouth shut in return for their support in getting him released and admitted to the priesthood?

How does a dangerous sex offender who shows no remorse get released into the community? The answers to that question lay in the records of the Parole Board of Canada. What did the representatives of the Catholic Church do to get Houston released? It seems that the Parole Board's records have disappeared or are not available. Oh, the long arm of the Catholic Church.

∞

We must remember that the Catholic Church is a hierarchical institution. At the top of the pyramid is the pope, who supposedly speaks for God. Why would God allow what happened to happen? No, the pope speaks only for the institution, not for God.

After the pope comes the cardinals, then the bishops, then the priests, then the brothers, then the nuns, then the lay workers, and finally, the great unwashed masses who kneel before the institution every day. The institution is held together by vows of obedience. Remember that Martin Houston told us that he had the authority of Father Ruyant. Remember also that Martin Houston told us that we must obey.

Remember, at the beginning of this book, I told you about Mama's frustration with her inability to get a higher education unless she agreed to become a nun. If she had become a nun, she would have been subject to a vow of obedience. Remember how I was rejected when I thought I had a vocation? The Church did not want anyone in the closed upper ranks above the great unwashed masses who might think for themselves and, maybe, disobey and call the Church to account.

The Church got itself caught in agreeing to educate us and then realized that it was putting a potent tool in our hands. We would be educated and would be free thinkers and could challenge the lies and hypocrisies. So, for those who showed some aptitude for higher education and showed independence, the Church had to do something.

It had to maintain its control. The answer, in my view, was to turn the Martin Houston's of the world loose upon us. This has clearly happened around the world. We have to recognize that what happened to us was and is a worldwide conspiracy being carried out by the Church in order to maintain its hierarchical power.

The individuals in the church hierarchy have no more close contact with God, than you or I do. I pray to the Creator that the Dene elders and chiefs stop believing that these people speak to and for what they call God.

How many insults and barbs will they direct to us? Credit: Anonymous.

How many are innocent? Credit: Anonymous.

PART VI

283

I know that there are Survivors still out there who have not yet told their stories. There are many reasons for this, including the ongoing shame that we all harbour and, in some cases, ongoing peer pressure not to disclose. If you are one of these Survivors, please do not be afraid. If this book serves no other purpose, I hope it shows you that baring your soul completely will not hurt you. In my case it has lifted a tremendous burden from me and may well have saved my life, once again.

LIST OF APPENDICES

Appendix A: Statement of Richard Irving Timothy Hardy – Taken at Fort Norman, NWT, 21 Aug 62 by "H. A. Feagan, Sgt., R. C. M. Police."

Appendix B: Confidential Memorandum for Mr. B. Gillis from Administrator of the Mackenzie on 31 August 1962.

Appendix C: Minutes of Meeting of Hostel Superintendents to pass on Confidential Information concerning Martin Houston held on 10 September, 1962.

Appendix D: Examination of Richard Irving Timothy Hardy by D. Searle on the 13th day of September AD 1962.

Appendix E: Part IV "Effects and Consequences" – *Grollier Hall Residential School Claims Phase II Validation Hearing Report*, September 28, 2001, Report of the Fact Finder, Katherine R. Peterson.

BIBLIOGRAPHY

BOOKS

Berger, Mr. Justice T. R. *Mackenzie Valley Pipeline Enquiry Transcripts, Volume 10.* 1975.

Bompas, William Carpenter, DD. *Diocese of Mackenzie River.* Society for Promoting Christian Knowledge. 1888.

Bown, Stephen R. *The Company – The Rise and Fall of the Hudson's Bay Company.* Toronto: Doubleday Canada, 2020.

Brown, Bern Will. *Arctic Journal.* Novalis, 2003.

Ibid. *End of the Earth People.* Dundurn Press and Parks Canada, 2014.

Camsell, Charles. *Son of the North.* Toronto: Ryerson Press, 1954.

Carrier, Roch. *The Hockey Sweater.* Toronto: House of Anansi Press Limited, 1979.

Cloughley, Maurice R. *The Spell of the Midnight Sun.* Victoria: Horsdal & Schubart Publishers Ltd., 1995.

Deans Cameron, Agnes. *The New North.* New York: D. Appleton and Company, 1909.

Fumoleau, Rene. *As Long As This Land Shall Last.* Toronto: McClelland and Stewart Limited, 1973.

Hardy, Jack. *From East to West: Drifting with the Wind,* 1993.

Harris Volden, Bridget. *If Only the Rod Had Been Round.* InstantPublisher.com, 2009.

Jean, Blair. *Clearwater River Fort McMurray to Methye Portage,* 2020.

Mackenzie, Sir Alexander. *The Journals of Alexander Mackenzie.* The Narrative Press, 2001.

McCarthy, Martha. *From the Great River to the Ends of the Earth.* Edmonton: University of Alberta Press, 1995.

McKnight, Lesley. *Davis & Company Partners in History.* Echo Memoirs Ltd., 2005.

Ogilvie, William G. *WAY . . . WAY Down North,* 1989.

Payment, Diane P. "Une Femme En Vaut Deux – Strong Like Two People," *Contours of a People – Métis Family, Mobility and History.* Norman, OK: University of Oklahoma Press, 2012.

Petitot, Emile. *Land Occupancy by the Amerindians of the Canadian Northwest in the 19th Century, as reported by Emile Petitot.* Ottawa: The Department of Indian and Northern Affairs, Canada, 2001.

Robertson, Heather. *A Gentleman Adventurer.* Toronto: Lester & Orpen Dennys Limited, 1984.

Searle, David H, CM, QC. *Gold, Diamonds and the Law,* 2015.

Simon, Sarah; Yakeleya, Elizabeth. *We Remember the Coming of the Whiteman.* Calgary: Durvile Publications Ltd., 2020.

Slobodin, Richard. *Métis of the Mackenzie District.* Ottawa: Canadian Research Centre for Anthropology, 1966.

Sutherland, Agnes. SGM. *The Bishop Who Cared*, 1995.

Trindell, Ted. *Métis Witness to the North*. Tillacum Library, 1986.

ARTICLES

Archer S.A. "A Heroine of the North," *Project Canterbury*, Chapter V.

Damas, David. "Richard Slobodin (1915–2005)," *Arctic* (Dec. 2005): 438-439.

Gaudet, J. L. "Chief Trader Charles Philip Gaudet," *The Beaver* (Sept., 1935): 45.

Hardy, Richard I. "Métis Rights in the Mackenzie River District of the Northwest Territories," *Canadian Native Law Reporter (1980) Volume 1*.

Hodgson, Joseph. "An H.B.C. Hercules," *The Beaver* (June 1924): 335-337.

THESIS

Fuchs, Denise. "Native Sons of Rupert's land 1760 to the 1860s." Department of History, University of Manitoba, 2000.

REPORTS

Tulít'a District Land Corporation. *Spirit of the Mountains*. December, 2009.

PART VI

APPENDIX A

STATEMENT OF RICHARD IRVING TIMOTHY HARDY (BD: 13 May 47) FORT NORMAN, N.W.T. – TAKEN AT FORT NORMAN 21 AUG 62

My home is in Fort Norman, N.W.T. but I attend school at Inuvik and stay at the Roman Catholic Hostel there during the school term. I was in grade 9 last school year.

During the 1960/61 term and the 1961/62 term, Martin HOUSTON was senior boys supervisor at the R.C. Hostel.

One Saturday afternoon during February or March, 1961, HOUSTON asked me into his room in the hostel to copy words of songs. While I was in his room, HOUSTON took hold of my private parts and he asked me to jerk him off. I refused to do it but he told me that he was the supervisor and it was his authority and he threatened to punish me if I didn't, so I took his prick in my hand and jerked him off.

HOUSTON never bothered me any more that year except that he grabbed me by the balls several times when I had occasion to go into his room for something.

Once in a while HOUSTON would line up all the boys naked in the shower room or in his own room and he would pull the foreskin back on each boy's penis. He claimed that Father RUYANT had given him authority to check the boys.

During the 1961/62 school term HOUSTON was worse. He asked me to go into his room lots of times but I refused. On two occasions though, I went into his room because he said it was not for that.

When HOUSTON took me into his room he played with my prick and balls and he tried to jerk me off and he made me jerk him off. He kept getting worse and worse and he made me go to bed with him, then he would try and take my clothes off and he would take his clothes off in bed. Twice he made me go to bed with him and he pushed his prick between my legs and when I tried to get out of bed, he would hold me there. The second time he actually put his prick in my ass. After he did this, he offered me money and warned me not to tell anybody. When I refused the money, he made me take it and said the money was not for that. He gave me around $15.00 all together.

One of the two times that HOUSTON had me in bed was last June and I can't remember when the other time was – it was sometime in the winter sometime, I think January, 1962.

HOUSTON never used his mouth on my penis and he never asked me to suck him off.

One time around January, 1962, when I was dying my hair in the washroom, HOUSTON was taking a shower and came out of the shower – that is the first time he got me in bed that I mentioned above.

All times when HOUSTON played with my private parts and made me jerk him off and when he made me go to bed with him, we were alone – there were no other boys with us but once he took Michael GLADUE and I both into his room together and tied our pricks together with string and made us pull.

Each time that HOUSTON did these things, he warned us not to say anything and he said he had authority as supervisor and not to resist his authority.

I was scared to tell anybody about it but Michael GLADUE and I have talked a little bit about it between ourselves.

One time when HOUSTON took us swimming, we went in the water with our under shorts on and after he told us to wring out our shorts and while we were naked he took our picture. All the senior boys from the Hostel were there.

Witness: "J. HARDY"   Sgd: "Richard HARDY"
         "H.A. FEAGAN, Sgt., R.C.M.Police"

APPENDIX B

DEPARTMENT OF NORTHERN AFFAIRS AND NATIONAL RESOURCES

NORTHERN ADMINISTRATION BRANCH

OUR FILE NO. 20-Norwegia
YOUR FILE NO. Rosie

CONFIDENTIAL

Fort Smith, N.W.T.,
31 August, 1962.

MEMORANDUM FOR MR. B. GILLIE
DISTRICT SUPERINTENDENT OF EDUCATION
FORT SMITH, N.W.T.

Attention: Mr. G. H. Needham

Robert Clement and Martin Houston

This will confirm our discussion held yesterday concerning the situation in the Roman Catholic Hostel at Inuvik.

I am attaching hereto copies of relevant correspondence which include a memorandum dated August 27 from Mr. Sivertz to the Administrator of the Mackenzie, a letter dated August 24 from Mr. Sivertz to Bishop Piche and a memorandum dated August 29 from the Administrator of the Mackenzie to the Director. You should review this material with Mr. Hodgkinson. You and Mr. Hodgkinson should then meet with two hostel superintendents at Inuvik and inform them of the details of the Houston case as they are known to you.

It is considered important that both hostel superintendents have factual information on this incident as there will undoubtedly be numerous rumours that will reach them that have no relationship to the facts of the case.

I would appreciate a report on your meeting together with any other pertinent information that you might have at your earliest convenience.

A/ Administrator of the Mackenzie.

CONFIDENTIAL

GNWT Archives G79 003 ~~Block~~ 600 box 244 file 4.

PART VI

289

APPENDIX C

MINUTES OF MEETING OF HOSTEL SUPERINTENDENTS TO PASS ON

CONFIDENTIAL INFORMATION CONCERNING MARTIN HOUSTON

Place: Sir Alexander Mackenzie School   Date: 10 September, 1962.

Persons present: 1. Father M. Ruyant   – Superintendent of Grollier Hall

2. Rev. L.P. Holman   – Superintendent of Stringer Hall

3. Mr. R. Hodgkinson   – A/Regional Administrator

4. Mr. G.H. Needham   – Superintendent of Schools

5. Mr. William Bock   – Principal of Sir Alexander
                           Mackenzie School – Recorder
                           of Meeting.

G.H. Needham briefly explained the purpose of the Meeting.

Mr. Hodgkinson read (a) Letter from the Director addressed to
                          Administrator of the Mackenzie concerning
                          Mr. Houston and the investigation.which
                          occurred in Ottawa.

                     (b) Other correspondence on the same topic.

Father Ruyant stated that the boys in Hostel were to retire at a
              quarter past ten and on occasion some were found in
              his room. This caused suspicion but on investigation
              nothing was discovered. The boys were afraid of Houston
              and would not speak out when asked.

Mr. Needham : What screening did he get before being hired?

Father Ruyant: Information came from the Father Provincial at Winnipeg
               and a school teacher. He had three recommendations which
               did not have any indication of this problem.

Mr. Needham: What are your plans for future screening?

Father Ruyant:Careful consideration of character reference as much as
              I can. At least three persons asked for references.

Mr. Needham: How far back should an applicant's record be checked?

Mr. Hodgkinson: There appears to be no record of any previous criminal
                offence in his case.

Father Ruyant:No, there is no evidence of it in the recommendations.
              The boys were afraid. They did not tell the truth.

Father Ruyant:Only two seniors out of ten had reservations about Mr.
              Houston.

Mr. Hodgkinson: Do you have the same screening process?

Rev. Holman: Three references. School principals, Doctors, former
             employers. Screened by central office. Record of
             employment passed to central office and available to all
             hostels.

Mr. Needham: Do you agree that the problem is difficult to detect?

CONFIDENTIAL   ..2

..2

Rev. Holman:	Yes, difficult to detect and very difficult to prove.
Mr. Needham:	What do you feel about the assistance of the Social Worker mentioned in the letter?
Rev. Holman:	The Social Worker is contacted as a matter of routine if problems are experienced.
Mr. Hodgkinson:	Is it agreeable to you then that the Social Worker comes in? Do you not feel that this will be interference in the internal affairs of the Hostels?
Rev. Holman!	Services of the Social Worker should be available when requested by the Hostels. This was agreed upon by all present.
Mr. Hodgkinson:	What were Mr. Houston's academic qualifications?
Father Ruyant:	Grade Eleven.
Mr. Needham:	Why did Mr. Houston wish to be tried in Inuvik?
Father Ruyant:	Maybe hoping to get defence in Inuvik.

CONFIDENTIAL

PART VI

291

APPENDIX D

```
        10

15    The Crown's first witness, sir.

16    Richard Irving Timothy HARDY, witness called on behalf

17    of the Crown, sworn, direct examination by Mr. Searle:

18  Q Where is your home, Richard?

19  A Fort Norman.

20  Q This ispresently your home?

21  A Yes.

22  Q And how old are you?

23  A Fifteen.

24  Q You are fifteen now.  Now did you at any time attend

25    the Roman Catholic educational institution here;  I

26    suppose the youth hostel; did you ever stay at the

27    youth hostel?
```

Hardy   11

1   A Yes.

2   Q When was this?

3   A 1959 to 1960, and 1960 to 1961, and 1961 to 1962

4   school years.

5   Q From the first half of 1959 to 1960 school year, right

6   through to the 1961-1962 school year?

7   A Yes.

8   Q Are you still attending the school here?

9   A No.

10 Q And you are not staying at the hostel?

11 A No.

12 Q Now at the time you were attending school here in

13   Inuvik, and at the time you were staying at the youth

14   hostel, during this time did you know the man who is

15   accused here today, Mr. Martin Houston?

16 A Yes.

17 Q And what was his position at that time; what did he do?

18 A He was the senior boys supervisor.

19 Q The senior boys supervisor, and where was that?

20 A At the hostel.

21 Q And this was the Roman Catholic hostel, was it?

22 A Yes.

23 Q You see, Richard, I can't lead you too much. You

24   are going to have to tell us. I can't put words in

25   your mouth. Now would you please relate in your own

26   words, and loud enough so that defence counsel and the

27   court can hear, exactly what your relationship was

PART VI

293

Hardy   12

1   with the accused, Martin Houston; how you knew him;

2   what happened between the two of you, that sort of

3   thing.

4 A (No answer)

5 Q Well, let's start, Richard, with when you first met

6   Mr. Houston?

7 A The beginning of the 60-61 school year when I came

8   to the school, and entered the hostel.

9 Q That's when you first met Mr. Houston?

10 A Yes.

11 Q Had he just begun his employment there at that time?

12 A Yes; I am not sure whether it was his first year as

13   supervisor.

14 Q Now you are aware of the charges that we have laid

15   against Mr. Houston?

16 A Yes.

17 Q Can you state whether or not any acts were committed

18   by Mr. Houston against yourself, and if so, would

19   you please describe when and where, and the type of

20   acts?

21 A The first time was .....

22 Q What was the year?

23 A 1961 I think.

24 Q Do you remember the month?

25 A No.

26 Q Was it summer or winter?

27 A Winter.

MOLAZHA

294

Hardy   13

1 Q Winter, and what happened in the winter of 1960-61,
2   the first association you had, the first time you
3   had anything to do with Mr. Houston. Just take your
4   time, and think back; when was that first time you
5   had anything to do with Mr. Houston?
6 A It was in the winter of 1961.
7 Q And can youdescribe what happened?
8 A He asked me to jerk him off.
9 Q Now where did this take place, Richard?
10 A In his room.
11 Q Now where is his room?
12 A The senior boys section in the hostel.
13 Q He lived right in the hostel, did he?
14 A Yes.
15 Q I will tell you what I will do, Richard. Just so
16   you don't talk low, too low, I will stand back here,
17   and then you will have to speak a little louder. So
18   Mr. Houston had a room in the youth hostel?
19 A Yes.
20 Q Was it very close to your room?
21 A Well, it was right beside our dorm.
22 Q Right beside your dorm; would it be connected with
23   hallways; in other words, could you easily come from
24   your room to his without going outside?
25 A It was right next to ours.
26 Q Right next to yours, in a separate building?
27 A No, the same building.

PART VI

295

Hardy   14

1 Q The same building; now would you please describe,
2   Richard, exactly what happened when Mr. Houston
3   asked you into his room?
4 A I was copying words from one song on the record
5   player, and he was laying down, and he asked me to come
6   and sit beside him.
7 Q This was in his room?
8 A Yes.
9 Q And did you go and sit beside him?
10 A Not right away.
11 Q Did you later?
12 A Yes.
13 Q And then what happened?
14 A Then he asked me to jerk him off.
15 Q (Mr. Williams) What was that again?
16 Mr. Searle: He asked him to jerk him off.
17 Q And did you comply with this request; in other words,
18   did you do this?
19 A Yes.
20 Q Why did you do this?
21 A First I didn't want to, but he kept .....
22 Q But then did you agree?
23 A Yes, I did.
24 Q Now let's just deal with the expression you used "He
25   asked you to jerk him off". Now it may sound ridicu-
26   lous to you to be asked to tell us about this,
27   Richard. We all have a good idea what it is, but
      s

MQLAZHA

296

Hardy   15

1   someone reading what has gone on today may not know
2   what we are talking about, so you will have to des-
3   cribe exactly what happened. We trust that you must
4   have had to touch the accused?
5   A Yes, I took his prick into my hand.
6   Q And just held it?
7   A No.
8   Q What did you do?
9   A (No answer)
10 Q So you took his private part in your hand; was that all?
11 A And moved it up and down.
12 Q Yes; now when you did this, Richard, would you explain
13   how you were persuaded to do this? Why you did it? Did
14   you do this out of your own free will?
15 A He said there's nothing wrong with it.
16 Q Are we to understand he said thereis nothing wrong
17   with this?
18 A I don't just recall, but it was something of that
19   nature.
20 Q Were there ever any threats of any kind?
21 A Not to me.
22 Q The accused never threatened you?
23 A Not that I recall.
24 Q He just persuaded you?
25 A Yes.
26 Q At this time, Richard, were you ..., was the accused
27   your supervisor?

PART VI

297

Hardy   16

1 A Yes.

2 Q What was his authority over you as a supervisor.

3   What were his functions. What would you have to do?1

4   As the supervisor of boys over twelve, he had a cer-

5   tain job?

6 A Yes.

7 Q What was his job with regard to these boys over

8   twelve?

9 A Well, he was supervisor, and was just looking after the

10   boys, I guess.

11 Q How did he look after them; could he tell you what to do?

12 A More or less.

13 Q More or less; what could he tell you to do?

14 A Well, practically anything, I guess.

15 Q You see, I can't lead you, Richard, and you have to

16   tell in your own words exactly what happened. You

17   have to answer my questions, because I can't put

18   words in your mouth. Now you say that Mr. Houston was

19   the supervisor, and he could make you do practically

20   anything; is that right?

21 A Yes.

22 Q Give us some examples of the type of thing you would

23   have to do as a result of Mr. Houston's orders. Can

24   you think of anything?

25 A (No answer)

26 Q Now Richard, you say this man asked you to sit down

27   on a bed and do this thing. Did this occur any other

Hardy   17

1   time?

2 A Not this particular thing.

3 Q Did anything else of a similar nature occur?

4 A Yes.

5 Q What was that. Did anything else like this occur?

6 A Yes.

7 Q Now would you please tell the court, Richard, what

8   that was?

9 A He made me go to bed with him.

10 Q Would you please say that louder?

11 A He made me go to bed with him.

12 Q And what happened when you went to bed with him. Did

13   anything happen?

14 A Yes.

15 Q What happened?

16 A (No answer)

17 Q What was the first time that you went to bed with Mr.

18   Houston?

19 A 1962.

20 Q In 1962?

21 A Yes.

22 Q Do you remember the month, Richard?

23 A No.

24 Q Winter, summer?

25 A Winter.

26 Q So the first time you went to bed with the accused was

27   the winter of 1962?

PART VI

299

Hardy   18

1   A Yes.

2   Q Did you do this any other time?

3   A Yes.

4   Q When was that?

5   A June 1962.

6   Q Any other time?

7   A No.

8   Q Only twice?

9   A Yes.

10 Q Now on each occasion, let's deal with the first one, let's

11   deal with the first time. Would you please explain

12   what happened then, when you went to bed. Was this

13   in the same bed?

14 A Yes.

15 Q And were you under the covers?

16 A I don't remember the first time.

17 Q Now what did Mr. Houston do when you were in bed?

18 A (No answer)

19 Q You know Richard you have to give me an answer?

20 A (No answer)

21 Q Let's deal with the first time. What did he do the

22   first time you went to bed with him?

23 A (No answer)

24 Q Are you unable to tell the court?

25 A He put his prick between my legs.

26 Q How were you lying when this happened?

27 A I was laying with my back to him, I guess.

MQLAZHA

Hardy   19

1   Q   On your back?

2   A   With my back to him.

3   Q   You were lying on your stomach then?

4   A   No, on my side.

5   Q   Were you clothed; did you have your clothes on?

6   A   My pyjamas, I did, I think.

7   Q   Did you keep them on?

8   A   Yes.

9   Q   What did these pyjamas look like; did they tie around

10   the waist?

11 A   I don't remember if they tied or had elastic; I don't

12   remember.

13 Q   But this first time when the accused ~~pulled~~ placed his

14   penis between your legs, you remained clothed, did you?

15 A   My pyjamas were down, but not off.

16 Q   Oh, your pyjamas were down. How far down were they,

17   to the knees?

18 A   About that I guess.

19 Q   And did Mr. Houston touch you with his prick, as you

20   call it?

21 A   Yes.

22 Q   Now could you describe this touching. Was it just a

23   touch?

24 A   No.

25 Q   What happened. I know this must be very difficult

26   for you Richard, but again we can't explain it for you.

27   You will have to tell us.

PART VI

301

| | | Hardy | 20 |

1   A   Well, he moved back and forth.

2   Q   He moved back and forth?

3   A   Yes, with his prick between my legs.

4   Q   Between your legs?

5   A   Yes.

6   Q   What part of the area between your legs was his prick

7   touching?

8   A   Crotch.

9   Q   Was there any pain caused to you?

10   A   No.

11   Q   Did Mr. Houston's prick penetrate you in any way,

12   enter into you?

13   A   No.

14   Q   This was the first time?

15   A   The first time.

16   Q   It didn't; now let's go to the second time. When was

17   that second time again?

18   A   June 1962.

19   Q   June 1962; did this occur in Mr. Houston's room

20   again, or your room, or where?

21   A   Yes, we used his room.

22   Q   And where did this occur?

23   A   In the bed.

24   Q   In his bed?

25   A   Yes.

26   Q   The two of you were in his bed?

27   A   Yes.

MQLAZHA

302

Hardy   21

1   Q   Would you describe now what happened the second time?

2   A   Well, I didn't want to stay, but he forced me to stay

3   there.

4   Q   How did he force you to stay there, Richard?

5   A   Just held me.

6   Q   Was there a struggle?

7   A   No, I was too scared.

8   Q   Were you afraid to struggle?

9   A   Yes.

10 Q   Did you call out; were you afraid to call?

11 A   Yes.

12 Q   Why were you afraid, of his authority?

13 A   Yes.

14 Q   Now just what did happen on this second time; you and

15   Mr. Houston are now in his bed. Exactly what happened

16   in that bed?

17 A   The same thing as the last time, except he put his

18   prick in my ass.

19 Mr. Williams: I am sorry; I didn't hear that at all.

20 A   He put his prick in my ass.

21 Q   And how long did it remain there, or did he just take

22   it out?

23 A   A few minutes.

24 Q   And at this time was there any motion, or were you just

25   lying still?

26 A   Well, I was moving around a little bit.

27 Q   Pardon me?

PART VI

303

Hardy   22

1 A I was moving slightly, yes.

2 Q Who was moving?

3 A Me, because I didn't want to stay there.

4 Q Were you trying to get away?

5 A I was trying to get out of bed.

6 Q You were trying to get outof bed. Where did Mr.

7   Houston have his hands, ~~txf~~ if he washolding you?

8 A Around like this, I guess.

9 Q Folded around your stomach?

10 A Or my chest.

11 Q You are going to have to speak a little louder,

12   Richard. Did you hear that, Mr. Williams?

13 Mr. Williams: No, I was busy.

14 Q Mr. Houston had his arms where?

15 A I don't remember exactly; it was around my stomach or

16   my chest, I think.

17 Q Now after this had been done, what did you do; did

18   you leave?

19 A Yes, he gave me j some things. I refused it, and he

20   said its not for this; I will give them to you because

21 8 you are a good monitor.

22 Q Because you are a good monitor; not because of this?

23 A Yes.

24 Q What were these things he gave you, Richard?

25 A Five dollars.

26 Q He gave you money?

27 A Yes.

Hardy   23

1 Q What else?

2 A A plate with the picture of the church on it.

3 Q A plate, yes. Did he give you money or gifts on the

4   first time?

5 A Yes.

6 Q Did you take this?

7 A Well, at first I refused, and then he said "Its not

8   for doing that, its a gift".

9 Q Yes; now did Mr. Houston ever do anything else to

10   you, other than request that you jerk him off, and

11   request that you go to bed with him. Did he ever do

12   anything else?

13 A Well, yes, me and another boy, he tied our pricks

14   together and made us pull.

15 Q Tied them together, what with?

16 A String.

17 Q Who was the other boy?

18 A Michael ~~Gorden.~~ *Gladue*   *EWJ*

19 Q Why did he do this?

20 A I don't know.

21 Q Did you do this freely; I mean, were you willing to

22   do this?

23 A No.

24 Q Why did you do it?

25 A He said it would be to resist his authority as super-

26   visor.

27 Q You did this because he said he was the supervisor, and

PART VI

Hardy 24

1 you weren't to resist his authority?

2 A Yes.

3 Q Now after he tied you and your friend's penes to-

4 gether, did he offer you any rewards?

5 A No.

6 Q No; when did this occur?

7 A I don't recall exactly.

8 Q Now we have these three acts that you have referred

9 to. Is there anything else that Mr. Houston ever

10 did to you at any time; is there anything else that

11 Mr. Houston would do?

12 A He used to check the boys' pricks sometimes.

13 Q Now Richard, we must be very sure that he did this

14 to yours, or that you saw it done?

15 A He did it to all the boys.

16 Q You saw this?

17 A Yes.

18 Q Did you see this done?

19 A He checked mine.

20 Q How do you mean, he checked?

21 A He used to check mine to make sure its clean.

22 Q What would he do when he did this?

23 A Just pulled the skin back on it, and looked at it.

24 Q And how often would he do this, more than once to you?

25 A Yes, more than once.

26 Q Ten times?

27 A No.

MQLAZHA

306

Hardy   25

1   Q How many times?

2   A I don't remember.

3   Q Approximately?

4   A Two or three times, maybe.

5   Q Now every time Mr. Houston did something like this,

6   were there any comments he would make. Did he ever

7   say anything to you about these things?

8   A I don't understand your question.

9   Q Yes, I will just re-state it. Richard, when these things

10   occurred, you must have wondered about whether they

11   were good or bad things to do?

12   A Yes.

13   Q Did you wonder about this?

14   A Yes.

15   Q Did you ever ask Mr. Houston about this?

16   A Yes.

17   Q What did he say?

18   A (No answer)

19   Q What did he say; that it was a good thing to do?

20   A (No answer)

21   Q Well, let's just leave that, Richard, for the time

22   being, and look at another point. Did you ever think

23   of speaking to the Father or the Sisters about this?

24   A Yes, I have thought about it.

25   Q And why didn't you speak to the Sisters and the Father?

26   Is there some reason why you didn't speak to them?

27   A (No answer)

PART VI

307

Hardy   26

Q Were you afraid of the Father?

A No.

Q Of the Sisters?

A I didn't feel like talking about these things with
the priest.

Q Did you ever talk to Mr. Houston about telling the
father or the priest?

A No.

Q Did he ever talk to you about telling anyone?

A After, he used to make me promise not to tell anybody.

Q How would he make you to promise this?

A He would ask me to promise, and he would start raising
his voice.

Q Raising his voice; how high; loud talk, or screaming?

A No, raised it so that it would scare me.

Q Raised it in such a way that it would scare you.
When you say he raised his voice to scare you, was
this fear from his authority because of his position,
or was it fear from what he could do to you physically,
what he could do to you with his strength?

A I was afraid of getting beat.

Q Did the accused at any time beat you or strike you?

A Yes, slapped and strapped.

Q Slapped and strapped; when he slapped you, was it with
the open hand?

A Yes.

Q Did he ever strike you with a closed fist?

Hardy 27

1 A No.

2 Q When he strapped you, was it with a belt, a strap?

3 A I forget now.

4 Q Now we just have to clear up one point, Richard?

5 A It was a piece of belting.

6 Q Thick?

7 A Yes, fairly thick.

8 Q Now why did he strap you and strike you, because of

9 these acts?

10 A No.

11 Q Or because of things you did in the school?

12 A Things I did at school, I guess.

13 Q Were you a bad boy in the school, and received lots of

14 strappings?

15 A No, I never received strappings any place else.

16 Q Did anyone else, other than Mr. Houston, strap you?

17 A No.

18 Q Was this his job to strap the boys?

19 A I don't think so.

20 Q Now, is there anything else that Mr. Houston may have

21 done that seemed to you peculiars I mean, did this

22 all occur in the hostel?

23 A Yes.

24 Q Did anything occur outside the hostel?

25 A Yes, one time when we went sqimming, went in in our

26 shorts, we were wringing them out, and he took pictures

27 of us naked.

PART VI

309

Hardy   28

1 Q Mr. Houston took pictures of you naked?

2 A Yes.

3 Q Just as you were swimming?

4 A We were wringing our shorts out.

5 Q How would he do this. Did he say ..., no, I can't

6   ask that. Would you describe how he took these

7   pictures?

8 A Our shirts were wet, and he said "You can wring them

9   out", so we took them off, and as we did that, he

10   took a picture.

11 Q Did you ever see those pictures later?

12 A Yes.

13 Q How many times did he show you these pictures later?

14 A I seen them only once.

15 Q When was this?

16 A I think it was the last week of June.

17 Q And did anything occur at the time that he showed

18   you these pictures?

19 A No.

20 Q Now the man who did these things to you, Richard, is

21   he here today?

22 A Yes.

23 Q Is he in the court room?

24 A Yes.

25 Q Would you please point him out?

26 A (The witness indicated the accused)

27 Mr. Searle: Would you please answer any questions that

Hardy 29

1   Mr. Williams may ask you.

2 Mr. Williams: I have no questions to ask, thanks.

3 Mr. Searle: That's all thank you, Richard.

4 (The witness withdrew)

PART VI

311

APPENDIX E

Grollier Hall Residence Claims
Phase Two Validation Hearing Report
Claimant: **Richard Hardy**
Hearing Date: **April 13, 2000**

12

PART IV   Effects and Consequences

During the course of the validation hearing, Rick was requested to provide some insight into his perspective of the effects and consequences of his Grollier Hall experiences. He was extremely articulate and candid in his evidence and he did not hesitate at times to indicate that it is difficult to determine in hindsight, exactly how his life would have been different had these events not occurred.

He stated that he felt that one major impact of the abuse was his loss of memories of significant periods of his life. This has left him in a position of having to piece together early parts of his life. While others around him have clear recollections of school years, teachers, activities and the like, his memory remains very fuzzy for large tracts of time. He has thus had to rebuild part of his early memories and he feels that this has occurred largely as a result of the trauma of events concerning Martin Houston.

He also suggests that his alcoholism has been related to these experiences, and more accurately the loss of self esteem and confidence and anger flowing from them. It is significant to him that his life only started to take a positive turn when he was first able to disclose these experiences at the Henwood program. It is clear that he was raised in a healthy and loving environment and he wonders therefore, with that background, why alcohol would have posed such a challenge for him starting in high school and for many years thereafter. However, I did note that both of his brothers appeared to struggle with alcohol as well, though they did not have the sexual abuse experiences that Rick had. It is almost impossible therefore to say with complete certainty the causal connection between sexual abuse and alcoholism. The effects of one and genesis of the other are still not well understood even by experts in the areas. However, from a lay point of view, it is hard to imagine that the experiences of abuse did not contribute in some significant way to the challenge of alcoholism.

Rick also stated that he has experienced difficulties in developing and maintaining healthy and long standing relationships with women. He attributes this to a lack of self confidence

Grollier Hall Residence Claims
Phase Two Validation Hearing Report
Claimant: **Richard Hardy**
Hearing Date: **April 13, 2000**

that plagues him still. This is in contrast to the evidence of his early activities in the community of Fort Norman. All of the material provided by Rick depicted him as confident, outgoing, energetic and a leader among his peers. There is no doubt that significant changes occurred to this bright and promising start.

Rick also indicated that for a great deal of his early adulthood, not only did he struggle with alcohol, but he was unable to control his anger and rage. He described himself as an "ugly" and violent drunk. There would no doubt be lingering effects from these experiences which contribute to the spiral of effects.

Rick feels that he has permanently lost his connection to the Catholic church and has struggled to find and retain a sense of spirituality in his life. It appeared at times during the hearing that he grieved for this loss and longed to replace it with a meaningful sense of the spiritual. He feels anger and disillusionment respecting the Church and finds it impossible to accept that it was not aware of the cruel and inappropriate treatment of the residents of Grollier. Its denial and lack of compassion in dealing with these matters leaves Rick with a profound sense of bitterness.

He feels that he has been sustained by his mother's unconditional love for him and by his being able finally to talk about being a victim of sexual abuse. With respect to the latter, he has done so fearlessly and publicly, not only for his own benefit, but for those who were dealing with a culture of denial and marginalization around the Paul Leroux proceedings. Rick courageously wrote a letter to the newspaper in which he spoke of his experiences as a survivor of sexual abuse. For a person with public standing in the community, this could not have been an easy step.

He has continued to suffer from and be treated for depression. With the aid of medical advice and drug therapy, he is hopeful that this problem will be conquered over the course of time.

PART VI

Grollier Hall Residence Claims
Phase Two Validation Hearing Report
Claimant: **Richard Hardy**
Hearing Date: **April 13, 2000**

14

I offer my apologies to Rick and others associated with this process for the lateness of this report. It does not in any way reflect how impressed I was with his demeanor and strength as an individual, as well as his candour and courage in dealing with issues that have been so painful and challenging for him.

Dated at the City of Yellowknife in the Northwest Territories this 28th day of September, 2001.

Katherine Peterson

Printed in the USA
CPSIA information can be obtained
at www.ICGtesting.com
LVHW021932270824
789469LV00009B/322